CliffsNotes®

GRE®
General Test
CRAM PLAN™

CliffsNotes®

GRE®
General Test
CRAM PLAN™

Carolyn Wheater and Catherine McMenamin

WILEY

Wiley Publishing, Inc.

About the Authors

Carolyn Wheater teaches middle-school and upper-school mathematics at the Nightingale-Bamford School in New York City. Educated at Marymount Manhattan College and the University of Massachusetts, Amherst, she has taught math and computer technology for 30 years to students from preschool through college. Catherine McMenamin has an M.A. in Art History from Columbia University. She lives and teaches in New York City.

Editorial

Acquisition Editor: Greg Tubach

Project Editor: Elizabeth Kuball

Copy Editor: Elizabeth Kuball

Technical Editor: Abraham Mantell

Composition

Proofreader: ConText Editorial Services, Inc.

Wiley Publishing, Inc., Composition Services

CliffsNotes® GRE® General Test Cram Plan™

Published by:
Wiley Publishing, Inc.
111 River Street
Hoboken, NJ 07030-5774
www.wiley.com

Published by Wiley, Hoboken, NJ
Published simultaneously in Canada

Library of Congress Cataloging-in-Publication Data

Wheater, Carolyn C., 1957–
    CliffsNotes GRE general test Cram Plan / by Carolyn Wheater and Catherine McMenamin.
        p. cm.
        ISBN-13: 978-0-470-46591-2
        ISBN-10: 0-470-46591-3
1. Graduate Record Examination—Study guides. I. McMenamin, Catherine. II. Title. III. Title: Cliffs Notes GRE general test Cram Plan.
    LB2367.4W53 2009
    378.1'.662—dc22
                            2009016231

Printed in the United States of America
10 9 8 7 6 5 4 3 2 1

For general information on our other products and services or to obtain technical support, please contact our Customer Care Department within the U.S. at 877-762-2974, outside the U.S. at 317-572-3993, or fax 317-572-4002.

Wiley also publishes its books in a variety of electronic formats. Some content that appears in print may not be available in electronic books. For more information about Wiley products, please visit our web site at www.wiley.com.

Table of Contents

Introduction

If you're preparing to take the GRE, this is not your first encounter with standardized testing. You've likely taken the SAT or ACT for your undergraduate admission, so you have some expectations for the GRE. From your previous test-taking experience, you probably realize that the goal is to test your reasoning and critical thinking skills, and the content, whether verbal or mathematical, is only the vehicle for that assessment. Without firm control of that vehicle, however, you won't be able to demonstrate your reasoning skills effectively. To approach the GRE with confidence, you need to review the content and practice the style of questions you'll find on the test. *CliffsNotes GRE General Test Cram Plan* is designed to help you achieve your best possible score on the GRE, whether you have two months, one month, or only one week to prepare.

About the Test

The GRE is comprised of three sections: Analytical Writing, Verbal Reasoning, and Quantitative Reasoning. Within the Analytical Writing section, you'll be asked to complete two writing tasks: an issue task and an argument task; you'll have 45 minutes to complete the issue task and 30 minutes for the argument. The Verbal Reasoning section includes critical reading, analogies, antonyms, and sentence completions; 30 minutes are allotted for this section. The Quantitative Reasoning questions may appear as multiple choice or quantitative comparison questions; you're given 45 minutes for this section.

Paper-based versions of the test were once the standard, but today they're used only in areas where computer-based testing is not available. They offered a predetermined number of questions of each type for the Verbal Reasoning and Quantitative Reasoning sections. The chart at the end of this section shows the breakdown of the paper-based test on which our final test was patterned.

The current computer adaptive version of the test allots a set time for each section and bases your score on the number of questions you answer in that time period and on their level of difficulty. You're presented first with medium-difficulty questions, which are scored immediately as you answer them. Based on your responses, the computer assigns you questions of higher, lower, or equal difficulty. It is difficult to predict exactly how many questions of each type you'll find on the computer adaptive test, but the chart at the end of this section gives you an idea of what to expect.

Because questions are scored as soon as you submit your answers, you can't return to previous questions. Unlike other testing situations, in which you might choose to skip over a question and return to it later, on the computer adaptive GRE you must answer each question as it is presented (or leave it unanswered permanently). Because you can't return to a previous question to change an answer, it may be wise to pause a moment before moving on to the next question, just to be certain that you're satisfied with your answer.

For the Analytical Writing section, you'll type your essays on the computer, using a simplified word processor that includes basic functions common to all word processing software (such as inserting, deleting, cutting, and pasting). The issue task presents you with a choice of two essay topics, while the argument task provides a single subject.

The GRE is administered year-round, by appointment, at computer test centers. When paper-based tests were used, they were administered to large groups of people simultaneously, but for the computer-based test, you'll be able to choose a day and time to take the test, subject to availability. Test centers may offer appointments at different times during the day, but whenever your appointment may be, you'll need to arrive at the test center 30 minutes before your appointment. Bring your admission ticket and a photo ID. Except for pens and pencils, no personal items may be brought into the testing room. You'll be provided with a place to store other items, including cellphones, calculators, and electronic devices, but you won't be able to access them again until the testing is over. You'll be given scratch paper, and you may not remove that paper from the testing room. You aren't permitted to use a calculator during the test.

About This Book

CliffsNotes GRE General Test Cram Plan is designed to guide you through a thorough and well-organized preparation for the GRE general test. Whether your test date is two months away, one month away, or just a week away, *CliffsNotes GRE General Test Cram Plan* will show you how to address your weaknesses and approach the test with confidence.

Begin with the diagnostic test, a compact simulation of the questions you can expect to find on the Verbal Reasoning and Quantitative Reasoning sections of the GRE general test. Check your work against the answers and solutions provided. The Verbal Reasoning questions are organized by type, allowing you to determine which style of question you need to practice. The Quantitative Reasoning questions are mixed by subject and the solutions include references to the section number that reviews the content of the question. After you've scored your diagnostic test, look for patterns of strength and weakness. As you begin your review, pay special attention to any areas of weakness you've identified.

After you've identified your target areas, the two-month, one-month, and one-week study plans will show you how to do a systematic study of the subject reviews, while practicing the question formats included in the test. The two-month study plan gives you seven weekly tasks and a day-by-day study plan for the week before the test. Like the two-month study plan, the one-month study plan includes weekly assignments and a daily breakdown for the last week, but it organizes the material and highlights key areas to make best use of the available time. If you have only one week to prepare for the test, the one-week study plan will guide you day by day through the essential topics and practice.

After you've had time to read and practice the material in the subject reviews, the final test will give you a clear assessment of your readiness. Patterned after the former paper-based GRE, this simulated GRE includes directions and timings that mimic the real test, as well as solutions and explanations to help you correct your errors.

With diagnosis, planning, practice, and assessment, *CliffsNotes GRE General Test Cram Plan* will provide the information, skills, and tactics you need to approach the GRE with confidence and to achieve your best possible score.

Paper-Based GRE

Section	Subject	Type of Question	Time Allotted
1	Writing	1 issue essay (2 essay topics presented) 1 argument essay (1 argument presented)	45 minutes 30 minutes
2	Quantitative (30 questions)	15 quantitative comparisons 15 multiple choice	30 minutes
3	Verbal (38 questions)	7 sentence completions 9 analogies 11 reading comprehension (1 long passage, 1 short passage) 11 antonyms	30 minutes
4	Verbal (38 questions)	7 sentence completions 9 analogies 11 reading comprehension (1 long passage, 1 short passage) 11 antonyms	30 minutes
5	Quantitative (30 questions)	15 quantitative comparisons 15 multiple choice	30 minutes
6	Experimental (verbal or mathematics section)		30 minutes

Computer-Adaptive GRE

Section	Subject	Type of Question	Time Allotted
1	Analytical Writing	1 issue task	45 minutes
2	Analytical Writing	1 argument task	30 minutes
3	Verbal (30 questions)	Multiple choice, including critical reading, sentence completions, analogies, and antonyms	30 minutes
4	Quantitative (28 questions)	Multiple choice and quantitative comparisons	45 minutes
5	Experimental	1 or 2 sections with varying content	Varies

Note: You will have 3 hours and 15 minutes in which to work on this test, which consists of two writing tasks and four multiple-choice sections. The sections are in any order. During the time allowed for one section, you may work only on that section. The time allowed for each section is printed at the top of the first page of the section.

Your scores for the multiple-choice sections will be determined by the number of questions for which you select the best answer from the choices given. Questions for which you mark no answer or more than one answer are not counted in scoring. Nothing is subtracted from a score if you answer a question incorrectly. Therefore, to maximize your scores, it is better for you to guess at an answer than not to respond at all.

Online Extras at CliffsNotes.com

As an added bonus to this *CliffsNotes GRE General Test Cram Plan,* you can get some additional practice by visiting www.cliffsnotes.com/go/GRECram. There, you'll find:

- Vocabulary practice exercises
- Antonym practice exercises
- Analogy practice exercises
- And more!

I. Diagnostic Test

Answer Sheet

Section 1

1	Ⓐ Ⓑ Ⓒ Ⓓ Ⓔ
2	Ⓐ Ⓑ Ⓒ Ⓓ Ⓔ
3	Ⓐ Ⓑ Ⓒ Ⓓ Ⓔ
4	Ⓐ Ⓑ Ⓒ Ⓓ Ⓔ
5	Ⓐ Ⓑ Ⓒ Ⓓ Ⓔ
6	Ⓐ Ⓑ Ⓒ Ⓓ Ⓔ
7	Ⓐ Ⓑ Ⓒ Ⓓ Ⓔ
8	Ⓐ Ⓑ Ⓒ Ⓓ Ⓔ
9	Ⓐ Ⓑ Ⓒ Ⓓ Ⓔ
10	Ⓐ Ⓑ Ⓒ Ⓓ Ⓔ
11	Ⓐ Ⓑ Ⓒ Ⓓ Ⓔ
12	Ⓐ Ⓑ Ⓒ Ⓓ Ⓔ
13	Ⓐ Ⓑ Ⓒ Ⓓ Ⓔ
14	Ⓐ Ⓑ Ⓒ Ⓓ Ⓔ
15	Ⓐ Ⓑ Ⓒ Ⓓ Ⓔ
16	Ⓐ Ⓑ Ⓒ Ⓓ Ⓔ
17	Ⓐ Ⓑ Ⓒ Ⓓ Ⓔ
18	Ⓐ Ⓑ Ⓒ Ⓓ Ⓔ
19	Ⓐ Ⓑ Ⓒ Ⓓ Ⓔ
20	Ⓐ Ⓑ Ⓒ Ⓓ Ⓔ

21	Ⓐ Ⓑ Ⓒ Ⓓ Ⓔ
22	Ⓐ Ⓑ Ⓒ Ⓓ Ⓔ
23	Ⓐ Ⓑ Ⓒ Ⓓ Ⓔ
24	Ⓐ Ⓑ Ⓒ Ⓓ Ⓔ
25	Ⓐ Ⓑ Ⓒ Ⓓ Ⓔ
26	Ⓐ Ⓑ Ⓒ Ⓓ Ⓔ
27	Ⓐ Ⓑ Ⓒ Ⓓ Ⓔ
28	Ⓐ Ⓑ Ⓒ Ⓓ Ⓔ

Section 2

1	Ⓐ Ⓑ Ⓒ Ⓓ Ⓔ
2	Ⓐ Ⓑ Ⓒ Ⓓ Ⓔ
3	Ⓐ Ⓑ Ⓒ Ⓓ Ⓔ
4	Ⓐ Ⓑ Ⓒ Ⓓ Ⓔ
5	Ⓐ Ⓑ Ⓒ Ⓓ Ⓔ
6	Ⓐ Ⓑ Ⓒ Ⓓ Ⓔ
7	Ⓐ Ⓑ Ⓒ Ⓓ Ⓔ
8	Ⓐ Ⓑ Ⓒ Ⓓ Ⓔ
9	Ⓐ Ⓑ Ⓒ Ⓓ Ⓔ
10	Ⓐ Ⓑ Ⓒ Ⓓ Ⓔ
11	Ⓐ Ⓑ Ⓒ Ⓓ Ⓔ
12	Ⓐ Ⓑ Ⓒ Ⓓ Ⓔ
13	Ⓐ Ⓑ Ⓒ Ⓓ Ⓔ
14	Ⓐ Ⓑ Ⓒ Ⓓ Ⓔ
15	Ⓐ Ⓑ Ⓒ Ⓓ Ⓔ
16	Ⓐ Ⓑ Ⓒ Ⓓ Ⓔ
17	Ⓐ Ⓑ Ⓒ Ⓓ Ⓔ
18	Ⓐ Ⓑ Ⓒ Ⓓ Ⓔ
19	Ⓐ Ⓑ Ⓒ Ⓓ Ⓔ
20	Ⓐ Ⓑ Ⓒ Ⓓ Ⓔ

21	Ⓐ Ⓑ Ⓒ Ⓓ Ⓔ
22	Ⓐ Ⓑ Ⓒ Ⓓ Ⓔ
23	Ⓐ Ⓑ Ⓒ Ⓓ Ⓔ
24	Ⓐ Ⓑ Ⓒ Ⓓ Ⓔ
25	Ⓐ Ⓑ Ⓒ Ⓓ Ⓔ
26	Ⓐ Ⓑ Ⓒ Ⓓ Ⓔ
27	Ⓐ Ⓑ Ⓒ Ⓓ Ⓔ
28	Ⓐ Ⓑ Ⓒ Ⓓ Ⓔ
29	Ⓐ Ⓑ Ⓒ Ⓓ Ⓔ
30	Ⓐ Ⓑ Ⓒ Ⓓ Ⓔ
31	Ⓐ Ⓑ Ⓒ Ⓓ Ⓔ
32	Ⓐ Ⓑ Ⓒ Ⓓ Ⓔ
33	Ⓐ Ⓑ Ⓒ Ⓓ Ⓔ
34	Ⓐ Ⓑ Ⓒ Ⓓ Ⓔ
35	Ⓐ Ⓑ Ⓒ Ⓓ Ⓔ
36	Ⓐ Ⓑ Ⓒ Ⓓ Ⓔ
37	Ⓐ Ⓑ Ⓒ Ⓓ Ⓔ
38	Ⓐ Ⓑ Ⓒ Ⓓ Ⓔ
39	Ⓐ Ⓑ Ⓒ Ⓓ Ⓔ
40	Ⓐ Ⓑ Ⓒ Ⓓ Ⓔ

41	Ⓐ Ⓑ Ⓒ Ⓓ Ⓔ
42	Ⓐ Ⓑ Ⓒ Ⓓ Ⓔ
43	Ⓐ Ⓑ Ⓒ Ⓓ Ⓔ
44	Ⓐ Ⓑ Ⓒ Ⓓ Ⓔ

45 _____

46 _____

47 _____

48 _____

49 _____

50 _____

Section 1: Verbal

Directions: Each of the following questions gives you a related pair of words or phrases. Select the lettered pair that best expresses a relationship similar to that in the original pair of words.

1. DEPOSE : CZAR ::

    A. checkmate : chess player
    B. howl : watchdog
    C. charge : employee
    D. manuscript : writer
    E. operate : doctor

2. TACTLESS : SENSITIVITY ::

    A. penurious : generosity
    B. imperturbable : assurance
    C. aggrieved : composure
    D. craven : cowardice
    E. bellicose : fear

3. ALTRUISM : LIBERALITY ::

    A. levity : stupidity
    B. autonomy : independence
    C. probity : dishonesty
    D. belief : temerity
    E. privation : suffering

4. NOSTAGLIA : PAST ::

    A. regret : deed
    B. yearning : eternity
    C. anticipation : future
    D. absence : presence
    E. memory : forgetfulness

5. SYCOPHANT : SINCERITY ::

    A. thief : cleverness
    B. deceiver : truth
    C. coward : fear
    D. friend : loyalty
    E. hero : courage

6. ASCETIC : PLEASURE ::

   A. politician : votes
   B. plant : light
   C. scientist : truth
   D. planner : water
   E. hermit : society

7. SQUARE : DIFFERENCES ::

   A. arbitrate : conflicts
   B. cast : fracture
   C. antagonize : amities
   D. compromise : negotiations
   E. forgive : troubles

8. TRAVAIL : CRY ::

   A. exercise : play
   B. lumber : toil
   C. malady : ail
   D. encore : join
   E. vacation : travel

Directions: Each blank in the following sentences indicates that something has been omitted. Considering the lettered words beneath the sentence, choose the word or set of words that best fits the whole sentence.

9. The _____ theory was one that not many people understand even though it gained gradual acceptance and picked up more supporters _____.

   A. arcane . . . incrementally
   B. proven . . . regularly
   C. known . . . esoterically
   D. disputable . . . mercurially
   E. protean . . . slowly

10. A _____ toward _____ acts occurs when one saves dollar by dollar each day during turbulent economic times.

   A. tendency . . . parsimonious
   B. ascription . . . greed
   C. asking . . . illiberal
   D. feeling . . . frugal
   E. thought . . . penurious

11. Despite a _____ effort, he had not understood the _____ meaning even after the hardest mental labor.

   A. tiring . . . innocuous
   B. laborious . . . obtuse
   C. protracted . . . liberal
   D. limited . . . frugal
   E. thoughtful . . . obvious

12. The novel's review was _____; it exaggerated minor faults and gave no credit at all for the author's style and humor.

   A. hypothetical
   B. hyperactive
   C. hypersensitive
   D. hyperbolic
   E. hyperopic

13. To the advocates of _____, the best form of government has no governing powers at all as opposed to a constitutional _____ in which the power of the king or queen is usually limited by a constitution and a legislature.

   A. anarchy . . . monarchy
   B. monarchy . . . oligarchy
   C. chaos . . . oligarchy
   D. patriarchy . . . monarchy
   E. anarchy . . . hierarchy

14. The iridescent acrobat gave a _____ performance despite irate opponents who tried to _____ him with false accusations of steroid use and improper conduct.

   A. incredible . . . accuse
   B. sparkling . . . flay
   C. excessive . . . malign
   D. proportionate . . . slander
   E. balanced . . . disparage

15. Even though it was so unlikely he would achieve his _____ goals, they appealed to his sense of _____.

   A. quixotic . . . romance
   B. irritating . . . fair play
   C. unrealistic . . . pragmatism
   D. ephemeral . . . humor
   E. realistic . . . whimsy

16. Pablo Picasso's painting *Guernica* portrays _____ Spanish citizens of a small city with machine gunfire _____ away and bombs blowing up, killing thousands of innocent people.

    A. unprotected . . . gunning
    B. frail . . . detonating
    C. defenseless . . . strafing
    D. strong . . . striving
    E. formidable . . . powering

Directions: Each word in capital letters is followed by five words or phrases. The correct choice is the word or phrase whose meaning is most nearly *opposite* the meaning of the word in capitals. You may be required to distinguish fine shades of meaning. Look at all choices before marking your answer.

17. MYOPIA

    A. hypersensitivity
    B. hyperopia
    C. hypertrophy
    D. farsightedness
    E. utopia

18. EXOTERIC

    A. wild
    B. exotic
    C. esoteric
    D. urgent
    E. perfidious

19. ALLOPATHY

    A. antipathy
    B. hyperactivity
    C. homeopathy
    D. impertinence
    E. irrelevance

20. LIST

    A. strive for
    B. stand erect
    C. falter
    D. omit
    E. prioritize

21. PINCHBECK

    A. alloy
    B. heroism
    C. genuine
    D. counterfeit
    E. copper

22. CHUTZPAH

    A. quick-tempered
    B. diffidence
    C. disconcerted
    D. therapeutic
    E. aggrieved

23. RECONDITE

    A. abstruse
    B. erudite
    C. understandable
    D. obtuse
    E. seismic

Directions: Questions follow each of the passages. Using only the stated or implied information in each passage, answer the questions.

Passage 1

The Vietnam War began in 1956 and ended in 1975. It had dire consequences for millions of Americans. The American military pushed forward to South Vietnam to assist its government against the communist regime, who were supported by North Vietnam. By the late 1960s, the United States entered this war in which almost 60,000 Americans would die. Two million Vietnamese lives may have been lost, including those of many thousands of civilians, due to intensive bombing by the opponents. Also, a highly toxic chemical caused defoliation, the elimination of vegetation. The Vietnam War is estimated to have cost approximately $200 billion.

Vietnam veterans, approximately 2.7 million in all, did not receive a positive welcome from American civilians. Instead, they returned to widespread public opposition. Their moral opposition to the war made it difficult for many Americans to show support for these veterans.

A few years after the Vietnam War, veterans started a fund for construction of a memorial to those who had died; they raised nearly $9 million. A competition was held for the proper design, with the proviso that the memorial should not express any political view of the war.

In a funerary design course at Yale University, 21-year-old architecture student Maya Lin submitted a proposal for the design competition for the memorial. The popular conception of a war memorial recalled the heroic equestrian statues of Civil War generals, but in Lin's opinion, such representations were too simplified. Her design consisted of two walls of polished black granite built into the earth, set in the shape of a shallow V. Carved into the stone are the names of all the men and women killed in the war or still missing, in chronological order by the date of their death or disappearance. Rising up 10 feet high, the names begin and continue to that wall's end, resuming at the point of the opposite wall and ending at the place where the names began. Visitors can easily access the wall and touch the names, an integral part of Lin's design.

After the judges evaluated thousands of entries for this competition in the spring of 1981, Maya Lin won. The public's reaction to this particular design was sharply divided, reflecting their opposing feelings about this war. Thus, a bronze statute of three larger-than-life soldiers was placed near the entrance; a second statute, of three servicewomen, was added later to silence critical opposition. Maya Lin's wall was dedicated in 1982. The Vietnam memorial attracts over a million visitors annually.

24. What is the author's primary purpose of the passage?

   A.   To propose ideas about Maya Lin's submission from Yale University
   B.   To dissect the Vietnam Memorial's proposition
   C.   To discuss the design competition for the Vietnam Memorial and its effects on American society
   D.   To critique the judges reviewing Lin's sculptural proposal
   E.   To discuss the history of the Vietnam war and its opposition in America

25. Based on this passage, how do you know that the war did not end in appeasement?

   A.   The war memorial is inscribed with this fact.
   B.   Many were killed during the debacle of the war's final days.
   C.   The animosity between its opponent and supporters created tension.
   D.   The competition highlighted how the war ended.
   E.   The war veterans did not receive a hero's welcome.

26. What details in the narrative suggest that it was possible to fulfill the requirement that the monument express no political view of the war?

   A.   Those opposing it said it degraded the memory of those who had given their lives to this cause.
   B.   The United States government wanted a memorial that would honor the dead.
   C.   Carved into the stone are the names of all the men and women killed in the war or still missing, in chronological order by the date of their death or disappearance.
   D.   One wall points toward the Washington Monument and the other wall points toward the Lincoln Memorial, bringing the Vietnam Memorial into proper historical reference.
   E.   Many Americans were unwilling to confront the war's many painful issues.

Passage 2

Alfred Tennyson was born August 6, 1809, at Somersby, a little village in Lincolnshire, England. His father was the rector of the parish; his mother, whose maiden name was Elizabeth Fytche, and whose character he touched in his poem "Isabel," was the daughter of a clergyman; and one of his brothers, who later took the name of Charles Turner, was also a clergyman. The religious nature in the poet was a constant element in his poetry, secrets to an observation that was singularly keen, and a philosophic reflection that made Tennyson reveal in his poetry an apprehension of the laws of life, akin to what Darwin was disclosing in his contemporaneous career.

In his early "Ode to Memory," Tennyson has translated into verse the consciousness that woke in him in the secluded fields of his Lincolnshire birthplace. For companionship, he had the large circle of his home, for one of eight brothers and four sisters; and in that little society there was not only the miniature world of sport and study, but a very close companionship with the large world of imagination.

Frederick Tennyson was already at Cambridge when Charles and Alfred went to that university in 1828 and were matriculated at Trinity College. Alfred Tennyson acquired there, as so many other notable Englishmen, not only intellectual discipline, but that close companionship with picked men that is engendered by the half-monastic seclusion of the English university.

Tennyson regarded his post as Poet Laureate in the light of a high poetic and patriotic ardor. Starting with his first laureate poem "To the Queen," the record of Tennyson's career from this time forward is marked by the successive publication of his works.

27. According to the passage, what role does religion play in Tennyson's poetry?

    A. It plays a significant role and is a subtle reference in many profound poems.

    B. It is a constant evocation in Tennyson's poetry based on nature.

    C. It plays a significant role based on religious nature and observation.

    D. It does not play a crucial role, even though Tennyson grew up among clergymen as relatives.

    E. Religion was studied at Trinity College and weaved into verse at that time.

28. It can be inferred from the passage that the author regards Tennyson as:

    A. Living a monastic style life with a society of intellectuals

    B. Being influenced by his family's role in society and religion as well as the patriotic fervor of peers

    C. Being influenced by his family's religious nature

    D. Being influenced by his peers at university

    E. Producing patriotic poetry that overrides the poetry's religious nature

IF YOU FINISH BEFORE TIME IS CALLED, CHECK YOUR WORK ON THIS SECTION ONLY. DO NOT WORK ON ANY OTHER SECTION IN THE TEST.

Section 2: Quantitative

Numbers: All numbers used are real numbers.

Figures: Figures are intended to provide useful positional information, but they are not necessarily drawn to scale. Unless a note states that a figure is drawn to scale, you should not solve these problems by estimating sizes or by measurement. Use your knowledge of math to solve the problem. Angle measures can be assumed to be positive. Lines that appear straight can be assumed to be straight. Unless otherwise indicated, figures lie in a plane.

Directions (1–16): You are given two quantities, one in Column A and one in Column B. You are to compare the two quantities and choose:

A if the quantity in Column A is greater
B if the quantity in Column B is greater
C if the two quantities are equal
D if the relationship cannot be determined from the information given

x and y are integers greater than 0.

$$\left(\frac{x}{y}\right)^2 > \frac{x}{y} \text{ and } \left(\frac{y}{x}\right)^2 < \frac{y}{x}$$

	Column A	**Column B**
1.	x	y

$$2.07 = \frac{x}{100}$$

	Column A	**Column B**
2.	x	270

The number 4.2953 is to be rounded to the nearest thousandth.

	Column A	**Column B**
3.	The digit in the thousandths place of the rounded number	The digit in the hundredths place of the rounded number

$$3 < a < b < 4$$

Column A

4. $33\frac{1}{3}\%$ of a

Column B

25% of b

$$\frac{n}{5} = \frac{p}{3}$$

Column A

5. $\dfrac{n+1}{5}$

Column B

$\dfrac{p+1}{3}$

Five times the difference between a and b is 25.

Column A

6. Six times the difference between a and b

Column B

36

$$n \geq 0$$

Column A

7. $\sqrt{n^2}$

Column B

$\left(\sqrt{n}\right)^2$

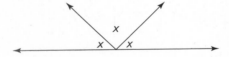

Column A

8. x

Column B

90

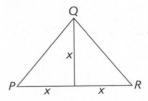

Column A

9. The area of $\triangle PQR$

Column B

Half the area of a circle of radius x

Column A	Column B
10. The length of a side of a square whose perimeter is 24	The length of the longer side of a rectangle whose perimeter is 24

A and B are points in the coordinate plane. A = $(-x, y)$ and B = $(x, -y)$.

Column A	Column B
11. The distance from the origin to point A	The distance from the origin to point B

Column A	Column B
12. $(x^3)^5(x^4)^5$	$(x^7)^5$

a and b are integers. $1 < a < b < 10$.

Column A	Column B
13. The number of multiples of a that are greater than 20 but less than 80	The number of multiples of b that are greater than 20 but less than 80

The mean of p, q, and r is 20.

Column A	Column B
14. The mean of p, q, r, and 40	30

Column A	Column B
15. The number of integers between 0 and 50 that are multiples of both 3 and 5	4

$$X = \{3, 4, 5\}$$
$$Y = \{4, 5, 6\}$$

Column A	Column B
16. The number of distinct products that can be formed by multiplying one element of X by one element of Y	The number of distinct sums that can be formed by adding one element of X and one element of Y

Directions (17–44): You are given five answer choices. Select the best choice.

---

17. Which of the following is equivalent to $b \cdot b \cdot b$?

   A. $3b$
   B. $b + 3$
   C. b^3
   D. $3b$
   E. $3b^3$

18. The length of a rectangle is four inches more than its width. If the perimeter is 20 inches, what is the area of the rectangle, in square inches?

   A.   20
   B.   96
   C.   64
   D.   21
   E.   32

19. A game booth at the carnival gave stuffed bears as prizes. The bears were identical except for color. Eight bears were brown, six were white, and four were black. A bear is selected at random for each winner. What is the probability that a winner will receive a black bear?

   A. $\dfrac{1}{4}$

   B. $\dfrac{2}{9}$

   C. $\dfrac{2}{7}$

   D. $\dfrac{1}{2}$

   E. $\dfrac{2}{3}$

20. $5.4 \times 10^{-3} =$

   A.   0.0054
   B.   0.054
   C.   0.54
   D.   540
   E.   5400

21. For all values of t for which it is defined, the expression $\dfrac{t^2 + 7t + 10}{t^2 - 4}$ can be simplified to

    A. $\dfrac{7t + 10}{-4}$

    B. $\dfrac{t + 5}{t - 2}$

    C. $\dfrac{t + 5}{t + 2}$

    D. $\dfrac{-5}{2}$

    E. $\dfrac{t + 3}{t}$

22. A right triangle has legs 15 cm and 20 cm long. Find the length of the hypotenuse.

    A. 25 cm
    B. 11.25 cm
    C. 33 cm
    D. 35 cm
    E. 18 cm

23. What is the area of the circle defined by the equation $(x - 4)^2 + (y + 9)^2 = 1$?

    A. π
    B. 2π
    C. 3π
    D. 4π
    E. 9π

24. How many solutions are there to the equation $4x^2 - 36 = 0$?

    A. 0
    B. 1
    C. 2
    D. 3
    E. 4

25. If $x|y - 3| < 0$, which of the following must be true?

    A. $x < 0$

    B. $y < 0$

    C. $y < 3$

    D. $y < -3$

    E. $xy < 3x$

26. In a sample of 2,000 computer chips, 0.2% were found to be defective. What is the ratio of defective to nondefective chips?

    A.   400 : 1,600

    B.   40 : 1,960

    C.   4 : 1,996

    D.   4 : 2,000

    E.   40 : 2,000

27. Which of the following is divisible by 9?

    A.   6,541

    B.   6,542

    C.   6,543

    D.   6,544

    E.   6,545

28. If a particle travels 2.4×10^7 cm/sec., how long will it take to travel 7.2×10^9 cm, in seconds?

    A. 3.0×10^{-2}

    B. 3.0×10^2

    C. 3.0×10^7

    D. 3.0×10^9

    E. 4.8×10^{63}

29. $\triangle XYZ$ is isosceles with $\overline{XY} \cong \overline{YZ}$. If $m\angle Y = 36°$, what is the measure of $\angle X$?

    A.   36°

    B.   54°

    C.   60°

    D.   72°

    E.   144°

30. If $5t = 3v - 9$, which of the following is an expression for v in terms of t?

    A. $v = 5t + 12$

    B. $v = \frac{5}{3}t + 9$

    C. $v = \frac{5t - 9}{3}$

    D. $v = \frac{5t + 9}{3}$

    E. $v = \frac{3t - 9}{5}$

31. If 70% of the senior class had part-time jobs and there are 480 seniors, how many seniors did not have jobs?

    A.   144
    B.   160
    C.   240
    D.   288
    E.   336

32. Find the area of the shaded region, if the rectangle is 24cm long and 8cm high.

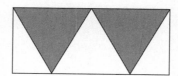

    A.   192
    B.   96
    C.   64
    D.   48
    E.   24

33. What is the length of the diagonal of a square whose area is 169 square inches?

    A. $169\sqrt{2}$

    B. $169\sqrt{3}$

    C. $13\sqrt{2}$

    D. $13\sqrt{3}$

    E. $\frac{43\sqrt{2}}{2}$

34. If n is divided by 5, the remainder is 1. What is the remainder when $7n$ is divided by 5?

    A.   0
    B.   1
    C.   2
    D.   3
    E.   4

35. Four children received a gift of candy, which they shared equally. The oldest child then gave half of his share to his youngest sister. Another brother kept three-fourths of his share and gave the rest to the youngest sister. What fraction of the candy did the youngest sister receive?

    A. $\dfrac{1}{16}$

    B. $\dfrac{3}{16}$

    C. $\dfrac{1}{2}$

    D. $\dfrac{5}{16}$

    E. $\dfrac{7}{16}$

36. A shoe store routinely sells shoes for 50% more than its cost. At the end of each season, it clears out the remaining stock by selling it at 10% below cost. If a pair of shoes regularly sold for $75, what would you pay for them at the end-of-season sale?

    A. $67.50
    B. $37.50
    C. $45.00
    D. $101.25
    E. $30.00

37. If the average (mean) of x and 10 is equal to the average (mean) of x, 3, 14, and 16, find the value of x.

    A.   10
    B.   11
    C.   12
    D.   13
    E.   14

38. The hollow cylinder shown has a radius of 3 and a height of 8.

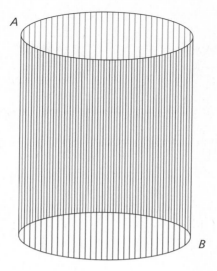

What is the straight-line distance from point A on the upper rim to point B on the lower rim?

A. $\sqrt{73}$
B. 11
C. 48π
D. 10
E. 20.5

Speed (mph)	Reaction Distance	Braking Distance
20	22	21
30	33	47
40	44	82
50	55	128
60	66	185

39. The previous table shows the distance required to stop a car at different speeds. The reaction distance is the distance the car travels in the time it takes the driver to realize that a stop is necessary and to apply the brakes. The braking distance is the additional distance the car will travel between the time the brake is applied and the time the car reaches a complete stop. Stopping distance is the total of reaction distance and braking distance. How much longer is the stopping distance for a car traveling at 60 mph than for one traveling at 40 mph?

A. 22
B. 55
C. 103
D. 125
E. 141

Building	Steps	Total Seconds
CN Tower, Toronto, Canada	1,776	687
Taipei 101, Taiwan	2,046	653
Sears Tower, Chicago, Illinois	2,109	822
Empire State Building, New York, New York	1,576	625
Hancock Tower, Chicago, Illinois	1,632	637
Boston Place, Boston, Massachusetts	697	272

40. Many tall buildings sponsor annual races in which participants run up the stairs to the building's top floor or observation deck. The table above lists the number of steps climbed and the first place finisher's time in seconds for some of these races. Based on the information in the table, which race's winner ran fastest?

    A. Sears Tower
    B. Taipei 101
    C. Empire State Building
    D. Hancock Tower
    E. Boston Place

41. In rectangle $QRST$, point P is the midpoint of side RS. If the area of quadrilateral $QRPT$ is 30, what is the area of rectangle $QRST$?

    A. 40
    B. 60
    C. 80
    D. 100
    E. 120

42. The difference between the measure of an interior angle of a regular hexagon and the measure of an external angles of a regular pentagon is

    A. 12°
    B. 36°
    C. 48°
    D. 60°
    E. 90°

43. If $290 \le 45 - 7w < 990$, all of the following could be true except

    A. $w > -135$
    B. $w < -35$
    C. $w = -35$
    D. $7w > -945$
    E. $-245 \le 7w$

44. Which of the following statements is true about the graph of $3x - 7y - 4 = 0$?

   I.   The x-intercept is $\left(\dfrac{4}{3}, 0\right)$

   II. The y-intercept is $\left(0, \dfrac{4}{7}\right)$

   III. The slope is 3

   A. I only
   B. II only
   C. III only
   D. I and II
   E. I and III

Directions (45–50): Give your answer as a number.

45. Let $x \otimes y$ be defined as the product of the integers from x to y. For example, $3 \otimes 7 = 3 \times 4 \times 5 \times 6 \times 7$. What is the value of $\dfrac{2 \otimes 5}{6 \otimes 8}$?

46. If a and b are integers with $5 < a < 8$ and $6 < b < 9$, what is the difference between the largest and smallest possible values of ab?

47. If the sum of two numbers is 12 and their difference is 2, what is their product?

48. A rectangular solid has two faces that are squares with sides of 5. The other four faces of the solid are rectangles that are 5 by 8. Find the volume of the solid.

49. The average grade of a class of N students is 80 and the average of a class of P students is 70. When the two classes are combined, the average is 76. What is $\dfrac{P}{N}$?

50. On Monday, Jennifer placed 1 cent in her piggy bank. On Tuesday, she put 2 cents in. On Wednesday, she added 4 cents, and on Friday, she added 8 cents. If Jennifer continues this saving pattern, how much will be in her piggy bank after 10 days?

IF YOU FINISH BEFORE TIME IS CALLED, CHECK YOUR WORK ON THIS SECTION ONLY. DO NOT WORK ON ANY OTHER SECTION IN THE TEST.

Scoring the Diagnostic Test

Answer Key

Section 1: Verbal

1. A	8. C	15. A	22. B
2. A	9. A	16. C	23. C
3. B	10. A	17. D	24. C
4. C	11. B	18. C	25. E
5. B	12. D	19. C	26. C
6. E	13. E	20. B	27. C
7. A	14. B	21. C	28. B

Section 2: Quantitative

1. A	14. B	27. C	40. B
2. B	15. B	28. B	41. A
3. B	16. A	29. D	42. C
4. A	17. C	30. D	43. E
5. B	18. D	31. A	44. A
6. B	19. B	32. B	45. $\frac{5}{14}$
7. C	20. A	33. C	46. 14
8. B	21. B	34. C	47. 35
9. B	22. A	35. E	48. 200
10. B	23. A	36. C	49. $\frac{2}{3}$
11. C	24. C	37. D	50. $10.23
12. C	25. A	38. D	
13. A	26. C	39. D	

Answer Explanations

Section 1: Verbal

1. **A** *To depose* means to remove a czar, so the right answer must fit this sequence of removal or ending a rule. In Choice A, to checkmate a chess player is to position the opponent's king so that it cannot escape, thus ending the chess game. In choices B, C, D, and E, the words do not share the same relationship. *(See Chapter VI.)*

2. **A** A tactless person lacks sensitivity just as, in Choice A, a penurious person lacks generosity. In Choice B, an imperturbable person is not easily excited but does not lack assurance. In Choice C, an aggrieved person may lack composure but primarily lacks joy. In Choice D, *craven* and *cowardice* are similar in meaning, not reflecting opposite traits as would occur in this type of analogy. In Choice E, a bellicose person is inclined to fight; he may or may not have fear. *(See Chapter VI.)*

3. **B** Liberality, in this case meaning generosity, is characteristic of altruism just as independence is characteristic of autonomy, making Choice B the correct answer. In choices A and C, the key words fit into the category "without" or "lack of," not "characteristic of." There is no relationship or logical bridge between belief and temerity in Choice D. In Choice E, privation or lack of comforts may, but does not have to, include suffering. *(See Chapter VI.)*

4. **C** Nostalgia is a positive feeling about the past just as anticipation is a positive feeling about the future, so Choice C is the best answer choice because it shows a similar relationship between the word pairs. In choices A and B, there is no clear relationship. In choices D and E, the words are antonyms. *(See Chapter VI.)*

5. **B** A sycophant lacks sincerity just as a deceiver lacks truth. In choices C, D, and E, the relationship is "with" not "without," which rules out these choices (a coward has fear, a friend has loyalty, and a hero has courage). In Choice A, a thief may or may not be clever. *(See Chapter VI.)*

6. **E** An ascetic denies pleasure just as a hermit shuns society, making Choice E the best answer. None of the other choices fits the category to be without or to lack; indeed, the relationship is quite the opposite (a politician seeks votes, and a scientist seeks the truth). *(See Chapter VI.)*

7. **A** To square differences means to make straight or settle small disputes or differences. In Choice A, to arbitrate (or settle) a conflict means exactly the same thing. In Choice B, to cast a fracture is the first step to fix it, but it's not close enough. In Choice C, to antagonize or to make an enemy or antagonist of amities or friendships does not fit. In Choice D, to compromise negotiations implies giving up something in the settlement. In Choice E, to forgive means to pardon or absolve, and the second word, *troubles,* does not fit as well as Choice A. *(See Chapter VI.)*

8. **C** In this analogy, *travail* is a noun meaning "tribulation" or "anguish." When you're creating a bridge sentence, you could say "A travail will cause one to cry." Choice C shares a similar relationship between words: "A malady will cause one to ail," making it the best choice. The other choices do not match the relationship. *(See Chapter VI.)*

9. **A** The key words in context in this sentence are *not many people understand* and *gradual,* which fit best with the words *arcane* and *incrementally* in Choice A. The other choices do not make sense in the sentence. *(See Chapter VII.)*

10. **A** Choice A is the best answer because *tendency* means "habit," which fits in the sentence. The second word, *parsimonious,* cinches it because it fits well with the key phrase that acts as a clue: "saves dollar by dollar," meaning not spending much or being parsimonious. *(See Chapter VII.)*

11. **B** In this sentence completion, Choice B is the best answer because *laborious* matches the key word in the sentence "hardest," and *obtuse* means "difficult to understand," which also makes sense in this sentence. The other answer choices do not make sense. *(See Chapter VII.)*

12. **D** Choice D is correct because the clue in the sentence is the word *exaggerated,* which makes the answer *hyberbolic* correct. The other answer choices are meant to be confusing since they all contain the prefix *hyper-. (See Chapter VII.)*

13. **E** Choice E is correct because the clue in the sentence is the phrase "king or queen is usually limited by a constitution and a legislature," which makes sense with the second word in the answer choice, *hierarchy.* The remaining answer choices are either *monarchy* or *oligarchy* and can be ruled out. When you check the first word, *anarchy,* it makes sense. *(See Chapter VII.)*

14. **B** The key word in the sentence is *iridescent,* making the first word in Choice B, *sparkling,* fit best. The next step is to check the second word, *flay,* which means, in this context, "to criticize." Before you check off Choice B as the correct answer, it's important to check the other answers. None fits as well as B. *(See Chapter VII.)*

15. **A** Choice A works best because the words *quixotic* and *romance* fit best in the context of this sentence. The clue in the sentence is "unlikely." The other answer choices do not work as well. *(See Chapter VII.)*

16. **C** In Choice C, the words *defenseless* and *strafing* fit best because *defenseless* means "without protection" and *strafing* means "to attack with airplanes with machine gunfire." In the sentence, the clues that make Choice C the best answer are "bombs blowing up" by machine gunfire. The other answer choices do not make sense. *(See Chapter VII.)*

17. **D** *Myopia* means "nearsightedness." The antonym is clearly answer Choice D: *farsightedness.* Here is a case where it pays to have a strong vocabulary. The other answer choices are not the opposite in meaning to the uppercase word. Choices B and E have the same suffix, but they don't fit as antonyms. *(See Chapter VII.)*

18. **C** *Exoteric* means "popular." The antonym of *popular* is not A *(wild),* B *(exotic),* D *(urgent),* or E *(perfidious).* The only clear antonym is Choice C, *esoteric,* meaning "understood by or meant only by the select few who have knowledge of it." *(See Chapter V.)*

19. **C** Allopathy is the method of treating disease by use of agents that produce effects different from the disease. Clearly, Choice C, *homeopathy,* works best. Choice A has the same suffix, but that's just to confuse you. And choices D and E are not the opposite in meaning. *(See Chapter V.)*

20. **B** This is a good example of the test writers using a secondary meaning of the word. Once you look at the answer choices, you see that, in this context, *list* is a verb, not a noun. *To list* means "to lean," so the antonym is Choice B. The other choices, D and E, are meant to confuse you, but they aren't the opposite in meaning. *(See Chapter V.)*

21. **C** *Pinchbeck* is not an everyday word, but you might know that it means "counterfeit." In that case, you'll know that Choice C is correct. If not, you can look at the answer choices and rule out the words that do not have antonyms. For example, choices A and E do not have opposite meanings. So, if you

don't know the meaning of *pinchbeck,* you're left only with choices B, C, and D (which happens to be a synonym), improving your odds. *(See Chapter V.)*

22. **B** The word *chutzpah* means "audacity," "gall," or "nerve," which is the antonym of Choice B, *diffidence,* which means "shyness" or "timidity." The other answer choices do not fit as antonyms. If you don't know what *chutzpah* means, you can look at the answer choices and ask yourself if you can rule out any ones that do not have antonyms. *(See Chapter V.)*

23. **C** *Recondite* means dealing with difficult or abstruse subject matter or something that is hard to understand. Choice C, *understandable,* is the opposite in meaning to this word. Choices A and D are closer to synonyms than antonyms. Choice B does not fit as an antonym, and it's meant to be confusing because it has the same suffix. And, clearly, Choice E doesn't work. *(See Chapter V.)*

24. **C** Choice C fits best as the primary purpose of the passage. Choice A is not correct because the passage is not about the proposal only. Choices B and E are too broad. Choice D is too specific. Thus, C is the best choice. *(See Chapter VIII.)*

25. **E** Choice E is the best answer. Choice A is too broad. Choice B is too specific and does not answer the question: "How do you know that the war did not end in appeasement?" Choices C and D do not make sense as answers. *(See Chapter VIII.)*

26. **C** Choice C is the best answer choice as the details in the narrative that suggest it was possible to fulfill the requirement that the monument express no political view of the war. Choice C is the only answer showing details on the monuments or specific names. *(See Chapter VIII.)*

27. **C** Based on the passage, religion plays a significant role in Tennyson's poetry from his upbringing and observation, making Choice C the correct answer. *(See Chapter VIII.)*

28. **B** Choice B is the correct answer because the passage is a biographical sketch of Tennyson and touches upon his religious influence, filial ties, and his university life as it relates to his work. The other answer choices are lacking. *(See Chapter VIII.)*

Section 2: Quantitative

1. **A** Since $\left(\dfrac{x}{y}\right)^2 > \dfrac{x}{y}$ and $\left(\dfrac{y}{x}\right)^2 < \dfrac{y}{x}$, $\dfrac{x}{y}$ must be greater than 1 and $\dfrac{y}{x}$ must be less than 1, so $x > y$. *(See Chapter X, Section D.)*

2. **B** Multiplying both sides by 100 gives $x = 207$. *(See Chapter X, Section E.)*

3. **B** The number 4.2953 rounded to the nearest thousandth is 4.295. The digit in the thousandths place is 5 and the digit in the hundreds place is 9. *(See Chapter X, Section F.)*

4. **A** If $3 < a < b < 4, 1 < 33\frac{1}{3}\%$ of $a < \frac{4}{3}$ and $\frac{3}{4} < 25\%$ of $b < 1. 25\%$ of $b < 1 < 33\frac{1}{3}\%$ of a. *(See Chapter X, Section G.)*

5. **B** $\dfrac{n}{5} = \dfrac{p}{3}$ $\quad 3n = 5p \quad n = \dfrac{5p}{3} \quad n+1 = \dfrac{5p}{3}+1 = \dfrac{5p+3}{3} \quad \dfrac{n+1}{5} = \dfrac{5p+3}{3 \cdot 5} = \dfrac{p + \frac{3}{5}}{3}$. *(See Chapter X, Section E.)*

6. **B** If 5 times the difference between a and b is 25, then the difference between a and b is 5, so 6 times the difference between a and b is 30. *(See Chapter XI, Section A.)*

7. **C** $\sqrt{n^2} = |n|$, which is just n, since $n \geq 0$ and $\left(\sqrt{n}\right)^2 = n$. *(See Chapter X, Section I.)*

8. **B** The three angles must total 180°, and since all three are equal, x must equal 60. *(See Chapter XII, Section B.)*

9. **B** The area of $\triangle PQR = \frac{1}{2}(2x)(x) = x^2$ and half the area of a circle of radius $x = \frac{1}{2}\pi \cdot x^2$. Since half of π is greater than one, $\frac{1}{2}\pi \cdot x^2 > x^2$. *(See Chapter XII, Sections B and F.)*

10. **B** The length of a side of the square can be determined to be $24 \div 4$ or 6, but the longer side of the rectangle will be greater than 6. In order to have a rectangle that is not a square and, thus, has a longer side, there must be a shorter side that is less than 6 and a longer side that is greater than 6. *(See Chapter XII, Section C.)*

11. **C** The distance from the origin to point $A = \sqrt{(-x-0)^2 + (y-0)^2} = \sqrt{x^2 + y^2}$. The distance from the origin to point $B = \sqrt{(x-0)^2 + (-y-0)^2} = \sqrt{x^2 + y^2}$. *(See Chapter XII, Section H.)*

12. **C** $(x^3)^5(x^4)^5 = x^{15}x^{20} = x^{35}$ and $(x^7)^5 = x^{35}$. *(See Chapter X, Section H.)*

13. **A** Since you're given little information about a and b, trying various possibilities won't be efficient. Instead, consider that the larger the number, the farther apart its multiples will fall, and so the fewer multiples will fall in a fixed range. For example, multiples of 9 between 20 and 80 include 27, 36, 45, 54, 63, and 72—a total of six—but multiples of 8 number seven: 24, 32, 40, 48, 56, 64, and 72. *(See Chapter X, Section C.)*

14. **B** If the mean of p, q, and r is 20, the sum of p, q, and r is 60; therefore the sum of p, q, r, and 40 is 100 and the mean of p, q, r, and 40 is $100 \div 4 = 25$. *(See Chapter XIII, Section A.)*

15. **B** Integers that are multiples of both 3 and 5 are multiples of 15, so they include 15, 30, and 45, a total of three. *(See Chapter X, Section C.)*

16. **A** Three elements in X and three elements in Y mean that there are nine products and nine sums, but they may not all be distinct. Products include 3×4, 3×5, 3×6, 4×4, 4×5, 4×6, 5×4, 5×5, and 5×6. Only 4×5 and 5×4 are duplicated; there are eight distinct products. Sums include $3 + 4$, $3 + 5$, $3 + 6$, $4 + 4$, $4 + 5$, $4 + 6$, $5 + 4$, $5 + 5$, $5 + 6$, giving only five distinct sums. *(See Chapter XIII, Section C.)*

17. **C** $b \cdot b \cdot b$ is the product obtained by using b as a factor three times, which would be written as b^3. *(See Chapter X, Section H.)*

18. **D** $L = 4 + W$ and $P = 2L + 2W = 2(4 + W) + 2W = 20$. Solving the equation $8 + 4W = 20$ gives $W = 3$ so $L = 7$ and the area is $L \cdot W = 21$ square inches. *(See Chapter XII, Section C.)*

19. **B** The probability that a winner will receive a black bear = the number of black bears divided by the total number of bears. $P(\text{black bear}) = \frac{4}{18} = \frac{2}{9}$. *(See Chapter XIII, Section C.)*

20. **A** Move the decimal point three places to the left. *(See Chapter X, Section F.)*

21. **B** $\dfrac{t^2 + 7t + 10}{t^2 - 4} = \dfrac{(t+5)(t+2)}{(t+2)(t-2)} = \dfrac{t+5}{t-2}$. *(See Chapter XI, Section D.)*

22. **A** Use the Pythagorean theorem: $c = \sqrt{a^2 + b^2} = \sqrt{15^2 + 20^2} = \sqrt{225 + 400} = \sqrt{625} = 25$. A quicker method is to recognize that these values are multiples of a Pythagorean triple. *(See Chapter XII, Section B.)*

23. **A** The equation describes a circle with center at $(4, -9)$ and a radius of 1. Only the radius is important to the question. Area is $\pi r^2 = \pi$. *(See Chapter XII, Sections F and H.)*

24. **C** $4x^2 - 36 = 0 \rightarrow 4x^2 = 36 \rightarrow x^2 = 9 \rightarrow x = \square 3$. *(See Chapter XI, Section D.)*

25. **A** The absolute value of any expression behaves as a positive, so the fact that $x|y - 3| < 0$ tells us that $x < 0$. We cannot make a determination about y. *(See Chapter XI, Section A.)*

26. **C** If 0.2% of 2,000 computer chips are defective, there are $0.002 \times 2,000 = 4$ defective chips, and 1,996 non-defective chips. *(See Chapter X, Sections E and G.)*

27. **C** Add the digits to determine divisibility quickly: $6 + 5 + 4 + 1 = 16$, $6 + 5 + 4 + 2 = 17$, $6 + 5 + 4 + 3 = 18$. Since 18 is divisible by 9, 6,543 is divisible by 9. *(See Chapter X, Section C.)*

28. **B** Distance divided by rate equals time, so $\dfrac{7.2 \times 10^9}{2.4 \times 10^7} = \dfrac{7.2}{2.4} \times \dfrac{10^9}{10^7} = 3 \times 10^2 = 300$ seconds. *(See Chapter X, Section F, and Chapter XIII, Section D.)*

29. **D** If $\triangle XYZ$ is isosceles with $\overline{XY} \cong \overline{YZ}$, $\angle Y$ is the vertex angle. If $m\angle Y = 36°$, then each of the congruent base angles measures $\dfrac{180 - 36}{2} = \dfrac{144}{2} = 72°$. *(See Chapter XII, Section B.)*

30. **D** $5t = 3v - 9 \Rightarrow 5t + 9 = 3v \Rightarrow \dfrac{5t + 9}{3} = v$. *(See Chapter XI, Section A.)*

31. **A** 70% of $480 = \dfrac{7}{10} \times 480 = 7 \times 48 = 336$ and $480 - 336 = 144$. Alternately, if 70% had jobs, 30% did not, so $\dfrac{3}{10} \times 480 = 3 \times 48 = 144$. *(See Chapter X, Section G.)*

32. **B** The area of the rectangle is $24 \times 8 = 192$ square centimeters, but each of the shaded triangles has a height of 8 and a base of half of 24. The combined area of the two triangles is $2 \times \dfrac{1}{2} \times \left(\dfrac{1}{2} \times 24\right) \times 8 = \left(\dfrac{1}{2} \times 24\right) \times 8$, which is 96cm², or half the area of the rectangle. *(See Chapter XII, Section E.)*

33. **C** If the area of the square is 169 square inches, each side is 13 inches, so the diagonal is $13\sqrt{2}$. *(See Chapter XII, Section D.)*

34. **C** N is one more than a multiple of five, a number of the form $5p + 1$, so multiplying N by 7 will produce a number of the form $35p + 7$. Dividing $35p + 7$ by 5 produces $\dfrac{35p + 7}{5} = 7p + 1$ with a remainder of 2. *(See Chapter X, Section C.)*

35. **E** If the four children shared the candy equally, each began with $\dfrac{1}{4}$ of the candy. The oldest brother gave $\dfrac{1}{2} \cdot \dfrac{1}{4} = \dfrac{1}{8}$ of the candy to the youngest sister. The other brother gave $\dfrac{1}{4} \cdot \dfrac{1}{4} = \dfrac{1}{16}$ of the candy to her. So the youngest sister had $\dfrac{1}{4} + \dfrac{1}{8} + \dfrac{1}{16} = \dfrac{4}{16} + \dfrac{2}{16} + \dfrac{1}{16} = \dfrac{7}{16}$ of the candy. *(See Chapter X, Section D.)*

36. **C** The regular price of $75 is 150% of cost, so cost is $75 \div 1.50 = \$50$. At the end of the season, it will sell for 90% of cost, or $0.90 \times 50 = \$45$. *(See Chapter X, Section G.)*

37. **D** The mean of x and 10 is equal to $\dfrac{x+10}{2}$ and the mean of x, 3, 14, and 16 is $\dfrac{x+3+14+16}{4} = \dfrac{x+33}{4}$. If $\dfrac{x+10}{2} = \dfrac{x+33}{4}$, then $\dfrac{2(x+10)}{4} = \dfrac{x+33}{4}$ and $2(x + 10) = x + 33$. Solving, $2x + 30 = x + 33 \rightarrow x = 13$. *(See Chapter XIII, Section A.)*

38. **D** A radius of 3 means a diameter of 6, and the diameter and height form the legs of a right triangle, whose hypotenuse, the straight line distance from A to B, can be found by the Pythagorean theorem. $c = \sqrt{a^2 + b^2} = \sqrt{6^2 + 8^2} = \sqrt{100} = 10$. *(See Chapter XII, Sections B and F.)*

39. **D** The stopping distance for a car traveling at 60 mph is $66 + 185 = 251$ feet. The stopping distance for a car traveling at 40 mph is $44 + 82 = 126$ feet. The difference is $251 - 126 = 125$ feet. *(See Chapter XIII, Section D.)*

40. **B** Actually calculating speeds would be time consuming. Using a rough estimation, most of the runners covered fewer than 3 steps per second, while the winner of the Taipei 101 climbed more than 3 steps per second. *(See Chapter XIII, Section D.)*

41. **A** Drawing the diagram will be helpful.

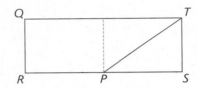

If a perpendicular were drawn to P, it would divide the rectangle in half, so the area of quadrilateral $QRPT$ is three-fourths of the area of the rectangle. *(See Chapter XII, Section C, and Chapter X, Section D.)*

42. **C** The measure of an interior angle of a regular hexagon is $\dfrac{180(6-2)}{6} = 120°$. The measure of an exterior angle of a regular pentagon is $\dfrac{360}{5} = 72°$. The difference is $120° - 72° = 48°$. *(See Chapter XII, Section D.)*

43. **E** $290 \le 45 - 7w < 990 \rightarrow 245 \le -7w < 945 \rightarrow -35 \ge w > -135$. *(See Chapter XI, Section A.)*

44. **A** When $y = 0$, $3x - 7(0) - 4 = 0 \Rightarrow 3x = 4 \Rightarrow x = \dfrac{4}{3}$, so I is true. When $x = 0$, however, $3(0) - 7y - 4 = 0 \Rightarrow -7y = 4 \Rightarrow y = -\dfrac{4}{7}$, so II is not true. Putting the equation in slope-intercept form, $-7y = -3x + 4 \Rightarrow y = \dfrac{3}{7}x - \dfrac{4}{7}$, shows that III is not true. *(See Chapter XII, Section H.)*

45. $\dfrac{5}{14}$ Applying the definition, $\dfrac{2 \otimes 5}{6 \otimes 8} = \dfrac{2 \cdot 3 \cdot 4 \cdot 5}{6 \cdot 7 \cdot 8_2} = \dfrac{5}{14}$. *(See Chapter XIII, Section B.)*

46. **14** a could be 6 or 7 and b could be 7 or 8, so the possible products are 42, 48, 49, and 56. The difference between the largest and the smallest is $56 - 42 = 14$. *(See Chapter XIII, Section C.)*

47. **35** If x and y represent the two numbers, $x + y = 12$ and $x - y = 2$. Adding the equations, $2x = 14$ and $x = 7$. $y = 12 - 7 = 5$. So the product $xy = 35$. *(See Chapter XI, Section B.)*

48. **200** The volume of a rectangular solid is length × width × height. Taking the square face as the base and 8 as the height, $V = 5 \times 5 \times 8 = 200$ cubic units. *(See Chapter XII, Section G.)*

49. $\frac{2}{3}$ If the average of N grades is 80, then the total of all the grades in that group is $80N$. The total of the grades in the class of P students is $70P$. When the classes are combined, $\frac{80N + 70P}{N + P} = 76$. While one equation is not sufficient to solve for N or P, it is enough to express the relationship between N and P. Cross-multiply and simplify, and work toward an equation with $\frac{P}{N}$ on one side. $80N + 70P = 76(N + P) \rightarrow 80N + 70P = 76N + 76P \rightarrow 4N = 6P$. Then $\frac{4N}{6} = \frac{6P}{6} \Rightarrow \frac{2N}{3} = P \Rightarrow \frac{2\cancel{N}}{3\cancel{N}} = \frac{P}{N}$. *(See Chapter XIII, Section A.)*

50. **$10.23** It's possible to calculate each day's addition to savings and then add, but it may be faster to look for a pattern in the cumulative sum. On day 1, she deposits 1¢, for a total of 1¢. On day 2, she deposits 2¢ for a total of 3¢. On day 3, she deposits 4¢ for a total of 7¢. Each day's total is 1 cent less than the next day's deposit. Calculate the deposit for the 11th day and subtract one to find the ten-day total. On the 11th day, she would deposit 2^{10} cents, or $10.24, so the ten-day total is $10.23. *(See Chapter XIII, Section F.)*

II. Two-Month Cram Plan

	Two-Month Cram Plan		
	Quantitative	**Verbal**	**Writing**
8 weeks before the test	**Study Time:** 2½ hours ❑ Take **Diagnostic Test** and review answer explanations. ❑ Based on your test results, identify difficult topics and their corresponding chapters. These chapters are your targeted chapters.		
	Study Time: 2 hours ❑ **Arithmetic:** Chapter X ❑ Read sections A, B, C, H, and I—one section per day. ❑ As you review, build a list of formulas and rules to memorize. ❑ Do practice questions 1–5.	**Study Time:** 1 hour ❑ **Antonyms:** Chapter V ❑ Read chapter. ❑ As you review, build a list of words that are new to you. ❑ Do practice questions 1–5. ❑ Practice more antonyms using word list.	**Study Time:** 1 hour ❑ **Analytical Writing:** Chapter IX ❑ Read chapter. ❑ Pay attention to the difference between the issue essay and the argument essay.
7 weeks before the test	**Study Time:** 2 hours ❑ **Arithmetic:** Chapter X ❑ Read sections D–G—one section per day. ❑ Add any new formulas to your list. ❑ Do practice questions 1–5. ❑ Review one of your target chapters. ❑ Do questions 6–10 in your target chapter.	**Study Time:** 1 hour ❑ **Analogies:** Chapter VI ❑ Read chapter. ❑ Practice building word relationships between two key words. ❑ As you review, build a list of words that are new to you and memorize. ❑ Do practice questions 1–5.	**Study Time:** 30 minutes ❑ **Analytical Writing:** Chapter IX ❑ Read chapter. ❑ Focus on the argument essay.
6 weeks before the test	**Study Time:** 2 hours ❑ **Algebra:** Chapter XI ❑ Read sections A–D—one section per day. ❑ Add any new formulas and rules to your list. ❑ Do practice questions 1–5. ❑ Review one of your target chapters. ❑ Do questions 6–10 in your target chapter.	**Study Time:** 1 hour ❑ **Sentence Completions:** Chapter VII ❑ Read chapter. ❑ As you review, build a list of words that are new to you. ❑ Do practice questions 1–5. ❑ Use word list to create your own sentence completions.	**Study Time:** 30 minutes ❑ **Analytical Writing:** Chapter IX ❑ Read chapter. ❑ Focus on the issue essay.

	Quantitative	Verbal	Writing
5 weeks before the test	**Study Time:** 2 hours ❏ **Geometry:** Chapter XII ❏ Read sections A–E—one section per day. ❏ Add any new formulas and rules to your list. ❏ Do practice questions 1–5.	**Study Time:** 1 hour ❏ **Reading Comprehension:** Chapter VIII ❏ Read chapter. ❏ As you review, build a list of words that are new to you. ❏ Do practice questions for Passage 1.	**Study Time:** 1½ hours ❏ **Analytical Writing:** Chapter IX ❏ Practice writing an issue essay.
4 weeks before the test	**Study Time:** 2 hours ❏ **Geometry:** Chapter XII ❏ Read sections F–H—one section per day. ❏ Add any new formulas and rules to your list. ❏ Do practice questions 1–5. ❏ Review one of your target chapters. ❏ Do practice questions 6–10 in your target chapter.	**Study Time:** 1½ hours ❏ **Antonyms:** Chapter V ❏ Read chapter. ❏ As you review, build a list of words that are new to you. ❏ Do practice questions 6–10. ❏ **Analogies:** Chapter VI ❏ Read chapter. ❏ As you review, build a list of words that are new to you. ❏ Do practice questions 6–10.	**Study Time:** 1½ hours ❏ **Analytical Writing:** Chapter IX ❏ Practice writing an argument essay.
3 weeks before the test	**Study Time:** 2 hours ❏ **Applications:** Chapter XIII ❏ Read sections A–C—one section per day. ❏ Add any new formulas and rules to your list. ❏ Do practice questions 1–5. ❏ Review one of your target chapters. ❏ Do practice questions 6–10 in your target chapter.	**Study Time:** 1½ hours ❏ **Sentence Completions:** Chapter VII ❏ Read chapter. ❏ As you review, build a list of words that are new to you. ❏ Do practice questions 6–10. ❏ **Reading Comprehension:** Chapter VIII ❏ Read chapter. ❏ Do practice questions for Passage 2. ❏ As you review, build a list of words that are new to you.	**Study Time:** 1 hour ❏ **Analytical Writing:** Chapter IX ❏ Analyze the argument essay to see how you could substantiate or back up your reasoning better with examples. ❏ Rewrite the essay based on what you discover.

	Quantitative	Verbal	Writing
2 weeks before the test	**Study Time:** 2½ hours ❏ Take **Practice Test** and review answer explanations. ❏ Based on your errors on the Practice Test, identify difficult topics and their corresponding chapters. These chapters are your targeted areas.		
	Study Time: 2 hours ❏ **Applications:** Chapter XIII ❏ Read sections D–F—one section per day. ❏ Add any new formulas and rules to your list. ❏ Do practice questions 1–5. ❏ Review one of your target chapters. ❏ Do practice questions 6–10 in your target chapter.	**Study Time:** 1 hour ❏ **Reading Comprehension:** Chapter VIII ❏ Read chapter. ❏ Do practice questions for Passage 2.	**Study Time:** 1 hour ❏ **Analytical Writing:** Chapter IX ❏ Analyze the issue essay to see how you could substantiate or back up your reasoning better with examples. ❏ Rewrite the essay based on what you discover.
7 days before the test	**Study Time:** 30 minutes ❏ **Arithmetic:** Chapter X ❏ Read sections C and G. ❏ Redo any problems you got wrong the first time.	**Study Time:** 1 hour ❏ **Antonyms:** Chapter V ❏ Read chapter. ❏ As you review, test yourself on your personal list of vocabulary words. ❏ Do practice questions 11–14.	**Study Time:** 1 hour ❏ **Analytical Writing:** Chapter IX ❏ Make sure you understand the difference between 6, 5, 4, 3, 2, and 1 scores on the essays. ❏ Review the topics of essay choices.
6 days before the test	**Study Time:** 30 minutes ❏ **Algebra:** Chapter XI ❏ Read Section B. ❏ Review your list of formulas. ❏ Rework any problems you got wrong the first time.	**Study Time:** 1 hour ❏ **Sentence Completions:** Chapter VII ❏ Read chapter. ❏ Do practice questions 11–13. ❏ As you review, test yourself on your personal list of vocabulary words.	**Study Time:** 30 minutes ❏ **Analytical Writing:** Chapter IX ❏ Write an argument essay and score yourself.
5 days before the test	**Study Time:** 30 minutes ❏ **Geometry:** Chapter XII ❏ Read sections B–C. ❏ Rework any problems you got wrong the first time.	**Study Time:** 1½ hours ❏ **Analogies:** Chapter VI ❏ Read chapter. ❏ Do practice questions 11–13. ❏ **Reading Comprehension:** Chapter VIII ❏ Read chapter. ❏ Do practice questions for Passage 3.	**Study Time:** 45 minutes ❏ **Analytical Writing:** Chapter IX ❏ Write an issue essay and score yourself.
4 days before the test	**Study Time:** 30 minutes. ❏ **Geometry:** Chapter XII ❏ Read section G. ❏ Rework any problems you got wrong the first time. ❏ Review your list of rules and formulas.	**Study Time:** 1 hour ❏ Reread your word list. ❏ **Reading Comprehension:** Chapter VIII ❏ Read chapter. ❏ Review any questions you answered incorrectly.	**Study Time:** 1 hour ❏ **Analytical Writing:** Chapter IX ❏ Read examples of score-6 essays.

	Quantitative	Verbal	Writing
3 days before the test	**Study Time:** 30 minutes ❑ **Applications:** Chapter XIII ❑ Read chapter. ❑ Rework any problems you got wrong the first time. ❑ Review your list of rules and formulas.	**Study Time:** 1 hour ❑ **Antonyms:** Chapter V ❑ Read chapter. ❑ Review any questions you answered incorrectly. ❑ **Sentence Completions:** Chapter VII ❑ Read chapter. ❑ Review any questions you answered incorrectly.	**Study Time:** 1 hour ❑ **Analytical Writing:** Chapter IX ❑ Read examples of score-6 essays.
2 days before the test	❑ **Applications:** Chapter XIII ❑ Read section D. ❑ Rework problems you got wrong the first time.	**Study Time:** 45 minutes ❑ **Analogies:** Chapter VI ❑ Read chapter. ❑ Review any questions you answered incorrectly.	**Study Time:** 30–45 minutes ❑ **Analytical Writing:** Chapter IX ❑ Pick the type of essay you need to work on most (either argument or issue), and write it with a timer.
1 day before the test	**Study Time:** 1 hour ❑ Review your target chapters. ❑ Review questions in your target chapters that you answered incorrectly on previous attempts and make sure you understand your errors. ❑ Review your rules and formulas one last time before bed.	**Study Time:** 1 hour ❑ Review your target chapters. ❑ Review your personal list of vocabulary words.	**Study Time:** 1 hour ❑ **Analytical Writing:** Chapter IX ❑ Read chapter. ❑ Rewrite your essay to a score-6 essay.

Morning of the test	**Reminders:**
	❑ Plan your day around your appointment.
	❑ Allow yourself enough time to reach the testing center with some time to spare, so that you have a chance to calm yourself before you're scheduled to begin testing.
	❑ Dress in layers so you can adjust if you find the testing room too hot or too cold.
	❑ Have a good meal before the test, but don't overeat.
	❑ Take the following items with you on test day:
	    ❑ Your admission ticket and photo ID
	    ❑ Several pens and #2 pencils
	    ❑ Scrap paper will be provided to you.
	    ❑ You may not bring anything else into the testing room.
	❑ Try to go outside for a few minutes and walk around before the test.
	❑ Most important: Stay calm and confident during the test. Take deep slow breaths if you feel at all nervous. You can do it!		

III. One-Month Cram Plan

	One-Month Cram Plan		
	Quantitative	**Critical Reading**	**Writing**
4 weeks before the test	**Study Time:** 2½ hours ❑ Take **Diagnostic Test** and review answer explanations. ❑ Based on your test results, identify difficult topics and their corresponding chapters. These chapters are your targeted chapters.		
	Study Time: 2 hours ❑ **Arithmetic:** Chapter X ❑ Read chapter. ❑ As you review, build a list of formulas and rules to memorize. ❑ Do practice questions 1–5.	**Study Time:** 1 hour ❑ **Antonyms:** Chapter V ❑ Read chapter. ❑ As you review, build a list of words that are new to you. ❑ Do practice questions 1–7.	**Study Time:** 1 hour ❑ **Analytical Writing:** Chapter IX ❑ Read chapter. ❑ Pay attention to the difference between the issue essay and the argument essay. ❑ Read essay topics.
3 weeks before the test	**Study Time:** 2 hours ❑ **Algebra:** Chapter XI ❑ Read chapter. ❑ Add any new formulas and rules to your list. ❑ Do practice questions 1–5.	**Study Time:** 1 hour ❑ **Analogies:** Chapter VI ❑ Read chapter. ❑ Practice building word relationships between two keywords. ❑ As you review, build a list of words that are new to you and memorize. ❑ Do practice questions 1–7	**Study Time:** 1 hour ❑ **Analytical Writing:** Chapter IX ❑ Practice writing an issue essay. ❑ Time yourself.
2 weeks before the test	**Study Time:** 2 hours ❑ **Geometry:** Chapter XII ❑ Read chapter. ❑ Add any new formulas and rules to your list. ❑ Do practice questions 1–5.	**Study Time:** 1 hour ❑ **Sentence Completions:** Chapter VII ❑ Read chapter. ❑ As you review, build a list of words that are new to you. ❑ Do practice questions 1–7.	**Study Time:** 1 hour ❑ **Analytical Writing:** Chapter IX ❑ Practice writing an argument essay. ❑ Time yourself.
7 days before the test	**Study Time:** 30 minutes ❑ **Applications:** Chapter XIII ❑ Read sections A–B. ❑ Add any new formulas and rules to your list. ❑ Do practice questions 1–5.	**Study Time:** 1 hour ❑ **Reading Comprehension:** Chapter VIII ❑ Read chapter. ❑ As you review, build a list of words that are new to you. ❑ Do practice questions for Passage 1.	**Study Time:** 30 minutes ❑ **Analytical Writing:** Chapter IX ❑ Write an argument essay and score yourself. ❑ Read through topics you will encounter on the GRE.

	Quantitative	Critical Reading	Writing
6 days before the test	**Study Time:** 1 hour ❏ **Applications:** Chapter XIII ❏ Read sections C–D. ❏ Add any new formulas and rules to your list. ❏ Do practice questions 1–5.	**Study Time:** 1 hour ❏ **Antonyms:** Chapter V ❏ Read chapter. ❏ As you review, build a list of words that are new to you. ❏ Do practice questions 8–14.	**Study Time:** 45 minutes ❏ **Analytical Writing:** Chapter IX ❏ Write an issue essay and score yourself.
5 days before the test	**Study Time:** 30 minutes ❏ **Applications:** Chapter XIII ❏ Read sections E–F. ❏ Add any new formulas and rules to your list. ❏ Do practice questions 1–5.	**Study Time:** 1 hour ❏ **Analogies:** Chapter VI ❏ Read chapter. ❏ As you review, build a list of words that are new to you. ❏ Do practice questions 8–13.	**Study Time:** 30 minutes ❏ **Analytical Writing:** Chapter IX ❏ Correct your essays, and add examples or rewrite awkward sentences.
4 days before the test	**Study Time:** 1 hour ❏ Review your target chapters. ❏ Rework questions you got wrong the first time. ❏ Study your list of rules and formulas.	**Study Time:** 1 hour ❏ **Sentence Completions:** Chapter VII ❏ Read chapter. ❏ As you review, build a list of words that are new to you. ❏ Do practice questions 8–13.	**Study Time:** 1 hour ❏ **Analytical Writing:** Chapter IX ❏ Read more score-6 examples.
3 days before the test	**Study Time:** 30 minutes ❏ Review your target chapters. ❏ Do practice questions 6–10. ❏ Study your list of rules and formulas.	**Study Time:** 1 hour ❏ **Reading Comprehension:** Chapter VIII ❏ Read chapter. ❏ Do practice questions for passages 2 and 3.	**Study Time:** 45 minutes ❏ **Analytical Writing:** Chapter IX ❏ Pick the type of essay you need to work on most (either argument or issue), and write it with a timer.
2 days before the test	**Study Time:** 2½ hours ❏ Take **Practice Test** and review answer explanations. ❏ Score your essay and rewrite if needed to make a 6 score. ❏ Correct your mistakes and make sure you understand your errors.		
1 day before the test	**Study Time:** 30 minutes ❏ Review your target chapters. ❏ Review your rules and formulas one last time before bed.	**Study Time:** 45 minutes ❏ Review your target chapters. ❏ Review your vocabulary list.	**Study Time:** 30 minutes ❏ **Analytical Writing:** Chapter IX ❏ Reread the score-6 essay samples. ❏ Revise your essays to improve score.

	Quantitative	Critical Reading	Writing

Morning of the test	**Reminders:**
	❏ Plan your day around your appointment.
	❏ Allow yourself enough time to reach the testing center with some time to spare, so that you have a chance to calm yourself before you're scheduled to begin testing.
	❏ Dress in layers so you can adjust if you find the testing room too hot or too cold.
	❏ Have a good meal before the test, but don't overeat.
	❏ Take the following items with you on test day:
	    ❏ Your admission ticket and photo ID
	    ❏ Several pens and #2 pencils
	    ❏ Scrap paper will be provided to you.
	    ❏ You may not bring anything else into the testing room.
	❏ Try to go outside for a few minutes and walk around before the test.
	❏ Most important: Stay calm and confident during the test. Take deep slow breaths if you feel at all nervous. You can do it!		

IV. One-Week Cram Plan

	Quantitative	Critical Reading	Writing
7 days before the test	**Study Time:** 2½ hours ❏ Take **Diagnostic Test** and review answer explanations. ❏ Based on your test results, identify difficult topics and their corresponding chapters. These chapters are your targeted chapters. Note: In one week, you can't study every detail of every chapter. Expect to give most material a quick reading and focus your efforts on your target chapters.		
6 days before the test	**Study Time:** 1 hour ❏ **Arithmetic:** Chapter X ❏ Read chapter. ❏ Build a list of rules and formulas as you read. ❏ Focus on your targets or on sections C and E. ❏ Do practice questions 1–10.	**Study Time:** 1 hour ❏ **Antonyms:** Chapter V ❏ Read chapter. ❏ As you review, build a list of words that are new to you. ❏ Do practice questions 1–14.	**Study Time:** 45 minutes ❏ **Analytical Writing:** Chapter IX ❏ Practice writing an issue essay. ❏ Time yourself.
5 days before the test	**Study Time:** 1 hour ❏ **Algebra:** Chapter XI ❏ Read chapter. ❏ Add rules and formulas to your list. ❏ Focus on your targets or on Section A. ❏ Do practice questions 1–10.	**Study Time:** 1 hour ❏ **Analogies:** Chapter VI ❏ Read chapter. ❏ Practice building word relationships between two key words. ❏ As you review, build a list of words that are new to you and memorize. ❏ Do practice questions 1–13.	**Study Time:** 30 minutes ❏ **Analytical Writing:** Chapter IX ❏ Practice writing an argument essay. ❏ Time yourself.
4 days before the test	**Study Time:** 1 hour ❏ **Geometry:** Chapter XII ❏ Read chapter. ❏ Add rules and formulas to your list. ❏ Focus on your targets or on sections C and G. ❏ Do practice questions 1–10.	**Study Time:** 1 hour ❏ **Sentence Completions:** Chapter VII ❏ Read chapter. ❏ As you review, build a list of words that are new to you. ❏ Do practice questions 1–13.	**Study Time:** 1 hour ❏ **Analytical Writing:** Chapter IX ❏ Analyze the issue essay to see how you could substantiate or back up your reasoning better with examples. ❏ Rewrite the essay based on what you discover.

	Quantitative	**Critical Reading**	**Writing**
3 days before the test	**Study Time:** 1 hour ❑ **Applications:** Chapter XIII ❑ Read chapter. ❑ Add rules and formulas to your list. ❑ Focus on your targets or on Section A. ❑ Do practice questions 1–10.	**Study Time:** 1 hour ❑ **Reading Comprehension:** Chapter VIII ❑ Read chapter. ❑ As you review, build a list of words that are new to you. ❑ Do practice questions for passages 1, 2, and 3.	**Study Time:** 1 hour ❑ **Analytical Writing:** Chapter IX ❑ Analyze the argument essay to see how you could substantiate or back up your reasoning better with examples. ❑ Rewrite the essay based on what you discover.
2 days before the test	**Study Time:** 2½ hours ❑ Take **Practice Test** and review answer explanations. ❑ Based on your errors on the Practice Test, identify difficult topics and their corresponding chapters. These chapters are your targeted areas.		
1 day before the test	**Study Time:** 1 hour ❑ Review your target chapters. ❑ Rework questions you got wrong the first time. ❑ Review your rules and formulas one last time before bed.	**Study Time:** 1 hour ❑ Review your target chapters. ❑ Rework questions you got wrong the first time. ❑ Review your word lists one last time before bed.	**Study Time:** 1½ hours ❑ **Analytical Writing:** Chapter IX ❑ Write an issue essay and an argument essay. ❑ Time yourself. ❑ Score your essays.

Morning of the test	**Reminders:**
	❑ Plan your day around your appointment.
	❑ Allow yourself enough time to reach the testing center with some time to spare, so that you have a chance to calm yourself before you're scheduled to begin testing.
	❑ Dress in layers so you can adjust if you find the testing room too hot or too cold.
	❑ Have a good meal before the test, but don't overeat.
	❑ Take the following items with you on test day:
	    ❑ Your admission ticket and photo ID
	    ❑ Several pens and #2 pencils
	    ❑ Scrap paper will be provided to you.
	    ❑ You may not bring anything else into the testing room.
	❑ Try to go outside for a few minutes and walk around before the test.
	❑ Most important: Stay calm and confident during the test. Take deep slow breaths if you feel at all nervous. You can do it!		

V. Antonyms

An *antonym* is a word opposite in meaning to another word. Antonym questions on the GRE test your vocabulary skills and your ability to choose a word's opposite. Each antonym question begins with a capitalized keyword and gives you five answer choices (all of which are the same part of speech as the keyword). Your job is to find the correct answer or the word that is the most nearly opposite in meaning to the keyword. Study your vocabulary!

If you think you know the word, use the association method and eliminate answer choices that are not the opposite in meaning.

To answer an antonym question, follow these steps:

1. **Read the keyword.**

2. **Simply define the keyword to avoid traps.** You need to define the keyword in order to find its opposite. When you first define the word, it helps you choose a word that is nearly or most opposite in meaning. The test creators expect that you'll read the keyword and jump right to the answer choices, so they set up trick words that *appear* to be opposites of the keyword but aren't. For example, the keyword *color* is tricky because it can be a noun or a verb. If you do not define it first, you may jump right to an answer choice and choose *outline* instead of the correct answer, "report accurately."

3. **Predict an antonym *before* you look at the answers.** Not only is it important to define the keyword, but it's a good strategy to predict the answer choice *before* you look at the answer choices. This will help you avoid traps or choose the first answer choice that feels right. This also enables you to find the correct antonym quickly and easily, because you've already come up with your own simple antonym. Then you just have to find it in the answer choices. The GRE also tests your vocabulary skills by making simple words challenging by using secondary meanings. That's why it's best to define the keyword and then predict your own antonym before you read the answer choices. You'll see quite clearly after you read the answer choices whether you need to redefine the word with a secondary meaning.

4. **Use process of elimination as you read the choices.** By using process of elimination, you narrow your answer choices, getting closer to the correct answer.

The antonym section of the GRE truly tests your vocabulary. You may not know the keyword or you may only be vaguely familiar with it. If so, don't give up. Read the answer choices and make an opposite for each of the answer choices. If you can't come up with an opposite, eliminate that answer choice. Compare your opposites to the keyword and try to see if this allows you to remember the keyword. Never eliminate words you don't know. Work with the words you know, make an educated guess after eliminating some answer choices, and move on.

If you *think* you know the word, use the association method and eliminate answer choices that are *not* the opposite in meaning. Clarify the idea of the association of the word: negative or positive sounding. It may help you find the right answer choice if you don't know the meaning of the keyword.

Here are a few examples to walk you through these strategies. Basically you're being tested on your vocabulary. You will find words you know, words you vaguely know, and words you don't know at all.

EXAMPLE:

ARREST

    A.   stop
    B.   seize
    C.   engage
    D.   progress
    E.   congratulate

First define *arrest* — to stop the movement or progress of. Then come up with your own antonym before reading the answer choices: to go or to move on. When you read the answer choices with a simple antonym in your head, you'll see that Choice A (stop), Choice B (seize), and Choice E (congratulate) need to be eliminated. Then you go back and examine closely Choice C (engage) and Choice D (progress). Choice C is a synonym for *arrest,* meaning "to catch and hold." When you have what you're looking for ahead of time, you'll choose the right answer, Choice D. It's the word most nearly the opposite of the keyword.

EXAMPLE:

ULTERIOR

    A.   exterior
    B.   outdoor
    C.   obvious
    D.   penultimate
    E.   premier

This is an example of a word that most people do not know: *ulterior.* So immediately read the answer choices and find the opposites. The antonym of *exterior* (Choice A) is *interior,* which is not the keyword, so you can eliminate Choice A. The opposite of *outdoor* (Choice B) is *indoor,* which is not the keyword, so you can eliminate Choice B. The opposite of *obvious* (Choice C) is *hidden;* don't rule out that one just yet, in case ulterior fits. Move on to Choice D, penultimate, which means "second to last"; it doesn't have an antonym, so you can eliminate it. *Premier* (Choice E) has two different meanings as an adjective: first in rank or earliest/oldest; this may work so you can now choose between C and E. You have a 50 percent chance of choosing the correct answer without even knowing what *ulterior* means. If you choose C, you're correct. *Ulterior* means hidden or intentionally concealed and the word most nearly opposite in meaning among the answer choices is *obvious.*

Practice

Directions: Each word in capital letters is followed by five words or phrases. The correct choice is the word or phrase whose meaning is most nearly *opposite* the meaning of the word in capitals. You may be required to distinguish fine shades of meaning. Look at all choices before marking your answer.

1. PERFIDY

    A. fidelity
    B. diffidence
    C. confusion
    D. affidavit
    E. infidel

2. DIFFIDENT

    A. incredible
    B. assuming
    C. credulous
    D. bona fide
    E. perfidious

3. CREDULOUS

    A. reflective
    B. flexible
    C. skeptical
    D. impertinent
    E. untenable

4. REFRACTORY

    A. fragmentary
    B. malleable
    C. fractious
    D. tortuous
    E. invincible

5. LANGUID

    A. insectivorous
    B. vivacious
    C. perishable
    D. languor
    E. carnivorous

6. APOGEE

   A. geography
   B. perigee
   C. georgic
   D. apathy
   E. pathos

7. BLASÉ

   A. bored
   B. tired
   C. happy
   D. excited
   E. bourgeois

8. INCONTROVERTIBLE

   A. disputable
   B. inverted
   C. obverse
   D. revert
   E. converted

9. OBVERSE

   A. perverse
   B. reverse
   C. diverse
   D. inverse
   E. verse

10. SATURNINE

   A. procrustean
   B. protean
   C. pyrrhic
   D. mercurial
   E. siren

11. ARBITRARY

   A. despotic
   B. individual
   C. legitimate
   D. organizational
   E. random

12. FRACTIOUS

    A. peaceable
    B. smooth
    C. divisible
    D. fragile
    E. refractory

13. FORTE

    A. weak
    B. timid
    C. piano
    D. runner
    E. ride

14. CAMEO

    A. performance
    B. intaglio
    C. canto
    D. libretto
    E. opera

Answers

1. **A** *Perfidy* means "faithlessness" or "treachery." Choice A is the correct answer, because *fidelity* means "loyalty," which is the opposite of *perfidy*. Choice B, *diffidence,* means "shyness." Choice C, *confusion,* means "bafflement." Choice D, *affidavit,* means "a written declaration upon oath." Choice E, *infidel,* means "a person who does not accept a particular faith."

2. **B** *Diffident* means "lacking confidence," "timid," or "shy." Choice B is the correct answer, because *assuming* means "bold or confident," which is the opposite of *diffident*. Choice A, *incredible,* means "fantastic." Choice C, *credulous,* means "gullible." Choice D, *bona fide,* means "made in good faith or without deceit." Choice E, *perfidious,* means "deceitful."

3. **C** *Credulous* means "gullible." Choice C is the correct answer, because *skeptical* means "questioning" or "not readily believing," which is the opposite of *credulous*. Choice A, *reflective,* means "contemplative." Choice B, *flexible,* means "easily bent." Choice D, *impertinent,* means "sassy or rude," "uncivil." Choice E, *untenable,* means "indefensible or incapable of being defended, as in an argument."

4. **B** *Refractory* means "stubbornly disobedient." Choice B is the correct answer, because *malleable* means "adaptable or capable of being extended or shaped," which is the opposite of *refractory*. Choice A, *fragmentary,* means "not whole, broken, disconnected." Choice C, *fractious,* means "unruly or readily angered." Choice D, *tortuous,* means "full of twists, turns, bends; twisting, winding, crooked." Choice E, *invincible,* means "incapable of being conquered or defeated."

5. **B** *Languid* means "lacking in vitality." Choice B is the correct answer, because *vivacious* means "lively, animated," which is the opposite of *languid.* Choice A, *insectivorous,* means "adapted to feeding on insects." Choice C, *perishable,* means it will not last. Choice D, *languor,* means "lacking in energy; sluggishness." Choice E, *carnivorous,* means "meat-eating."

6. **B** *Apogee* means "climax" or "highest point." Choice B is the correct answer, because *perigee* means "the point in orbit of a planet nearest to Earth," which is the opposite of *apogee.* Choice A, *geography,* means "study of earth." Choice C, *georgic,* means "agricultural in nature." Choice D, *apathy,* means "hatred." Choice E, *pathos,* means "pity."

7. **D** *Blasé* means "indifferent" or "unimpressed." Choice D is the correct answer, because *excited* means "feeling passion," which is the opposite of *blasé.* Choice A, *bored,* means "not challenged or happy." Choice B, *tired,* means "lacking in energy." Choice C, *happy,* means "content." Choice E, *bourgeois,* means "a member of the middle class."

8. **A** *Incontrovertible* means "something that is not disputable." Choice A is the correct answer, because *disputable* means "capable of being disputed, questionable," which is the opposite of *incontrovertible.* Choice B, *inverted,* means "something turned inside out or upside down," reversing the position. Choice C, *obverse,* means "the front or principal side of anything, usually a coin or flag; a counterpart." Choice D, *revert,* means "to return to a former habit; go back." Choice E, *conversion,* means "change."

9. **B** *Obverse* means "side turned toward the observer" or "the front of a coin." Choice B is the correct answer, because *reverse* means "the opposite direction of going forward," which is the opposite of *obverse.* Choice A, *perverse,* means "contrary, or wayward or cantankerous." Choice C, *diverse,* means "varied." Choice D, *inverse,* means "reversed in position." Choice E, *verse,* means "a line in writing or a stanza."

10. **D** *Saturnine* means "heavy," "dull," "sullen," or "morose." Choice D is the correct answer, because *mercurial* means "quickly changing," which is the closest opposite of *saturnine.* Choice A, *procrustean,* means "tending to produce conformity by violent means." Choice B, *protean,* means "extremely variable; changeable in shape or form." Choice C, *pyrrhic,* means "consisting of two unaccented syllables." Choice E, *siren,* means "one of several sea nymphs or a luring, beautiful woman."

11. **C** *Arbitrary* means "despotic" or "tyrannical." Choice C is the correct answer, because *legitimate* means "genuine, real," which is the opposite of *arbitrary.* Choice A, *despotic,* means "autocratic, tyrannical." Choice B, *individual,* means "single, one." Choice D, *organizational,* means "being neat and tidy." Choice E, *random,* means "not systematic."

12. **A** *Fractious* means "unruly or irritable." Choice A is the correct answer, because *peaceable* means "not argumentative or hostile," which is the opposite of *fractious.* Choice B, *smooth,* means "not rough." Choice C, *divisible,* means "capable of being divided, without a remainder." Choice D, *fragile,* means "easily breakable." Choice E, *refractory,* means "stubbornly disobedient, hard to manage."

13. **C** *Forte* means "loud." Choice C is the correct answer, because *piano* (as an adjective) means "soft," which is the opposite of *forte.* Choice A, *weak,* means "not strong." Choice B, *timid,* means "shy." Choice D, *raucous,* means "loud and unruly." Choice E, *ruly,* means "not unruly."

14. **B** Cameo means "a medallion cut in relief with the carved figure standing out." Choice B is the correct answer, because *intaglio* means "incised carving," as opposed to a relief, which is the opposite of *cameo.* Choice A, *performance,* means "an action on stage or public acting." Choice C, *canto,* means "one of the main or larger divisions of a long poem." Choice D, *libretto,* means "the text or words of an opera." Choice E, *opera,* means "an extended dramatic composition."

VI. Analogies

There are about ten analogies in the verbal section of the GRE. For each question, you will be given a pair of two capitalized words separated by a colon. Your job is to determine the relationship or connection between the two keywords at the top and then choose the pair of words with the same relationship as the answer choices. The meaning of the two words is less important than how the words are related.

Here are typical categories of relationships between keywords:

- **Degree:** For example, HAPPINESS : ELATION :: ANGER : WRATH. In this example, *elation* is an extreme form of happiness, and *wrath* is an extreme form of anger.
- **Type:** For example, SONNET : POEM :: WHEAT : GRAIN. In this example, a *sonnet* is a type of poem, and *wheat* is a type of grain.
- **Characteristic:** BELLICOSE : HOSTILITY :: CYNICAL : SKEPTICISM. In this example, someone who is bellicose has hostility (he is quick to anger and to fight) and someone who is cynical is skeptical and doubting. Being bellicose is characteristic of being hostile, and being cynical is characteristic of a skeptic.
- **Use:** LADLE : SCOOP :: PEN : WRITE. In this example, a ladle is used to scoop, and a pen is used to write.
- **Lack:** PERFECTION : DEFECT :: APATHY : PASSION. In this example, something or someone that is perfect lacks any defects, and someone who is apathetic lacks passion.
- **Secondary meaning:** LIST : BOAT :: FLY : PLANE. The GRE will sometimes try to trick you by using a less common meaning of a word. In this example, *list* is being used as a verb (to lean) rather than as a noun. A boat lists, and a plane flies.

Here are the steps to solving analogies:

1. **Construct your own sentence with the two keywords.** Make a bridge sentence—a sentence you create that uses the two keywords and attempts to establish the relationship between the two words. Keep it simple! In your sentence, make a specific declarative statement. (**Hint:** Avoid ambiguous words like *may, could, might,* and so on.) By making your own sentence before you read the answer choices, you establish how the two words fit together and thus finding the correct answer will be easier.
2. **Place each set of answers into your bridge sentence, using the process of elimination until you find the answer choice that has the same relationship between the words.**

For each analogy, part of speech is consistent. For example, the first word of the keywords will be the same part of speech as the first words in the answer choices. The same holds true for the second word in each analogy: it will match the part of speech for all second words in the answer choices.

EXAMPLE:

RESERVOIR : WATER::

Before you go on to read the answer choices, construct a bridge sentence using the two keywords. An example would be: "A reservoir holds water." The sentence is simple and makes it evident that the first word is something that holds or contains the second word. Now look at the choices:

A. FLOWERS : GARDEN
B. CHATTEL : FARM
C. PITHY : SHORT
D. PRISTINE : WILDERNESS
E. URN : ASHES

Plug them into the sentence you created and see if they make sense:

- **Choice A:** "A flower holds a garden." This does not make sense, so you can rule it out.
- **Choice B:** "A chattel holds a farm." This does not make sense.
- **Choice C:** "Pity holds short." This does not make sense.
- **Choice D:** "Pristine holds wilderness." This does not make sense.
- **Choice E:** "An urn holds ashes." This makes sense.

The answer is E, because it is the only set of words that fits into the bridge sentence as the keywords do.

Sometimes you know the meaning of only one word in the pair of two capitalized words. In this case, try to make a bridge sentence from the answer choices and eliminate any answer choices that don't fit into a bridge sentence.

Remember: The stronger your vocabulary, the better. Practicing analogies is critical to improving your score on this portion of the GRE.

Practice

Directions: Each of the following questions gives you a related pair of words or phrases. Select the lettered pair that best expresses a relationship similar to that in the original pair of words.

1. UTOPIAN : DEFECT ::
   A. continuous : endeavor
   B. accidental : injury
   C. voluntary : motive
   D. immediate : delay
   E. urgent : aid

2. ARRAY : FRIPPERY ::

   A. crochet : creation
   B. empower : increase
   C. replenish : reaffirmation
   D. furbish : absorption
   E. soak : saturation

3. INIMICAL : DELETERIOUS ::

   A. ascetic : austere
   B. unrestricted : confined
   C. repugnant : palatable
   D. dimorphous : diabolical
   E. demure : unduly

4. FORTHRIGHT : DECEIVER ::

   A. brilliant : genius
   B. deleterious : onlooker
   C. beloved : outcast
   D. magnanimous : companion
   E. empathy : master

5. FLAUNT : OSTENTATIOUS ::

   A. gall : pompous
   B. cower : servile
   C. sputter : fastidious
   D. flinch : indolent
   E. waver : arrogant

6. HUBS : WHEELS ::

   A. radii : circles
   B. eyes : hurricanes
   C. knots : ties
   D. tops : spins
   E. vertices : triangles

7. WINCE : AGONY ::

   A. growl : green
   B. learn : aplomb
   C. tremble : fright
   D. grovel : embarrassment
   E. glower : disquiet

8. HEIRLOOM : SAFE ::

   A.   water : droplet
   B.   confection : dish
   C.   corn : granary
   D.   fish : brine
   E.   jewelry : gemstone

9. RAVINE : CHASM ::

   A.   breeze : hurricane
   B.   blizzard : avalanche
   C.   valley : earthquake
   D.   puddle : downpour
   E.   rock : waterfall

10. TALK : DRAWL ::

   A.   discover : find
   B.   fly : tour
   C.   listen : disagree
   D.   walk : amble
   E.   jump : marvel

11. WEAVE : FABRIC ::

   A.   write : narrative
   B.   call : messenger
   C.   droop : trees
   D.   destroy : barricade
   E.   reduce : statue

12. MAGICIAN : FOOLS ::

   A.   complainer : annoys
   B.   comedian : amuses
   C.   potentate : obeys
   D.   swimmer : strides
   E.   welder : rivets

Answers

1. **D** Something that is utopian lacks defect, and something that is immediate lacks delay. If you try to apply this bridge sentence with the incorrect answers, it doesn't work. In Choice C, you could try to say, "Something voluntary lacks motive," but it doesn't work.

2. **E** The secondary definition of *array* is a verb meaning "to dress in finery or adorn," and the noun *frippery* is an extreme degree of this concept. To soak something until it is saturated is an extreme. Choices A and B are the only other choices that have a relationship, but they don't share the same relationship as the keywords.

3. **A** *Deleterious* and *inimical* are synonyms. You're looking for an answer choice with synonyms. In the correct choice, *ascetic* is a synonym of *austere*.

4. **C** A deceiver is not forthright, so you're looking here for a similar relationship. In the correct choice, an outcast is not beloved. This is an example of working backward with the key words. Order matters—you have to be consistent when you apply the bridge sentence to the answer choices.

5. **B** The bridge sentence can be: An ostentatious person flaunts. Thus, a servile person cowers. Choice A is close, because a pompous person can have gall, but it's not as clear as Choice B. The remaining answer choices don't make sense.

6. **B** A *hub* is the center of a wheel. Similarly, the eye is the center of a hurricane. The rest of the answer choices don't share the same relationship.

7. **C** A person winces when in pain or agony and trembles when in fright. The other answer choices may be characteristics of an attribute, but they aren't a matter of degree.

8. **C** An heirloom is stored in a safe and corn is stored in a granary.

9. **A** A ravine is minute compared to a chasm, and a breeze is tiny compared to a hurricane. Both the keywords and the correct answers show words that are related by degree. The first choice is a smaller version, or degree, of the second word.

10. **D** To talk slowly is to drawl and to walk slowly is to amble. This is a clear example of a matter of degree.

11. **A** You weave to create a fabric and you write to create a story or a narrative. This is an example of purpose of use of an action.

12. **B** A magician deludes or fools an audience and a comedian amuses an audience. The other answer choices may be characteristic of a type of person, but the action is not the primary one.

VII. Sentence Completion

There are nine sentence completion questions in the verbal section of the GRE. This portion of the test measures your ability to logically complete the meaning of a sentence by choosing the words that best fit in the sentence. You're tested on your vocabulary, context skills, and language usage.

Read through the sentence and fill in the blanks with words that you think make the sentence complete and logical, before reading the answer choices. Then read through the answers and choose the words that most closely match *your* words. This technique isn't foolproof, but it can quickly help you narrow down the correct answer.

The correct answer must fit the sentence, not just in proper usage but grammatically. For example, if it's clear that the blank word is an adjective, the answer will not be a noun. The tense must also be consistent—if the sentence is in the present tense, the correct answer will not be in the past tense, even if the word appears to fit with the rest of the sentence.

With sentences that contain two blanks, make sure that both answer choices fit grammatically and logically into the sentence. Cross off answer choices if one of the two words doesn't fit. If one word fits perfectly, but the other doesn't make sense, move on.

Don't rush. Read all answer choices even if you think you've found the best answer at the beginning. Sometimes the differences between the answer choices are subtle.

Look for transitional words that link the sentence. These words will highlight which direction the sentence is going. Words such as *hence, so, as a result, thus, therefore, likewise, in addition,* and so on indicate that the sentence is continuing in the same direction, so the best answer is a word that supports or enforces the idea of the sentence. Transitional words such as *yet, however, but, although,* and so on are clues that the sentence is changing direction and the appropriate answer choice will enforce the new direction, tone, or idea.

You can narrow down the correct answer by determining if the missing word or words has a negative or positive connotation, and then looking for answers that are either negative or positive. If it's obvious that the missing word is a positive word, look for the answer choices that are positive and cross off the negative choices. This process of elimination is helpful if you don't know the meaning of some of the answer choices.

After you've selected the best possible answer, plug the word or words into the sentence and do a final read through and make sure the sentence makes sense in content, grammar and syntax.

Practice

Directions: Each blank in the following sentences indicates that something has been omitted. Considering the lettered words beneath the sentence, choose the word or set of words that best fits the whole sentence.

1. The complex merger was credited to the business woman's _____.

   A. acumen
   B. approval
   C. poise
   D. supposition
   E. crux

2. People often misinterpreted his _____ sense of humor and allowed their feelings to be hurt.

   A. arbitrary
   B. axiomatic
   C. eclectic
   D. fallible
   E. mordant

3. Many chief officers have been _____ after a(n) _____ of the corporation due to accusations of fraudulent activity.

   A. impugned . . . investigation
   B. promoted . . . objection
   C. debated . . . remonstrance
   D. spurned . . . promotion
   E. subjected . . . poll

4. She was _____ about her current financial profits in the stock market, so she felt she could be more _____ than usual during the holidays.

   A. sanguine . . . munificent
   B. unruffled . . . zany
   C. unwieldy . . . residual
   D. salutary . . . nettlesome
   E. excruciated . . . oblivious

5. The remote, _____ moors in Bronte's gothic novel *Wuthering Heights* are the ideal backdrop to the _____ love story.

    A. lugubrious . . . tumultuous
    B. acquiescent . . . passionate
    C. mellifluous . . . mundane
    D. foreboding . . . insouciant
    E. dreary . . . parsimonious

6. The blight of locusts nearly _____ the _____ corn crop.

    A. ameliorated . . . person's
    B. extolled . . . equestrian's
    C. decimated . . . farmer's
    D. acquitted . . . agriculturalist's
    E. consigned . . . tender's

7. The king resolutely refused to _____ the throne to his _____, thinking them to be too dimwitted to handle the demands of the high position.

    A. appropriate . . . archetypes
    B. abnegate . . . subordinates
    C. acquit . . . complexities
    D. exalt . . . servants
    E. sublimate . . . progenitors

8. She diligently studied quantum physics with the intention of joining the _____ of elite scientists who would confer on important issues in this field of study.

    A. posse
    B. coterie
    C. chasm
    D. zenith
    E. acclivity

9. The chef delighted the food critic's _____ expectations with a(n) _____ chocolate tart.

    A. gustatory . . . ambrosial
    B. delicious . . . acrid
    C. severe . . . abysmal
    D. palatable . . . expected
    E. paramount . . . relevant

10. She considered her boyfriend's _____ stance on only seeing action movies one of his many irritating _____.

    A. unequivocal . . . foibles
    B. unrelenting . . . rectitudes
    C. obdurate . . . vicissitudes
    D. blasé . . . talents
    E. typical . . . outcomes

11. The friends decided to delay their annual trip to Las Vegas due to their _____ situation.

    A. solvent
    B. impecunious
    C. fragile
    D. dangerous
    E. involuntary

12. The student's simple _____ at noon consisted of an apple and a piece of bread, which left him _____ by dinnertime.

    A. repast . . . ravenous
    B. meal . . . ingratiated
    C. banquet . . . carnivorous
    D. craving . . . empty
    E. feast . . . peckish

13. Many restrictions on the use of water will end as soon as our reservoirs are _____ after a _____ time of conservation.

    A. replenished . . . protracted
    B. refreshed . . . lengthy
    C. restored . . . short
    D. depleted . . . long
    E. replaced . . . serious

14. The _____ judge listened to the arguments of both attorneys before _____ her decision.

    A. liberal . . . making
    B. judicious . . . rendering
    C. civil . . . ceding
    D. prejudiced . . . supplying
    E. magisterial . . . yielding

15. We moved into first place but our glory was _____, because the next day we experienced _____ in both games of a doubleheader.

    A.   episodic . . . win
    B.   temporary . . . tragedy
    C.   ephemeral . . . defeat
    D.   impermanent . . . loss
    E.   everlasting . . . disappointment

16. Construction workers safely _____ the road before the explosive _____.

    A.   vindicated . . . dismantled
    B.   opened . . . blasted
    C.   cleared . . . detonated
    D.   extricated . . . fulminated
    E.   emancipated . . . discharged

Answers

1. **A** The best choice is A, because *acumen* means "keenness" and "shrewdness," and in order to successfully accomplish a complex task, the business woman would need these traits. Be on the lookout for keywords that can help you answer the question correctly. The keyword in this question is *complex.* Knowing that the business woman's task was complex helps you narrow down what type of skills she needed in order to perform her job well.

2. **D** The best choice is D, because *mordant* means "bitingly sarcastic," which is the type of remark most likely to hurt people's feelings.

3. **A** You don't need to know that *impugned* means to be attacked as questionable or false to know that A is the correct answer because the second word, *investigation,* makes sense. When the rest of the answer choices are plugged in, the sentence no longer makes sense. In Choice D, *spurned* may fit in the first blank, but *promotion* doesn't work in the second—a corporation is not promoted, an individual is.

4. **A** The best choice is A, because *sanguine* means "content" and *munificent* means "very generous." Someone who is feeling content about her finances will feel better able to be more generous during the holidays.

5. **A** The best choice is A, because *lugubrious* means "gloomy" or "dreary," and *tumultuous* fits within the context using both words in the blanks. You don't need to know the story of *Wuthering Heights* to know that Choice A is correct. Although the word *passionate* fits in the second blank, moors are not "acquiescent." Also, the love story could be mundane but moors are not mellifluous (which means sweetly flowing or sweet sounding). It helps if you know that gothic novels are characterized by a bleak setting and mysterious or violent events.

6. **C** *Decimated* means to be destroyed or wiped out, and, obviously, a farmer (not an equestrian) grows corn.

7. **B** The best choice is B, because *abnegate* means "to give up as a right or claim" and *subordinates* are inferior persons. The king may be able to appropriate a throne, but it doesn't make sense that he would hand over the throne to an archetype, which is not a real person but refers to a model or prototype.

8. **B** The best choice is B, because a *coterie* is an exclusive group of people. The word *elite* in the sentence reaffirms that the group of scientists is exclusive. A posse is a group as well but not necessarily an elite or exclusive group of people. Choices C, D, and E do not fit at all.

9. **A** The best choice is A, because both *gustatory* and *ambrosial* are positive words, and clearly something positive, not negative, would delight the critic. *Gustatory* relates to the sense of taste and *ambrosial* means "pleasing to taste and smell."

10. **A** The best choice is A, because *unequivocal* means "unyielding" or "unforgiving" and a *foible* is a small fault or weakness in a person's character (something a girlfriend might find irritating).

11. **B** The best choice is B, because *impecunious* means "penniless" and a trip to Las Vegas would require money.

12. **A** The best choice is A, because *repast* means "meal" and such a small meal would cause someone to be ravenous, or really hungry, by dinner. Although *peckish* would fit in the second blank, because it means to be a little hungry, the first word is incorrect—an apple and a piece of bread can hardly be called a "feast."

13. **A** The best choice is A, because *protracted* means "drawn out or extended," and a water supply would be *replenished* after a period of conservation.

14. **B** The best choice is B, because *judicious* means wise and fair. A good judge is fair and listens equally to the arguments of both attorneys, and the word *render* means to deliver something formally or officially, to hand down. The judge is rendering her decision for the courtroom. Although the answers in Choice D would work, it makes less sense—a prejudiced judge has already made up her mind and would not truly listen to the arguments presented by both sides.

15. **C** The best choice is C, because something that is ephemeral is fleeting or short lived. The transitional word *because* clues you in to the fact that the sentence is shifting, that a change is occurring—you can glean that the glory is going to change so something negative is most likely going to happen. The team was defeated, ending their brief stay in first place.

16. **C** The best choice is C, because, where explosives are involved, construction workers would be most likely to clear the road, and *detonated* is a word used to refer to the setting off of explosives. If you used the tactic of filling in your own words before reading the answers, your sentence might look something like this: "Construction workers safely blocked off the road before the explosive went off." By looking through the answer choices, you can see that the words *cleared* and *detonated* are the best matches with "blocked off" and "went off."

VIII. Reading Comprehension

The reading comprehension portion of the GRE is designed to test your ability to recall and sometimes infer (or read between the lines) to find facts and analyze concepts from a dense and often uninteresting reading passage. Even though it can be tedious, here's the good news: everything you need to know to answer the questions is contained in the passage! You don't need any outside knowledge of the subject in order to do well on this section of the GRE.

Being able to read and understand information is obviously a big part of graduate school regardless of your course of study. This section will test your ability to comprehend and make sense of information on topics that may or may not be familiar to you or of interest to you.

Reading comprehension topics tend to come from the social sciences, physical sciences, and arts and humanities. The passages are purposefully tedious and not very succinct. The questions will test your ability to draw inferences and evaluate the meaning of the passage and to be able to refer back to the passage and search for specific information. You'll encounter two to four passages, each of which will be followed by two to four questions, with one question on the screen at a time. The passage stays in view on the screen until you've answered all related questions for that passage so that you can refer to it as you work through the questions.

Here are some helpful hints to tackle reading comprehension:

- Read the passage quickly without getting bogged down in details. Notice the tone of the writing and the overall theme or general idea. Can you glean the author's main point, or hypothesis?
- Read the first question, and then reread the passage carefully, jotting down key points from each paragraph.
- Read each question and answer carefully and thoroughly. An answer choice or two may jump out at you as being obviously incorrect. Use the process of elimination to find the correct answer. Be wary of answer choices that may be true statements based on the passage, but are not accurate answers to the question that's being asked.

In this chapter, you'll find sample reading passages to help improve your reading comprehension score.

Practice

Directions: Questions follow each of the passages. Using only the stated or implied information in each passage, answer the questions.

Passage 1

The planet's largest terrestrial ecosystem is an environment that completely encircles the Earth's northern pole. Called the Taiga Forest in the northern region (closest to the Arctic) and the Boreal Forest in the southern region, this immense area covers 4.6 million square miles and includes much of Russia, Canada, and parts of Norway, Sweden, Finland, and the United Sates. Conifer forests dominate this region. The paucity of nutrients in the soil keeps the types of trees rather limited; there are only about 30 types of trees in the Boreal and Taiga forests, in contrast with the highly diversified tropical rainforests, which can have hundreds of different species of trees in small areas. The unique, challenging environment leads to a somewhat homogenous forest.

The soil content of this region is ideal for conifer trees that are well suited for this harsh environment. These efficient gymnosperms are highly adapted to conserving nutrients, an important characteristic in a land where the soil is highly acidic, thin, often frozen for much of the year, and lacking in nutrients. Conifers need fewer nutrients than other trees do, because they shed their needles every three or four years or more and, thus, are less dependent on nutrients for annual needle growth.

Water conservation is another adaptive technique employed by coniferous trees. Because they can't access water from the soil for much of the year, retaining the water they do have is crucial for survival. Conifer needles are encased in a protective, waxy coat that retards evaporation, and the *stomata* (the pores on the needles' surface) are depressed rather than flush with the surface, so less moisture is lost due to wind and evaporation, a process called transpiration.

1. An appropriate title for this passage could be:

   A. Conifers Thrive and Dominate in the Boreal and Taiga Forests
   B. Life in the Boreal Forest
   C. Harsh Conditions in the Northern Regions of the Planet Result in Limited Flora and Fauna
   D. Conifers Require Limited Amounts of Water and Nutrients for Growth
   E. Lack of Nutrients in Forests

2. What adaptive techniques are particular to conifer trees in the region discussed above?

   A. A waxy coating on the needles protect against moisture loss requiring less water.
   B. Conifers shed their needles annually.
   C. These trees have stomata that don't store nutrients.
   D. Conifers require more than average rainwater and nutrients.
   E. None of the above.

Passage 2

The fungal kingdom is enormous and has a unique and vital ecological niche. Mushrooms are the fruiting bodies of fungi, and some form beneficial relationships with living plants. Others degrade, colonize, and sometimes kill their hosts. Fungi, along with bacteria, fulfill the role in nature of breaking down and recycling material by reducing complex organic compounds into simple building blocks, thus enabling plants to reuse them. Fungi are divided into three categories based on their relationship to their substrate.

Parasitic fungi are mushrooms that feed on living organisms. A comparatively small amount of fungi fall into this category, including the *Cordyceps, Asterophora,* and *Sparassis crispa* species. Although these mushrooms are pernicious and can do great damage to their hosts, they are now recognized for their ability to create new habitats for other organisms. Some mushrooms are parasitic only under certain conditions and saprophytic under others; honey mushrooms are one example.

Saprophytic fungi subsist on dead or decaying matter such as wood, soil, grass, dung, and debris. By utilizing their mycelial network to weave between the cell walls of plants and secrete enzymes and acids, they are able to transform the large molecular complexes into simpler ones. After the matter has been decomposed, the result is a return of carbon, hydrogen, nitrogen, and minerals back into the ecosystem. Most saprophytes are woodland species such as Shiitakes and Oysters. Primary decomposers are the first to begin the decomposition process; secondary decomposers arrive after previous fungi have partially broken down the substrate to a condition in which they can thrive. The common cultivated button mushroom is an example of a secondary saprophytic mushroom.

Mycorrhiza is the term to describe the symbiotic associations between fungi and the rootlets of trees and plants. Ecologists recognize that the health of a forest is directly related to the presence, abundance, and variety of mycorrhizal associations. These rootlets provide the fungus with organic compounds and moisture while the fungus assists the roots in the absorption of inorganic nitrogen and other minerals, and essential elements including phosphorus, copper, and zinc. This process is believed to aid in the resistance of certain diseases. Improved plant growth and reproductive fitness are other ways that plants and trees benefit from this relationship.

3. What is the primary point of the article?

   A. There is a variety of mushrooms that play different ecological roles.
   B. Fungii are a critical part of the ecosystem.
   C. Mushrooms are healthy to eat because they contain enzymes and they can contribute carbon, hydrogen, and nitrogen minerals.
   D. *Mycorrhiza* is the term to describe the symbiotic relationship between fungi and the rootlets of trees and plants.
   E. Organic compounds and moisture assist the roots of all fungi.

4. What is the result after saprophytic matter has been decomposed?

   A. Hydrogen, carbon, nitrogen, and minerals return to the ecosystem.
   B. Mushrooms secrete enzymes and acids.
   C. Nutrient-dense soil is created.
   D. Matter such as wood, grass and soil is regenerated.
   E. Simple molecular complexes are transformed into more complex ones.

Passage 3

A seminal piece of music widely regarded as a masterpiece of the 20th century had an inauspicious debut. Igor Stravinsky's ballet score *Le Scare du Printemps,* or *Rite of Spring,* premiered in 1913 at Paris's Theatre des Champs-Élysées to a woefully unprepared audience. Both the music and the performance of the dancers, choreographed by Vaslav Nijinksy, were a radical departure from what the audience had come to expect and they responded by laughing, hissing, cat calling, and causing a near riot. Stravinsky's story of a pagan sacrificial ritual was accompanied by ferociously dissonant, avant-garde music, unusual dance costumes, and strange choreography. It was an abrupt, decisive break from the harmonious, melodious past and a brazen introduction to the modern era. The audience had a visceral reaction from the moment of the bassoon's opening notes, the instrument pushed jarringly to its highest register. The string section playing a single dissonant chord 23 times in succession in a loud, pulsating manner, and the large percussion section pounded out primitive rhythms.

5. Which of the following is *not* true:

    A. Igor Stravinsky intended to shock his audience.

    B. The audience responded negatively to the piece.

    C. The audience quickly appreciated the dissonant music.

    D. The score was a cacophony of sound.

    E. The score was a cacophony of rhythm.

6. The main point of this paragraph can be summed up as:

    A. *Rite of Spring* was a good representation of a typical ballet score of that era.

    B. Stravinsky was a rebel.

    C. The audience of 1913 France was not prepared for this avant-garde style of music.

    D. Classical ballet music is normally accompanied by melodious music.

    E. Classical ballet music is normally accompanied by rhythmic music within a mathematical framework.

Answers

1. **A** Given the options, Choice A would be the most appropriate title for this reading passage. Although some of the other options may be true statements based on the information presented, Choice A is the best, because the passage is primarily about how conifers adapt and thrive in this environment.

2. **A** Conifer needles have a waxy coating that protects against moisture loss, so these trees can live in an environment without a lot of rain water. The other answers are not true—conifers shed their needles every three or four years, not annually; the stomata does store nutrients; and conifers require *less* than average water and nutrients, not more.

3. **B** Although all the answer choices are true, Choice B is the correct answer because the *main* point of this passage is that fungii play a critical role in the ecosystem.

4. **A** After the matter has been decomposed by the saprophytic mushrooms, hydrogen, carbon, nitrogen, and minerals are returned to the ecosystem. This is clearly stated in the passage.

5. **C** The audience did not quickly learn to appreciate the dissonant music.

6. **C** It is clear from the passage that the audience at the premiere of the *Rite of Spring* was not accustomed to this type of music and choreography.

IX. Analytical Writing

The analytical writing section of the GRE, introduced in October 2002, tests your critical thinking skills and analytical writing. It assesses your ability to express and substantiate complicated ideas, analyze an argument, and write a clear and cogent essay. It does not assess specific content knowledge, but rather it tests your ability to think on the spot, form a thesis, and substantiate that thesis with evidence.

The analytical writing section consists of two separately timed analytical writing tasks:

- **A 45-minute "Present Your Perspective on an Issue" task:** You'll be given a choice between two Issue topics, each of which states an opinion on an issue of broad interest. You can discuss the issue from any perspective(s) you choose, as long as you provide relevant reasons and specific examples to clarify and substantiate your views.

- **A 30-minute "Analyze an Argument" task:** Unlike the Issue essay, the Argument essay does not give you a choice of topics. It requires you to critique a given argument by discussing how well reasoned you find it. You have to consider the logic of the argument rather than agree or disagree with the position it presents.

The two tasks are complementary in that one requires you to construct your own argument by taking a stance and giving evidence to support your views on the issue, whereas the other requires you to critique someone else's argument by assessing its claims and evaluating the evidence given. This requires critical thinking and persuasive writing skills that university faculty value as important for success in graduate school.

Before you take the GRE, you need to spend at least three weeks preparing for the analytical writing section. Review the list of possible essay topics, how the analytical writing section is scored, test-taking strategies, and scored sample essay responses and reader commentary.

In the analytical writing section, the topics relate to a broad range of subjects from humanities to fine arts to the social and/or physical sciences. *Remember:* No topic requires specific content knowledge. Topics only test analytical writing and critical thinking rather than a particular subject matter. Practice writing and organizing an essay with specific examples, as well as analyzing a position's reasoning and evidence.

Analytical Writing Topics

The GRE analytical writing topics are published on the GRE Web site. Go to www.gre.org/pracmats.html, scroll down to the "Test Preparation Materials" section, and under "General Test," you'll see an item that says, "View the entire pool of Issue topics and Argument topics," with links to both types of topics.

There are too many topics for us to list them all here, but in the following sections, we provide a sampling of some of the topics you may see on the GRE. *Remember:* Be sure to go online to the complete list of topics and study them in advance of taking the GRE. You can even print all the topics to make the studying easier.

Issue Topics

For the Issue essay, you'll be given the following instructions:

> Present your perspective on the issue below, using relevant reasons and/or examples to support your views.

Here are some of the general topics or ideas you might find:

- Politics should not be about pursuing ideals, but instead its aims should be to find a common thread among people and reach a reasonable argument.
- Technology enables one to access information immediately; however, it steals humans of the ability to contemplate deeply since we feel unable to compete with computers.
- Artistic innovations are more valuable than scientific inventions in modern-day civilization.
- Contemporary technology in today's society gives us fractious information at rapid speed, and society can lose perspective in this fast-moving, fragmented world.
- The intellect—such as analytical reasoning and cognitive ability—deserves more attention today.
- One can be a healthier and happier companion to others after experiencing important time on one's own.
- Productivity is effective and teamwork thrives when people work together toward a common goal.
- The past does not help when one is looking for guidance in our new and complex world.
- Society values artists more than critics because artists create something worthy of praise. (*Note:* A *critic* is one who evaluates works of art, such as novels, films, music, paintings, and so on.)
- Only experts, not generalists, can provide a valuable critique.

Argument Topics

For the Argument essay, you'll be given the following instructions:

> Discuss how well reasoned you find this argument.

Here are some of the topics you might find:

- The following appeared in a letter from the owner of the Shadeland Station apartment complex to its manager:

  "One month ago, all the sinks on the first ten floors of Shadeland Station were changed to restrict the water flow to half of its original force. Although actual readings of water usage before and after the adjustment are not yet available, this modification will obviously result in a considerable savings for Shadeland Corporation, because the corporation pays for the water. Except for a few complaints about low water pressure in the bathrooms and kitchens, no problems with sinks have been reported since the change. Clearly, restricting water flow throughout all the 30 floors of Shadeland Station will increase our profits further."

- The following recommendation was presented by the human resources department to the trustees of the Best Jeans Company:

  "In the last two quarters of this fiscal year, under the leadership of our president, J. Y. Kearney, our profits have fallen considerably. Thus, we should ask for his resignation in return for a munificent severance package. In Jeff's place, we should appoint Catherine Mack. Catherine is currently president of Starlight Hot Jewelry, a company whose profits have increased considerably over the past several years. Although we will have to pay twice the salary for this replacement, it will be well worth it because we can expect our profits to increase significantly."

The Scoring of the Analytical Writing Section

Each essay response is scored on a 6-point scale with holistic scoring, which means that each response is judged as a whole: readers don't separate the response into sections and award a certain number of points for a particular component (such as organization, grammar, and so on), but they do assign scores based on the quality of the response taking into account its characteristics overall. Organization (or the lack thereof) will be part of the readers' general impression of the response and will, therefore, contribute to the score.

GRE readers are college and university faculty experienced in teaching courses with an emphasis on writing and critical thinking skills. All GRE readers have undergone careful training, passed qualifying tests, and demonstrated that they are able to maintain scoring accurately.

Responses are randomly distributed to two readers who independently score responses. The test takers do not know the readers. Each reader does not know the other reader's scores, and the scoring procedure requires that each response either receive scores that are identical scores from the two readers or receive scores that differ by only one point. Any other score combination requires a third GRE reader to score the response. The primary emphasis in scoring the analytical writing section is on critical thinking and analytical writing skills.

Following is a breakdown of the various score ranges.

5.5 to 6: Superb Essay

- Supports an opinion on the issue with insightful examples and organization or a fine critique of the argument.
- Generally well written and organized with strong vocabulary, logical reasoning, and clarity of style.
- Mechanics of writing are solid with proper grammar and spelling.

4.5 to 5: Solid Essay

- Supports an opinion on the issue with solid examples or a strong critique of the argument.
- Generally well written and organized with varied vocabulary, logical reasoning, and clarity of style.
- Mechanics of writing are good with only minor flaws in grammar and spelling.

3.5 to 4: Good Essay

- Supports an opinion on the issue with good examples.
- Generally well written and organized with logical reasoning and a clear style.
- Mechanics are okay.

2.5 to 3: Fair Essay

- Partially supports an opinion on the issue with insightful examples and organization or a fine critique of the argument.
- Generally disorganized with an unclear style and lacking organization.
- Poor mechanics of writing or awkward grammatical structure and weak spelling.

1.5 to 2: Poor Essay

- Barely supports an opinion on the issue with few or no examples and weak organization or a poor argument.
- Generally poorly written and lacking in organization and clarity.
- Many grammar and spelling mistakes.

0.5 to 1: Deficient Essay

- Fails to support an opinion on the issue with examples and lacks any organization or logic of the argument.

0: No Score Essay

- Irrelevant or missing topic or argument.
- Copies or plagiarizes writing.
- Undecipherable language or written in another language.

Test-Taking Strategies for the Analytical Writing Section

It is very important to budget your time wisely. Within the 45-minute time limit for the Issue essay, you need to give yourself enough time to select one of the two topics, think about the issue you've chosen, outline or plan a response, and then compose an essay. Within the 30-minute time limit for the Argument essay, you need to allow enough time to analyze the argument, organize a critique, and compose your response.

Here are specific strategies to help you write a cohesive essay within the time allotted:

1. **Brainstorm.** Take five minutes to think about as many ideas as you can to support your position. On a separate piece of paper, list your ideas, definitions, theories, reasons, and examples that support and refute your point. Then read over your notes and choose the best three to five ideas as a foundation for your essay.

2. **Outline.** Now that you have your ideas, organize them in a logical sequence. *Remember:* Good organization is key. Think about how a GRE reader will grade it and make sure you include essential examples that support your thesis.

3. **Draft or write.** Use the standard format: introduction, supporting paragraphs, and conclusion. It is important that your composition is focused and well substantiated. Write the introduction and conclusion first, and then draft the body paragraphs.

4. **Proofread and edit.** Leave five minutes to reread for errors of spelling, grammar, and organization and make sure you have clear transitions.

Edit and proofread at the end of each timed task to check for obvious errors. Although an occasional spelling or grammatical error will not significantly affect your score (GRE readers who grade your writing understand the time constraints of this section and will consider your response a "first draft"), obvious and persistent errors will weaken the overall effectiveness of your writing and lower your score.

Following the analytical writing section, you'll have the opportunity to take a 10-minute break. There is a one-minute break between the other test sections. You might want to get up, stretch, and replenish any materials such as scratch paper during each scheduled break.

In the following sections, I provide more specific strategies for each type of essay.

The Issue Essay

Because the Issue essay is meant to assess writing skills and not a specific knowledge on one subject area, it is best to prepare for it by practicing writing responses and critiquing your response based on these tips:

- Use solid reasons, evidence, and examples to support your position on an issue.
- Use critical thinking skills. Remember it is not your position on the issue that matters but rather how you substantiate it.

A smart way to prepare for the Issue essay is to practice writing on some of the published topics and read the commentary about sample responses along with scoring.

Think about these questions:

- What is the primary or main issue?
- Why is the argument sound (or why is it not sound)? Do you agree with the argument?
- Does the issue make reasonable or unreasonable assumptions?
- Are the conditions of the claim reasonable?
- Is further explanation needed to explain terms for the reader?
- Are the reasons that support it sound?
- What are some strong examples—both hypothetical and real—to substantiate the argument? Which are the best examples?

Read through both topics and choose one that interests you and that you can support with solid examples.

The Argument Essay

The Argument essay differs from the Issue essay in that your task is to critique and analyze the writer's argument, not present your own opinion or ideas on the subject. You'll be given one short passage and you'll have 30 minutes to write an essay on how well the argument is supported. These passages intentionally contain assumptions and holes in their arguments; you need to identify these assumptions and holes. Then you need to present your case on why you think the author has erroneously reached his conclusion and offer your suggestions on how to write a better response.

This section tests two skills that are crucial for success in graduate school: your analytical writing skills and your critical thinking. Regardless of your course of study in school, the ability to utilize critical thinking and analytical writing are tools you'll use and rely upon often.

Your score will be based on

- How well you identify and analyze the argument
- The structure of your response (how well organized it is, how well your ideas are developed, and supported and how well you present your case)
- Your use of standard written English

Prepare ahead of time for this portion of the GRE by giving yourself 30 minutes to write critiques to argument essays. With each practice critique you write, you'll learn how to wisely divide your half-hour into reading the essay, making notes, writing your response, and proofreading your work.

The main components of an Argument essay are the following:

- **Premise:** The premise, or proposition, is what the author concludes from the information given.
- **Assumptions:** Assumptions are what the author assumes, drawing inferences and insinuations based on the material.
- **Conclusion:** This is the conclusion that the author arrives at based on the facts and assumptions.

Use your scratch paper to organize yourself before you begin writing. Ask yourself:

- Are there any holes in the author's logic? Is he jumping to conclusions based on the evidence presented, or are there valid assumptions being made based on the material?
- What is the author's premise, or point? Is the premise logically convincing?
- Why does the author reach the conclusion that he does? What evidence or proof supports the author's claims?
- Can you think of an alternate explanation that may also be true given the material presented? Does this explanation confirm or contradict the author's?
- Are there any gaps—assumptions or faulty logic in the argument? Is the author over-generalizing? How specifically is the author's premise weakened?
- Is the author jumping to conclusions? Is he assuming causal relationships between two pieces of evidence that aren't necessarily true? What can one logically conclude based on the information provided in the passage?
- What are your ideas for strengthening the author's argument?

Make an outline using the standard format.

- **First paragraph (introduction):** What is the author's premise? Explain that the argument isn't well reasoned.

- **Supporting paragraphs:** Highlight the most obvious flaws in the author's argument. Why is the author wrong? What crucial piece of information is missing for the author to be able to confidently make that claim? Support your critique well.

  Continue on with another paragraph or two identifying other mistakes. Would additional information strengthen the author's premise, or weaken it?

- **Summary:** Summarize your assessment of the argument. Use good examples on how you would suggest the author improves his point.

Be direct and concise. This is not the place for flowery language or to showcase your large vocabulary. You will be graded on how well you argue your case, present facts that support your case, and express yourself. Your response should be well articulated and insightful and highlight your command and facility of English.

Remember: Give yourself a few minutes at the end to go back and reread your essay. Edit and proofread and, most important, ensure that your ideas are supported well and that your writing is well organized and clear.

Sample Essay Responses

In this section, we provide examples of varying levels of argument essays, all written in response to the following:

A recent five-year study of the sleeping habits of a selection of people challenges the belief that receiving at least eight hours of sleep a night is healthy. People in this study who reported sleeping eight or more hours a night had a higher rate of specific health problems than the subjects who slept seven hours of sleep a night on average. People who reported sleeping five hours a night had only a minimal increase in health issues compared to those who slept eight hours a night. It is apparent that people should try to sleep seven hours each night; therefore, too much sleep is worse for one's health than getting too little sleep.

Sample Level-6 Essay

The passage above claims that people should aim to get seven hours of sleep each night because, in the cited study, those who reported sleeping more than eight hours or less than seven had higher rates of health issues. There is not sufficient data presented here for the author to draw the conclusion that all people should sleep for seven hours to get maximum health benefits. Numerous important variables are absent from the information presented that would substantiate the author's conclusion.

The author does not give crucial facts regarding the study; without this information, it is impossible to safely state that people should sleep seven hours per night. When was the study conducted? How many people were involved? What were the ages and genders of the subjects? These are all critical pieces of information. We are also unaware of other health risk factors such as diet, stress levels, alcohol consumption, whether the person smoked; all of these variables have a major impact on a person's overall health, and sleep is but one variable. Only comparing the number of hours of sleep people received and ignoring these other factors is specious logic.

Another glaring omission is the health of the subjects prior to the study beginning. People who are healthier tend to need less sleep than people whose health is compromised in some way, so it is not clear which came first: Did the participants who slept longer do so because they had health problems, or did the fact that they slept longer than eight hours make them unhealthy? It can't be determined based on the limited information given.

In addition, we are not privy to what kind of health problems the study's subjects suffer from. It is not clear if the health issues are mental or physiological. Sleep clearly impacts both mental and physical health, but the causal relationship between health and sleep is not evident based on this particular study. There is also no mention of the degrees of health problems between those who slept for eight hours or more versus those who slept less than seven hours, other than saying that the difference was "slight." It is too simplistic to suggest that people are better off sleeping too little rather than too much as it ignores other important factors.

The author is not necessarily incorrect in his conclusion, but as mentioned above, there isn't enough information present to adequately prove his thesis. The writer needs to present more facts about the study and its participants in order to substantiate the idea that seven hours of sleep is ideal for most people. It is a mistake to make such a sweeping generalization based on the limited information presented.

Reader Commentary: The above essay was graded a 6 based on the fact that it is well organized, the writer has a mastery of English, and the ideas are well supported. The language is clear and concise, it follows the standard essay format (opening paragraph, supporting paragraphs, conclusion) and is well executed in its critique of the author's argument.

Sample Level-4 Essay

The author claims that people need seven hours of sleep each night in order to be healthy based on a study of people who reported higher rates of health problems if they slept more than eight hours, or less than seven. The author draws the conclusion based on scant evidence and makes assumptions on insufficient facts.

In order to give more credence to the statement that people would be healthiest if they slept for seven hours each night but it is too black and white. The study leaves out crucial information that would make his argument more valid. A sound study would include more information about the subject's lifestyle including their age, sex, stress levels, and eating and drinking habits.

The author is also assuming a cause-and-effect relationship between health and sleep that is not well supported. One can't conclude that those who slept the most were unhealthy because they slept longer, perhaps they slept longer because they were depressed, didn't feel well, didn't have to be up early in the morning—and it could be merely coincidental that this group reported higher rates of health problems.

For the author's premise to be valid more information is necessary. The logic is somewhat faulty and conclusions are being drawn based on a lot of assumptions and guesses versus being supported by solid data.

Reader Commentary: The above essay was graded a 4 because it showed competent use of English, had some mistakes but not enough to confuse the reader, and had valid critiques of the argument that were satisfactorily supported. To be a stronger critique there should be fewer grammatical errors and a stronger critique of the errors in the argument.

Sample Level-2 Essay

I think that in order for this authors argument to be stronger it should give more background information on the subjects so we'd know if he was comparing apples with apples. There's a lot of stuff missing. From the information presented it is not clear why some people, who were unhealthy slept more, maybe they were not health to begin with or maybe sleeping more did make them unhealthier. It is hard to say.

This argument isn't very convincing. It should have more information so we can have a clue as to why the author is making the claims he makes. It would also be helpful to now some facts about the people in the study, such as what was their health like, what they suffered from and why sleeping less than seven hours made them unhealthy. Maybe sleeping more really is better for us if we are healthy to begin with but it's hard to say.

We'd need better facts for this to be a stronger argument. Right now its weak.

Reader Commentary: This essay is graded a 2 because it is disorganized and contains too many spelling, punctuation, and grammatical errors (subjects don't agree with the verbs, the possessive is not used when it should be, and so on). The errors are enough to create a major distraction, and the writer does not demonstrate any critical thinking or analytical writing skills.

X. Arithmetic

A. Order of Operations

Arithmetic problems can involve many operations, and if those operations are performed in different orders, the resulting answers could be different. Because only one answer can be correct, there are rules about the order in which arithmetic operations should be performed. The order of operations is a set of rules that tells us how to evaluate expressions. Some people remember this order by the acronym **PEMDAS;** others use a sentence to help them remember. *Please Excuse My Dear Aunt Sally* is one favorite.

The letters in **PEMDAS** are meant to help you remember to:

- Simplify expressions inside **P**arentheses.
- Evaluate powers, or numbers with **E**xponents.
- **M**ultiply and **D**ivide, moving from left to right.
- **A**dd and **S**ubtract, moving from left to right.

Multiplication and division have the same priority. Do multiplication or division as you meet them as you work across the line, rather than doing all the multiplication and then all the division. The same is true for addition and subtraction. Do them as you come to them. Do not give addition a higher rank than subtraction.

EXAMPLE:

Find the simplest value for $8 \times [2 \times (4 + 3)^2 - 20 + 12] \div 4$.

Grouping symbols take precedence. So, working from the inside out:

$8 \times [2 \times (4 + 3)^2 - 20 + 12] \div 4$ Add 4 + 3.

$8 \times [2 \times (7)^2 - 20 + 12] \div 4$ Square 7.

$8 \times [2 \times 49 - 20 + 12] \div 4$ Multiply 2×49.

$8 \times [98 - 20 + 12] \div 4$ Subtract 98 − 20.

$8 \times [78 + 12] \div 4$ Add 78 + 12.

$8 \times [90] \div 4$ Multiply 8×90.

$720 \div 4$ Divide $720 \div 4$.

180   You get the answer: 180.

Practice

Directions (1–2): You are given two quantities, one in Column A and one in Column B. You are to compare the two quantities and choose:

A if the quantity in Column A is greater
B if the quantity in Column B is greater
C if the two quantities are equal
D if the relationship cannot be determined from the information given

	Column A	**Column B**
1.	$4 - 3 \times 4 + 3$	$(4 - 3) \times (4 + 3)$

	Column A	**Column B**
2.	$4 - 3(4 + 3)$	$(4 - 3) \times 4 + 3$

Directions (3–10): You are given five answer choices. Select the best choice.

3. $5 \cdot 3 - 7 \cdot 2 =$

    A. −3
    B. −40
    C. 1
    D. 16
    E. 29

4. $5^2 - 2 \times (7 - 3) =$

    A. 19
    B. 18
    C. 17
    D. 5
    E. 2

5. $[(66 - 54) \div 3 + 10 \div 5 - (6 - 2^2)] =$

    A. 14
    B. 4
    C. 3
    D. 0.8
    E. −10

6. The product of 15 and 4, minus the quotient of 30 and 5, is equal to

   A.   25
   B.   35
   C.   54
   D.   17
   E.   66

7. Eight times 9, plus 10 times 11, minus the product of 2 squared and 5 squared is

   A.   81
   B.   82
   C.   153
   D.   873
   E.   802

8. $5 - 2 + 2(8 - 5) \div 2 =$

   A.   19.5
   B.   7.5
   C.   6
   D.   1.5
   E.   −1

9. $17 - (8 - 3)(2 + 1) \div 5 =$

   A.   0.4
   B.   2.6
   C.   7.1
   D.   14
   E.   16

10. $7 + 3^2 \div 2 - 6 =$

   A.   −4
   B.   −25
   C.   2
   D.   5.5
   E.   44

Answers

1. **B** The correct answer is B, because $(4 - 3) \times (4 + 3) = 1 \times 7 = 7$, which is greater than $4 - 3 \times 4 + 3 = 4 - 12 + 3 = -8 + 3 = -5$.

2. **B** The correct answer is B, because $(4 - 3) \times 4 + 3 = 1 \times 4 + 3 = 4 + 3 = 7$, which is greater than $4 - 3(4 + 3) = 4 - 3(7) = 4 - 21 = -17$.

3. **C** The correct answer is C, because $5 \cdot 3 - 7 \cdot 2 = 15 - 14 = 1$.

4. **C** The correct answer is C, because $5^2 - 2 \times (7 - 3) = 25 - 2(4) = 25 - 8 = 17$.

5. **B** The correct answer is B, because $[(66 - 54) \div 3 + 10 \div 5 - (6 - 2^2)] = [(66 - 54) \div 3 + 10 \div 5 - (6 - 4)]$ $= [12 \div 3 + 10 \div 5 - 2] = [4 + 10 \div 5 - 2] = [4 + 2 - 2] = 4$.

6. **C** The correct answer is C, because the product of 15 and 4 is 60 and the quotient of 30 and 5 is 6, so $60 - 6 = 54$. (**Remember:** The product is the result of multiplication, and the quotient is the result of division.)

7. **B** The correct answer is B, because 8 times 9, plus 10 times 11, minus the product of 2 squared and 5 squared is $8 \times 9 + 10 \times 11 - (2^2 \times 5^2) = 72 + 110 - (4 \times 25) = 182 - 100 = 82$.

8. **C** The correct answer is C, because $5 - 2 + 2(8 - 5) \div 2 = 5 - 2 + 2(3) \div 2 = 5 - 2 + 6 \div 2 = 5 - 2 + 3 = 3 + 3 = 6$.

9. **D** The correct answer is D, because $17 - (8 - 3)(2 + 1) \div 5 = 17 - (5)(3) \div 5 = 17 - 15 \div 5 = 17 - 3 = 14$.

10. **D** The correct answer is D, because $7 + 3^2 \div 2 - 6 = 7 + 9 \div 2 - 6 = 7 + 4.5 - 6 = 11.5 - 6 = 5.5$.

B. Integers

Integers are positive and negative whole numbers and zero. The rules for arithmetic with integers apply to other positive and negative numbers as well, like $+4\frac{3}{5}$ or -7.5. Remember that larger numbers are farther to the right on the number line. For negative numbers, larger means closer to zero (-4 is larger than -5).

1. Absolute Value

The *absolute value* of the number is the distance of the number from zero, without regard to direction. Absolute value is often thought of as "the number without its sign." The symbol for the absolute value of x is $|x|$. Both 5 and -5 have an absolute value of 5, because both are five units from zero, so $|5| = 5$ and $|-5| = 5$. One number is positive and one is negative because one is above zero and one is below zero, but absolute value is not concerned with direction.

2. Addition

To add integers, you need to look at the signs and at the absolute values. If the signs are the same, add the absolute values and keep the sign.

$+3 + +5 = +8$

In the preceding equation, both numbers are positive, so add $3 + 5$ and make the answer positive.

$-9 + -2 = -11$

In the preceding equation, both numbers are negative, so add $9 + 2$ and make the answer negative.

If the signs are *different,* subtract the absolute values, and take the sign of the number with the larger absolute value.

$+3 + -5 = -2$

In the preceding equation, the signs are different, so subtract 5 – 3 = 2. Because | –5 | > | +3 |, take the sign of –5.

$$-14 + +25 = +11$$

In the preceding equations, the signs are different, so subtract 25 – 14 = 11. Because | +25 | > | –14 |, take the sign of +25.

3. Subtraction

Do not subtract. When a problem calls for subtraction, change the sign of the second number and follow the rules for adding.

$-5 - +3 = -5 + -3 = -8$	Subtracting a positive is adding a negative.
$-4 - -5 = -4 + +5 = +1$	Subtracting a negative is adding a positive.

4. Multiplication and Division

The rules for signs are identical whether you're multiplying or dividing. If the signs are the same, the answer is positive. If the signs are different, the answer is negative.

$+2 \times +5 = +10$	Positive × positive = positive
$+4 \times -7 = -28$	Positive × negative = negative
$-3 \times +9 = -27$	Negative × positive = negative
$-6 \times -8 = +48$	Negative × negative = positive

Practice

Directions (1–2): You are given two quantities, one in Column A and one in Column B. You are to compare the two quantities and choose:

A if the quantity in Column A is greater
B if the quantity in Column B is greater
C if the two quantities are equal
D if the relationship cannot be determined from the information given

	Column A	Column B
1.	-12×4	12×-4

	Column A	Column B
2.	$\dfrac{-16}{8}$	$\dfrac{16}{-2 \times 4}$

Directions (3–10): You are given five answer choices. Select the best choice.

3. Which of the following is not equal to –18?

   A. $-8 - 10$
   B. -3×6
   C. $-4 + 14$
   D. 2×-9
   E. $\dfrac{36}{-2}$

4. $4 + -3 - -5 - 8 =$

   A. -2
   B. -1
   C. 0
   D. 1
   E. 2

5. $-4 - 5 - -5 - 8 + 12 - -4 =$

   A. -4
   B. -2
   C. 0
   D. 2
   E. 4

6. Each day, Jon records the temperature at 2 p.m. On Monday, the temperature was 62°. On Tuesday, it was 4° higher, but on Wednesday, it dropped 7°. On Thursday, there was no change, but on Friday, the temperature rose 10°. What was the temperature on Friday?

   A. 59°
   B. 62°
   C. 65°
   D. 69°
   E. 73°

7. When Carl went out for the wrestling team, he started a program of diet and exercise. In the first month of the season, he gained 9 pounds. In the second month, he lost 3 pounds. In the third month, he gained 6 pounds. What was the average monthly change in Carl's weight?

   A. +12 pounds per month
   B. –6 pounds per month
   C. +6 pounds per month
   D. –4 pounds per month
   E. +4 pounds per month

8. The sum of –7 and –4 times the quotient of –8 and +2 is equal to which of the following?

    A. 0
    B. –23
    C. 9
    D. 44
    E. –44

9. Simplify: $\dfrac{(5 \times -7) - (2 \times -10) + 1}{(-3 \times 5) + (-2 \times -4)} =$

    A. 2
    B. –2
    C. $7\dfrac{5}{7}$
    D. $\dfrac{14}{23}$
    E. 8

10. The expression $x \pm y$ is defined as follows:

    ■ If the sum of x and y is positive, add –7 to the sum.
    ■ If the sum of x and y is negative, divide the sum by –2.
    ■ If the sum of x and y is 0, subtract 3 from the sum.

    Find -4 ± 3.

    A. 6
    B. $\dfrac{1}{2}$
    C. $\dfrac{7}{2}$
    D. –8
    E. –14

Answers

1. **C** The correct answer is C, because $-12 \times 4 = -48$ and $12 \times -4 = -48$.

2. **C** The correct answer is C, because $\dfrac{-16}{8} = -2$ and $\dfrac{16}{-2 \times 4} = \dfrac{16}{-8} = -2$.

3. **C** The correct answer is C, because $-4 + 14 = 10$. Checking the other answer choices, you find that $-8 - 10 = -8 + -10 = -18$, $-3 \times 6 = -18$, $2 \times -9 = -18$ and $\dfrac{36}{-2} = -18$.

4. **A** The correct answer is A, because $4 + -3 - -5 - 8 = 4 + -3 + 5 + -8 = 4 + 5 + -3 + -8 = 9 + -11 = -2$.

5. **C** The correct answer is C, because $-4 - 5 - -5 - 8 + 12 - -4 = -4 + -5 + 5 + -8 + 12 = -4 + -5 + -8 + 5 + 12 = -17 + 17 = 0$.

6. **D** The correct choice is D, because $62° + 4° - 7° + 0° + 10° = 66° - 7° + 0° + 10° = 59° + 0° + 10° = 69°$.

7. **E** The correct choice is E, because the average monthly change in Carl's weight is $+9 - 3 + 6 = +12$ pounds, divided by 3 months, which equals $+4$ pounds per month.

8. **D** The correct choice is D, because the sum of -7 and -4 times the quotient of -8 and $+2$ is equal to $(-7 + -4) \times (-8 \div +2) = (-11) \times (-4) = +44$.

9. **A** The correct choice is A, because
$$\frac{(5 \times -7) - (2 \times -10) + 1}{(-3 \times 5) + (-2 \times -4)} = \frac{-35 - -20 + 1}{-15 + +8} = \frac{-35 + 20 + 1}{-15 + 8} = \frac{-15 + 1}{-7} = \frac{-14}{-7} = +2.$$

10. **B** The correct choice is B. Because $-4 + 3 = -1$, you follow the second rule and divide the sum by -2, so $-1 \div -2 = \frac{1}{2}$.

C. Number Theory

1. Odds and Evens

Integers can be classified as odd or even. An even number is a number that is a multiple of 2. It can be expressed as $2n$, for some integer n. Numbers that are not even are called odd numbers. Odd numbers fall just before and just after even numbers, so they can be expressed as $2n + 1$ or $2n - 1$.

Here are the rules to keep in mind when you're adding odd and even numbers:

- Even + even = even (for example, $12 + 14 = 36$).
- Odd + odd = even (for example, $13 + 19 = 32$).
- Even + odd = odd (for example, $14 + 15 = 29$).

Here are the rules to keep in mind when you're multiplying odd and even numbers:

- Even × even = even (for example $8 \times 6 = 48$).
- Odd × odd = odd (for example, $7 \times 9 = 63$).
- Even × odd = even (for example, $6 \times 11 = 66$).

EXAMPLE:

If r is even and t is odd, which of the following is odd?

- **A.** rt
- **B.** $5r^2t$
- **C.** $6r^2t$
- **D.** $5r + 6t$
- **E.** $6r + 5t$

In Choice A, because r is even and t is odd, rt is even. In Choice B, r^2 is even × even, which is even, and r^2t is even × odd, which is even; so $5r^2t$ is odd × even, which is even. In Choice C, you already know that r^2t is even, so $6r^2t$ is even × even, which is even. In Choice D, $5r$ is odd × even, which is even, and $6t$ is even × odd, which is even, so you're adding even + even, which is even. In Choice E, $6r$ is even × even, which is even, and $5t$ is odd × odd, which is odd, so you're adding even + odd, which is odd. This makes Choice E the correct answer.

2. Factors

When you multiply two numbers, each number is called a *factor,* and the answer you produce is called the *product. Factorization* is the process of expressing a number as a multiplication problem or rewriting it as a product of factors.

Sometimes you want to consider different factor pairs for a number. The number 24, for example, can be expressed as 1×24, or 2×12, or 3×8, or 4×6. Each of these is a pair of factors that equal 24. Other times, you'll want to find the prime factorization of a number, expressing it as a product of prime numbers.

3. Primes

Whole numbers can be classified as prime or composite. Prime numbers are numbers whose only factors are themselves and one. The number 41, for example, is a prime number, because the only factor pair that will produce 41 is 1×41. Composite numbers have other factor pairs. For example, 51 could be written as 1×51 or 3×17, so 51 is composite.

Small prime numbers (like 2, 3, 5, and 7) are usually easy to recognize and remember, but you may come across a test question that asks about larger primes. To locate primes quickly, list all the numbers in the range and then cross out multiples of small primes. This should leave just a few numbers that require further testing. For example, if you're looking for all the primes between 40 and 60, make a list of the integers from 40 to 60:

40 41 42 43 44 45 46 47 48 49 50 51 52 53 54 55 56 57 58 59 60

Now cross out all the multiples of 2:

~~40~~ 41 ~~42~~ 43 ~~44~~ 45 ~~46~~ 47 ~~48~~ 49 ~~50~~ 51 ~~52~~ 53 ~~54~~ 55 ~~56~~ 57 ~~58~~ 59 ~~60~~

Next cross out the multiples of 3. (Check to see if a number is a multiple of 3 by adding the digits. If they add to a number that's divisible by 3, the number is a multiple of 3.)

~~40~~ 41 ~~42~~ 43 ~~44~~ ~~45~~ ~~46~~ 47 ~~48~~ 49 ~~50~~ ~~51~~ ~~52~~ 53 ~~54~~ 55 ~~56~~ ~~57~~ ~~58~~ 59 ~~60~~

Cross out the multiples of 5, which end in 0 or 5, and you'll have narrowed the list down quite a bit:

~~40~~ 41 ~~42~~ 43 ~~44~~ ~~45~~ ~~46~~ 47 ~~48~~ 49 ~~50~~ ~~51~~ ~~52~~ 53 ~~54~~ ~~55~~ ~~56~~ ~~57~~ ~~58~~ 59 ~~60~~

The only numbers left are 41, 43, 47, 49, 53, and 59. You probably realize 49 is a multiple of 7. The rest of the numbers are prime.

Remember that 2 is the only even prime. All other primes are odd. Note, too, that 1 is neither prime nor composite.

4. Divisors

Questions about number relationships will often require that you determine whether one number is divisible by another, or whether one is a factor of another. You may be asked that question directly, or you may need to determine that in the process of finding a common denominator or factoring a polynomial. Several quick tests can help you:

- **Divisible by 2:** Any number divisible by 2 ends in 0, 2, 4, 6, or 8. These are the even numbers.
- **Divisible by 3:** To determine if a number is divisible by 3, add the digits. If the sum of the digits is divisible by 3, so is the original number. (Not sure whether the sum is divisible by 3? Add its digits until you get to a small enough number that you can tell whether it's divisible by 3.)
- **Divisible by 4:** Just test the last two digits. If the final two digits form a number that is divisible by 4, then the entire number is divisible by 4 as well.
- **Divisible by 5:** All numbers divisible by 5 end in either 5 or 0.
- **Divisible by 6:** A number will only be divisible by 6 if it is divisible by both 2 and 3.
- **Divisible by 9:** You can test for divisibility by 9 the same way you test for divisibility by 3. Add the digits of the number. If the sum is divisible by 9, so is the original number.
- **Divisible by 10:** All numbers divisible by 10 end in 0. (And all numbers divisible by powers of 10 end in zeros. The number of zeros is the power.)

Practice

Directions (1–2): You are given two quantities, one in Column A and one in Column B. You are to compare the two quantities and choose:

A if the quantity in Column A is greater
B if the quantity in Column B is greater
C if the two quantities are equal
D if the relationship cannot be determined from the information given

Column A	Column B
1. The smallest prime greater than 20	The largest prime less than 30

Column A	Column B
2. The number of primes between 10 and 15	The number of primes between 15 and 20

Directions (3–10): You are given five answer choices. Select the best choice.

3. All of the following are divisors of 270 except

   A. 2
   B. 3
   C. 5
   D. 7
   E. 9

4. The largest prime factor of 121 minus the largest prime factor of 49 is

   A. 0
   B. 1
   C. 2
   D. 3
   E. 4

5. All of the following are prime except

   A. 31
   B. 41
   C. 51
   D. 61
   E. 71

6. Marilyn baked brownies to give as gifts at holiday time. If she packaged the brownies 5 to a package, she had 3 brownies left over, and if she put 7 in a package, she had 3 left over, but if she put 6 in a package, there were only 2 left over. How many brownies did Marilyn bake?

   A. 35
   B. 36
   C. 37
   D. 38
   E. 39

7. Which of the following is divisible by 6?

   A. 826
   B. 723
   C. 624
   D. 555
   E. 428

8. The sum of the primes greater than 30 and less than 40 is

   A. 31
   B. 37
   C. 68
   D. 64
   E. 1,011

9. Find a prime number that divides both 35 and 98.

   A. 2
   B. 5
   C. 7
   D. 35
   E. 49

10. Find the smallest number divisible by both 11 and 17.

    A. 11
    B. 17
    C. 28
    D. 170
    E. 187

Answers

1. **B** The smallest prime greater than 20 is an odd number (because 2 is the only even prime), but it's not 21, because 21 is divisible by 3 and 7. Therefore, the smallest prime greater than 20 is 23. The largest prime less than 30 is also an odd number in the 20s. Working back from 30, the first odd number is 29, which is prime. Therefore, B is the correct answer, because 29 is larger than 23.

2. **C** The prime numbers between 10 and 15 are 11 and 13, so there are two primes between 10 and 15. The prime numbers between 15 and 20 are 17 and 19, so there are also two primes between 15 and 20 as well. This makes C the correct answer.

3. **D** To figure out the answer, you can factorize 270 as follows: $270 = 2 \times 135 = 2 \times 5 \times 27 = 2 \times 5 \times 9 \times 3 = 2 \times 5 \times 3 \times 3 \times 3$. This prime factorization makes it clear that 2, 3, 5, and 9 are factors or divisors of 270. That leaves 7 as the only answer choice that *isn't* a factor of 270.

   You could also arrive at this answer by using divisibility tests: 270 ends in 0, which is even, so 270 is divisible by 2. The final 0 is also a sign that 270 is divisible by 5. Finally, adding up the digits of 270, $2 + 7 + 0 = 9$, and 9 is divisible by both 3 and 9, so 270 is divisible by 3 and 9. That leaves 7 as the correct choice.

4. **E** The prime factorization of 121 is 11×11, so the largest (and only) prime factor of 121 is 11. The prime factorization of 49 is 7×7, so the largest prime factor of 49 is 7. Subtracting $11 - 7 = 4$.

5. **C** To figure out which number isn't prime, divisibility tests are the best method. None of the choices is even, and none ends in 0 or 5, so try adding the digits: $3 + 1 = 4$, $4 + 1 = 5$, $5 + 1 = 6$, $6 + 1 = 7$, and $7 + 1 = 8$. Because 6 is divisible by 3, 51 is divisible by 3, which means it isn't prime.

6. **D** The question tells you that if Marilyn packaged the brownies 5 to a package, she had 3 brownies left over, so the number of brownies is 3 more than a multiple of 5. If Marilyn put 7 brownies in a package, she had 3 left over, so the number of brownies is 3 more than a multiple of 7. And, if she put 6 brownies in a package, there were only 2 left over, so the number of brownies was 2 more than a multiple of 6. If you look at the answer choices, 35 is a multiple of 5 and a multiple of 7, not three more than those multiples, and 36 and 37 are only one more and two more, respectively. The best choice looks like 38, which is 3 more than 35, and is also 2 more than 36, a multiple of 6.

7. **C** A number is divisible by 6 if it is divisible by 2 and by 3. So, you can eliminate Choice B and Choice D right off the bat, because they're odd and, therefore, not divisible by 2. Then check the remaining choices for divisibility by 3 by adding the digits: $8 + 2 + 6 = 16$, $6 + 2 + 4 = 12$, and $4 + 2 + 8 = 14$. Because 12 is divisible by 3, but 14 and 16 are not, only 624 is divisible by 2 and by 3. So only 624 is divisible by 6.

8. **C** To find the primes greater than 30 and less than 40, start by eliminating the even numbers. That leaves 31, 33, 35, 37, and 39. You can eliminate 35, which is a multiple of 5 (so not prime), and you can eliminate 33 and 39, both of which are multiples of 3 (so not prime). That leaves you with 31 and 37, and $31 + 37 = 68$.

9. **C** To find a prime number that divides both 35 and 98, start by listing the prime factors of 35, which are 5 and 7. You know that 98 is not divisible by 5. But $98 \div 7 = 14$, so the prime that divides both 35 and 98 is 7.

10. **E** Because 11 and 17 are both prime, the smallest common multiple is their product: $11 \times 17 = 187$.

D. Fractions

1. Equivalent Fractions

Equivalent fractions have the same value, but their appearance is altered by multiplying by a fraction equal to 1. Changing the appearance of a fraction without changing its value requires that the numerator and denominator of the fraction be multiplied by the same number. The fraction $\frac{3}{4}$ is equivalent to $\frac{3}{4} \cdot \frac{5}{5} = \frac{15}{20}$. The fraction $\frac{8}{14} = \frac{2}{2} \cdot \frac{4}{7}$, so $\frac{8}{14}$ is equivalent to $\frac{4}{7}$.

2. Comparing Fractions

If you're asked to compare fractions, first be sure the fractions have a common denominator. When you're working with fractions in longer calculations, it's wise to choose the lowest common denominator, but if all you're asked to do is compare, any common denominator will do. Often, the common denominator that is quickest to find is the product of the two denominators.

EXAMPLE:

Which of the following statements is true?

A. $\dfrac{5}{8} < \dfrac{19}{32}$

B. $\dfrac{7}{16} < \dfrac{3}{8}$

C. $\dfrac{5}{8} < \dfrac{7}{16}$

D. $\dfrac{3}{8} < \dfrac{19}{32}$

E. $\dfrac{19}{32} < \dfrac{7}{16}$

Changing all the fractions to a denominator of 32 simplifies the comparison. Your choices then become:

A. $\dfrac{5}{8} < \dfrac{19}{32} \Rightarrow \dfrac{20}{32} < \dfrac{19}{32}$

B. $\dfrac{7}{16} < \dfrac{3}{8} \Rightarrow \dfrac{14}{32} < \dfrac{12}{32}$

C. $\dfrac{5}{8} < \dfrac{7}{16} \Rightarrow \dfrac{20}{32} < \dfrac{14}{32}$

D. $\dfrac{3}{8} < \dfrac{19}{32} \Rightarrow \dfrac{12}{32} < \dfrac{19}{32}$

E. $\dfrac{19}{32} < \dfrac{7}{16} \Rightarrow \dfrac{19}{32} < \dfrac{14}{32}$

You can see that only D is true.

3. Addition and Subtraction

Adding and subtracting fractions requires that the fractions have the same denominator. When they do, you simply add the numerators and keep the denominator. Your real work comes if they do not have a common denominator to start out.

A common denominator is a number that is a multiple of each of the denominators you were given. Ideally, you should choose the lowest number that all your denominators divide evenly, but larger multiples will work—you'll just have to reduce to lowest terms at the end.

EXAMPLE:

Add $\dfrac{1}{3} + \dfrac{2}{7}$.

The lowest common multiple of 3 and 7 is 21. Multiply $\dfrac{1}{3} \cdot \dfrac{7}{7} = \dfrac{7}{21}$ and $\dfrac{2}{7} \cdot \dfrac{3}{3} = \dfrac{6}{21}$. Then $\dfrac{1}{3} + \dfrac{2}{7} = \dfrac{7}{21} + \dfrac{6}{21} = \dfrac{13}{21}$.

EXAMPLE:

Add $\dfrac{7}{30} + \dfrac{5}{42}$.

To find the lowest common denominator, take a moment first to factor each denominator:

$$30 = \boxed{2} \cdot 5 \cdot \boxed{3}$$
$$42 = \boxed{2} \cdot 7 \cdot \boxed{3}$$

The factors in the boxes are already common to both denominators, so they should be factors of the common denominator, but each of them only needs to appear once. In addition, the 5 and 7 that are *not* in boxes should be factors of the common denominator.

So, the lowest common denominator = $2 \times 3 \times 5 \times 7 = 210$.

Multiply $\dfrac{7}{2 \cdot 3 \cdot 5} \cdot \dfrac{7}{7} = \dfrac{49}{210}$ and $\dfrac{5}{2 \cdot 3 \cdot 7} \cdot \dfrac{5}{5} = \dfrac{25}{210}$ and the problem becomes $\dfrac{49}{210} + \dfrac{25}{210} = \dfrac{74}{210} = \dfrac{2 \cdot 37}{2 \cdot 105} = \dfrac{37}{105}$.

You don't always need to find the lowest common denominator. Sometimes you simply want to add or subtract the fractions as quickly as possible. In these cases, you can fall back on a strategy commonly referred to as the bow tie and symbolized by this set of three arrows:

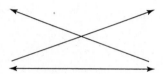

Each arrow represents a multiplication that needs to be done, and the place to put that answer.

EXAMPLE:

Add $\dfrac{5}{8} + \dfrac{5}{6}$.

The double-pointed arrow at the bottom tells you to multiply the two denominators for a common denominator:

$$\dfrac{5}{8} \underset{\leftrightarrow}{+} \dfrac{5}{6} = \dfrac{}{48}$$

The arrow slanting from the lower right to the upper left tells you to multiply the second denominator by the first numerator and put the result in the first numerator's position:

$$\dfrac{5}{8} \nwarrow \dfrac{5}{6} = \dfrac{30 + ?}{48}$$

The arrow slanting from the lower left to the upper right tells you to multiply the first numerator times the second denominator and put the result in the second numerator's position:

$$\dfrac{5}{8} \nearrow \dfrac{5}{6} = \dfrac{30 + 40}{48} = \dfrac{70}{48}$$

4. Multiplication

The basic rule for multiplication of fractions calls for multiplying numerator × numerator and denominator × denominator and reducing if possible.

EXAMPLE:

Multiply $\frac{1}{9} \times \frac{3}{7}$.

Multiply 1×3 and 9×7. This gives you $\frac{3}{63}$, which reduces to $\frac{1}{21}$.

Much of the work of multiplying and dividing fractions can be made easier by canceling before multiplying. *Canceling* is dividing the numerator and the denominator by the same number. You can think of it as reducing before you multiply instead of after.

EXAMPLE:

Multiply $\frac{3}{8} \cdot \frac{4}{9}$.

The basic rules says to multiply 3 times 4 and 8 times 9, giving the fraction $\frac{12}{72}$, which reduces to $\frac{1}{6}$.

However, you can cancel before multiplying. Divide 3 into both 3 and 9, and divide 4 into both 4 and 8:

$$\frac{3}{8} \cdot \frac{4}{9} = \frac{\overset{1}{\cancel{3}}}{8} \cdot \frac{4}{\underset{3}{\cancel{9}}} = \frac{\overset{1}{\cancel{3}}}{\underset{2}{\cancel{8}}} \cdot \frac{\overset{1}{\cancel{4}}}{\underset{3}{\cancel{9}}} = \frac{1 \cdot 1}{2 \cdot 3} = \frac{1}{6}.$$

5. Division

To divide fractions, multiply by the reciprocal. In other words, invert the divisor and multiply. The divisor is the second fraction. Invert only the divisor.

EXAMPLE:

Divide $\frac{1}{8} \div \frac{3}{4}$.

The fraction $\frac{3}{4}$ is the divisor. Invert $\frac{3}{4}$ to get $\frac{4}{3}$ and then multiply $\frac{1}{8} \cdot \frac{4}{3} = \frac{4}{24} = \frac{1}{6}$.

EXAMPLE:

Divide $\frac{15}{14} \div \frac{3}{7}$.

Invert the divisor, $\frac{3}{7}$, and multiply, so the problem becomes $\frac{15}{14} \cdot \frac{7}{3}$. Divide 3 into both 15 and 3, and divide 7

into both 7 and 14: $\frac{15}{14} \cdot \frac{7}{3} = \frac{\overset{5}{\cancel{15}}}{14} \cdot \frac{7}{\underset{1}{\cancel{3}}} = \frac{\overset{5}{\cancel{15}}}{\underset{2}{\cancel{14}}} \cdot \frac{\overset{1}{\cancel{7}}}{\underset{1}{\cancel{3}}} = \frac{5 \cdot 1}{2 \cdot 1} = \frac{5}{2} = 2\frac{1}{2}.$

6. Mixed Numbers and Improper Fractions

A number like $2\frac{1}{2}$, which involves both a whole number and a fraction, is called a *mixed number*. A fraction in which the numerator is larger than the denominator is called an *improper fraction*. The mixed number represents a whole number plus a fraction: $2\frac{1}{2} = 2 + \frac{1}{2} = \frac{2}{1} + \frac{1}{2} = \frac{4}{2} + \frac{1}{2} = \frac{5}{2}$. The common shortcut for changing a mixed number to an improper fraction is to multiply the denominator of the fraction times the whole number, add the numerator of the fraction part, and place that result as a numerator over the denominator of the fraction part.

EXAMPLE:

Change $3\frac{2}{7}$ to an improper fraction.

Multiply the denominator, 7, by the whole number, 3: $7 \times 3 = 21$. To the product, 21, add the 2 that is the numerator of the fraction: $21 + 2 = 23$. The result, 23, goes over the denominator, 7: $3\frac{2}{7} = \frac{7 \times 3 + 2}{7} = \frac{23}{7}$.

To change an improper fraction to a mixed number, divide the numerator by the denominator. The quotient becomes the whole number, and the remainder goes over the divisor to form the fraction part.

EXAMPLE:

Change $\frac{43}{5}$ to a mixed number.

Divide 43 by 5. The quotient of 8 is the whole number. The remainder of 3 goes over the 5 to make the fraction: $\frac{43}{5} = 8\frac{3}{5}$.

Adding mixed numbers is as simple as adding the whole number parts and adding the fraction parts: $3\frac{2}{7} + 2\frac{6}{7} = 3 + 2 + \frac{2}{7} + \frac{6}{7} = 5\frac{8}{7}$. If this results in an improper fraction, as in this example, change the improper fraction to a mixed number: $\frac{8}{7} = 1\frac{1}{7}$. Add this to the 5 that was the whole number part: $5\frac{8}{7} = 5 + 1\frac{1}{7} = 6\frac{1}{7}$.

Subtracting mixed numbers can often be done by subtracting whole number from whole number and fraction from fraction as in $4\frac{7}{10} - 2\frac{3}{10}$. Subtracting $4 - 2 = 2$ and subtracting $\frac{7}{10} - \frac{3}{10} = \frac{4}{10} = \frac{2}{5}$, so $4\frac{7}{10} - 2\frac{3}{10} = 2\frac{4}{10} = 2\frac{2}{5}$. But in some cases, this strategy runs into a problem.

EXAMPLE:

Subtract $8\frac{3}{10} - 4\frac{7}{10}$.

In this case, the previous strategy leads to trying to subtract $\frac{7}{10}$ from $\frac{3}{10}$. One way to work around this problem is to do some regrouping: $8\frac{3}{10} = 7 + 1 + \frac{3}{10} = 7 + \frac{10}{10} + \frac{3}{10} = 7\frac{13}{10}$. When the first number is re-expressed this way, you can subtract $7\frac{13}{10} - 4\frac{7}{10}$ by subtracting $7 - 4 = 3$ and $\frac{13}{10} - \frac{7}{10} = \frac{6}{10}$.

The need for regrouping can be avoided, however, by simply changing both mixed numbers to improper fractions, subtracting, and changing back to a mixed number:

$$8\frac{3}{10} - 4\frac{7}{10} = \frac{83}{10} - \frac{47}{10} = \frac{36}{10} = 3\frac{6}{10} = 3\frac{3}{5}$$

Don't try to multiply or divide mixed numbers. Change mixed numbers to improper fractions before multiplying or dividing.

Practice

Directions (1–4): You are given two quantities, one in Column A and one in Column B. You are to compare the two quantities and choose:

A if the quantity in Column A is greater
B if the quantity in Column B is greater
C if the two quantities are equal
D if the relationship cannot be determined from the information given

	Column A	**Column B**
1.	$\dfrac{5}{12}$	$\dfrac{3}{7}$

	Column A	**Column B**
2.	$\dfrac{7}{20}$	$\dfrac{1}{3}$

	Column A	**Column B**
3.	$\dfrac{5}{7}+\dfrac{1}{2}$	$\dfrac{2}{3}+\dfrac{5}{8}$

	Column A	**Column B**
4.	$\dfrac{4}{9}\cdot\dfrac{3}{5}$	$\dfrac{3}{5}\div\dfrac{4}{9}$

Directions (5–10): You are given five answer choices. Select the best choice.

5. $\dfrac{4}{5}-\dfrac{1}{6}+\dfrac{1}{4}=$

    A. $3\dfrac{1}{4}$

    B. $\dfrac{23}{60}$

    C. $\dfrac{5}{8}$

    D. $\dfrac{53}{60}$

    E. $1\dfrac{1}{6}$

6. $\dfrac{1}{10} \div \dfrac{3}{5} \times \dfrac{12}{13} =$

    A. $\quad\dfrac{1}{13}$

    B. $\quad\dfrac{2}{13}$

    C. $\quad\dfrac{13}{72}$

    D. $\quad\dfrac{4}{13}$

    E. $\quad\dfrac{1}{2}$

7. $\left(\dfrac{3}{4} - \dfrac{2}{3}\right) \div \left(\dfrac{1}{2} + \dfrac{1}{5}\right) =$

    A. $\quad\dfrac{5}{6}$

    B. $\quad\dfrac{5}{7}$

    C. $\quad\dfrac{6}{7}$

    D. $\quad\dfrac{5}{42}$

    E. $\quad\dfrac{7}{120}$

8. Hector's uncle gave him a baseball card collection from the 1950s. Half of the cards were from the Brooklyn Dodgers, and one-fourth of the cards were from the New York Giants. The rest were evenly divided among the Philadelphia Athletics, the St. Louis Browns, and the Washington Senators. If there were 15 cards from the Browns, how many Dodgers cards did Hector's uncle give him?

    A.   15
    B.   45
    C.   60
    D.   90
    E.   180

9. During contract negotiations, $\frac{7}{8}$ of the union members voted on a new contract proposal. Of those voting, $\frac{2}{3}$ voted to approve the contract. If there are 3,600 members in the union, how many voted to approve?

    A.   1,200
    B.   1,500
    C.   2,100
    D.   2,400
    E.   3,150

10. Half a number minus $3\frac{3}{4}$ is equal to $\frac{5}{4}$. Find the number.

    A. $1\frac{1}{4}$

    B. $2\frac{1}{2}$

    C.   5
    D.   10
    E.   20

Answers

1. **B** To determine which is larger, change the fractions to a common denominator, and compare the numerators: $\frac{5}{12}?\frac{3}{7} \Rightarrow \frac{5\times7}{12\times7}?\frac{3\times12}{7\times12} \Rightarrow \frac{35}{84} < \frac{36}{84}$.

2. **A** To determine which is larger, change the fractions to a common denominator, and compare the numerators: $\frac{7}{20}?\frac{1}{3} \Rightarrow \frac{7\times3}{20\times3}?\frac{1\times20}{3\times20} \Rightarrow \frac{21}{60} > \frac{20}{60}$.

3. **B** To determine which is larger, first you have to add the pairs of fractions. To add the first pair of fractions, change to a common denominator of 14: $\frac{5}{7}+\frac{1}{2} = \frac{5\times2}{7\times2}+\frac{1\times7}{2\times7} = \frac{10}{14}+\frac{7}{14} = \frac{17}{14}$. To add the second pair of fractions, change to a common denominator of 24: $\frac{2\times8}{3\times8}+\frac{5\times3}{8\times3} = \frac{16}{24}+\frac{15}{24} = \frac{31}{24}$. Comparing the answers requires changing $\frac{17}{14}$ and $\frac{31}{24}$ to a common denominator, but it doesn't have to be the *lowest* common denominator—it may be faster to multiply each fraction by the denominator of the other: $\frac{17}{14}?\frac{31}{24} \Rightarrow \frac{17\times24}{14\times24}?\frac{31\times14}{24\times4} \Rightarrow \frac{408}{14\times24} < \frac{434}{24\times14}$. You don't need to know the simplified value of the denominator, just that the denominators of both fractions are the same. Once they have a common denominator, comparing the numerators will tell you the relationship of the fractions.

4. **B** To determine which is larger, first you have to multiply the first pair of fractions and divide the other. Multiplying allows for cancellation: $\frac{4}{9} \cdot \frac{3}{5} = \frac{4}{3\,\cancel{9}} \cdot \frac{\cancel{3}}{5} = \frac{4}{15}$. Dividing requires inverting and multiplying, and the inversion eliminates the opportunity to cancel: $\frac{3}{5} \div \frac{4}{9} = \frac{3}{5} \times \frac{9}{4} = \frac{27}{20}$. You don't

have to find a common denominator to see that the first equation is less than 1 and the second equation is greater than 1, which gives you the answer you need.

Beware of the assumption that multiplying makes bigger answers and dividing makes smaller ones. That pattern may be true for numbers greater than 1, but not for fractions less than one.

5. **D** To solve the equation, you need to find the lowest common denominator for all three fractions, and multiply each fraction by the equivalent of 1 to change its appearance: $\frac{4}{5} - \frac{1}{6} + \frac{1}{4} = \frac{48}{60} - \frac{10}{60} + \frac{15}{60}$.

Take note of the signs and perform the subtraction and addition as you encounter them from left to right: $\frac{48}{60} - \frac{10}{60} + \frac{15}{60} = \frac{38}{60} + \frac{15}{60} = \frac{53}{60}$.

6. **B** To solve the equation, start by changing the division to multiplying by the reciprocal: $\frac{1}{10} \div \frac{3}{5} \times \frac{12}{13} = \frac{1}{10} \times \frac{5}{3} \times \frac{12}{13}$. Then take advantage of the opportunities to cancel before multiplying:

$\frac{1}{10} \times \frac{5}{3} \times \frac{12}{13} = \frac{1}{{}_2 \cancel{10}} \times \frac{\cancel{5}^1}{{}_1 \cancel{3}} \times \frac{\cancel{12}^4}{13} = \frac{4^2}{{}_1 2 \times 13} = \frac{2}{13}$.

7. **D** To subtract the fractions in the first set of parentheses, use a common denominator of 12: $\left(\frac{3}{4} - \frac{2}{3}\right) \div \left(\frac{1}{2} + \frac{1}{5}\right) = \left(\frac{9}{12} - \frac{8}{12}\right) \div \left(\frac{1}{2} + \frac{1}{5}\right) = \left(\frac{1}{12}\right) \div \left(\frac{5}{10} + \frac{2}{10}\right)$. To add the fractions in the second set

of parentheses, use a common denominator of 10: $\left(\frac{1}{12}\right) \div \left(\frac{5}{10} + \frac{2}{10}\right) = \left(\frac{1}{12}\right) \div \left(\frac{7}{10}\right)$. To divide, multiply

$\frac{1}{12}$ by the reciprocal of $\frac{7}{10}$: $\left(\frac{1}{12}\right) \div \left(\frac{7}{10}\right) = \frac{1}{{}_6 \cancel{12}} \times \frac{\cancel{10}^5}{7} = \frac{5}{42}$.

8. **D** If there were 15 cards from the Browns, then there were also 15 from the Athletics and 15 from the Senators. Half of the cards were Dodgers, one-fourth were Giants, and $\frac{1}{2} + \frac{1}{4} = \frac{2}{4} + \frac{1}{4} = \frac{3}{4}$, so the

other 45 cards are the remaining one-fourth. If 45 cards are $\frac{1}{4}$ of the collection, then $2 \times 45 = 90$ cards

would be $\frac{2}{4}$ or $\frac{1}{2}$ of the collection. The Dodgers cards were half of the collection, so there were 90 Dodgers cards.

9. **C** The question tells you that $\frac{7}{8}$ of the membership voted, and $\frac{2}{3}$ of those present voted to approve:

$\frac{2}{3} \times \frac{7}{8} = \frac{\cancel{2}^1}{3} \times \frac{7}{\cancel{8}_4} = \frac{7}{12}$, so $\frac{7}{12}$ of the 3,600 members voted to approve. Multiplying, $\frac{7}{{}_1 \cancel{12}} \times \frac{\cancel{3,600}^{300}}{1} = 2,100$

members who voted to approve.

10. **D** Half a number minus $3\frac{3}{4}$ is equal to $\frac{5}{4}$, so half the number is equal to $\frac{5}{4} + 3\frac{3}{4}$. Don't worry about

the fact that $\frac{5}{4}$ is an improper fraction; take advantage of the common denominator to add and then

simplify: $\frac{5}{4} + 3\frac{3}{4} = 3\frac{8}{4} = 3 + 2 = 5$. Half the number is 5, so the whole number is 10.

E. Ratio and Proportion

1. Ratio

A *ratio* is a comparison of two numbers by division. If one number is three times the size of another, we say the ratio of the larger to the smaller is "3 to 1." This can be written as 3:1 or as the fraction $\frac{3}{1}$.

When you're told that the ratio of one number to another is 5:2, you aren't being told that the numbers are 5 and 2, but that when you divide the first by the second, you get a number equal to $\frac{5}{2}$. This means that the first number was 5 times some number and the second was 2 times that number. You can represent the numbers as $5x$ and $2x$.

EXAMPLE:

Two numbers are in ratio 7:3 and their sum is 50. Find the numbers.

First, represent the numbers as $7x$ and $3x$. Then, $7x + 3x = 50$, so $10x = 50$ and $x = 5$. Don't forget to find the numbers! $7x = 7 \times 5 = 35$ and $3x = 3 \times 5 = 15$, so the numbers are 35 and 15.

2. Extended Ratios

An *extended ratio* compares more than two numbers. Extended ratios are usually written with colons.

EXAMPLE:

A punch contains grapefruit juice, orange juice, and ginger ale, in a ratio of 2:5:3. If 20 gallons of punch are needed for a party, how much orange juice is required?

Represent the amounts as $2x$ (grapefruit juice), $5x$ (orange juice), and $3x$ (ginger ale). So, $2x + 5x + 3x = 20$, which means that $10x = 20$ and $x = 2$. Be sure you answer the right question. Orange juice is $5x = 5 \times 2 = 10$ gallons.

3. Cross-Multiplication

A *proportion* is statement that two ratios are equal. The equation $\frac{1}{3} = \frac{2}{6}$ or 1:3 = 2:6 is an example of a proportion.

In any proportion, the product of the *means* (the two middle terms) is equal to the product of the *extremes* (the first and last terms). For example, in the proportion 5:8 = 15:24, $8 \times 15 = 5 \times 24$. This means that whenever you have two equal ratios, you can cross-multiply, and solve the resulting equation to find the unknown term.

EXAMPLE:

If $\frac{7}{4} = \frac{x}{14}$, find x.

Cross-multiplying produces $4x = 7 \times 14$. Solving this equation gives $x = \frac{7 \cdot 14}{4} = \frac{98}{4} = 24.5$.

Practice

Directions (1–2): You are given two quantities, one in Column A and one in Column B. You are to compare the two quantities and choose:

A if the quantity in Column A is greater
B if the quantity in Column B is greater
C if the two quantities are equal
D if the relationship cannot be determined from the information given

---

Fruit is packed in crates so that the ratio of lemons to limes is 2:1.

Column A	**Column B**
1. The number of limes in a crate containing 54 pieces of fruit	The number of lemons in a crate containing 27 pieces of fruit.

$$\frac{x}{7} = \frac{y}{12}$$
$$x > 0, \ y > 0$$

Column A	**Column B**
2. $24x$	$15y$

Directions (3–8): You are given five answer choices. Select the best choice.

---

3. In a certain town, the ratio of Democrats to Republicans is 5:4. If there are 18,000 people in the town, how many are Democrats?

    A. 3,600
    B. 4,500
    C. 2,000
    D. 5,000
    E. 10,000

4. Miriam's CD collection includes 42 operas and 36 Broadway shows. The ratio of shows to opera is

    A. 3:4
    B. 3:2
    C. 6:7
    D. 18:39
    E. 21:39

5. Each gallon of Callie's lemonade is 2 parts lemon juice, 2 parts sugar, and 3 parts water. What fraction of the lemonade mixture is sugar?

A. $\dfrac{2}{7}$

B. $\dfrac{2}{5}$

C. $\dfrac{1}{2}$

D. $\dfrac{2}{3}$

E. $\dfrac{3}{2}$

6. $\dfrac{8}{15} = \dfrac{x}{3}$

A. 0.8
B. 1
C. 1.2
D. 1.4
E. 1.6

7. Rick's favorite salad dressing calls for vinegar and oil in a ratio of 3:2. If he wants to make 2 quarts of salad dressing for a picnic, how much oil will he need?

A. $\dfrac{1}{2}$ quart

B. $\dfrac{2}{5}$ quart

C. $\dfrac{1}{3}$ quart

D. $\dfrac{3}{5}$ quart

E. $\dfrac{4}{5}$ quart

8. Charles determined that the time he spent on homework was divided between math and physics in a ratio of 4:5. If Charles spent one and a half hours on homework last night, how many minutes did he spend on math?

A. 18
B. $22\dfrac{1}{2}$
C. 40
D. 50
E. 90

Directions (9–10): Give your answer as a number.

9. The ratio of girls to boys on the math team is 8:3. If there are 24 girls on the team, how many people are on the team?

10. The ratio of blue marbles to red ones in a certain jar is 7:5. If there are 60 marbles in the jar, how many are blue?

Answers

1. **C** The number of lemons is $2x$ and the number of limes is x. If the total is 54, $2x + x = 54$, so $3x = 54$ and $x = 18$. There are 18 limes and 36 lemons. If the total is 27, $2x + x = 3x = 27$, so $x = 9$. There are 9 limes and 18 lemons. The number of limes in a crate containing 54 pieces of fruit is equal to the number of lemons in a crate containing 27 pieces of fruit.

2. **B** Cross-multiplying, $\frac{x}{7} = \frac{y}{12} \Rightarrow 12x = 7y$. Multiplying both sides of that equation by 2 give you $2(12x) = 2(7y) \Rightarrow 24x = 14y$. Because $24x$ is equal to $14y$, $24x$ is less than $15y$.

3. **E** If the ratio of Democrats to Republicans is 5:4, the number of Democrats can be represented by $5x$ and the number of Republicans can be represented by $4x$. Then $5x + 4x = 18,000$ people in the town; $9x = 18,000$ means that $x = 2,000$. So the number of Democrats is $5 \times 2,000 = 10,000$ people.

4. **C** The ratio of shows to operas is 36:42, but ratios, like fractions, can be reduced to lowest terms. Dividing both numbers by 6, 36:42 = 6:7.

5. **A** Each gallon is 2 parts lemon juice, 2 parts sugar, and 3 parts water, for a total of 7 parts. Sugar is 2 of the seven parts, or $\frac{2}{7}$ of the mixture.

6. **E** Cross-multiplying, $\frac{8}{15} = \frac{x}{3} \Rightarrow 15x = 8 \cdot 3 \Rightarrow x = \frac{8 \cdot \cancel{3}^{1}}{{}_{5}\cancel{15}} = \frac{8}{5} = 1\frac{3}{5} = 1.6$.

7. **E** The dressing is 3 parts vinegar and 2 parts oil, so oil is 2 of a total of 5 parts, or $\frac{2}{5}$ of the mixture. Don't forget to convert it to quarts: $\frac{2}{5}$ of 2 quarts is $\frac{4}{5}$ of a quart.

8. **C** Let $4x$ represent the number of minutes spent on math and $5x$ represent the number of minutes spent on physics. One and a half hours is equivalent to $60 + 30 = 90$ minutes, so $4x + 5x = 90$, $9x = 90$, and $x = 10$. The number of minutes spent on math is $4x = 4(10) = 40$ minutes.

9. **33** If the ratio of girls to boys on the math team is 8:3, then $8x$ represents the number of girls and $3x$ represents the number of boys. If there are 24 girls, $8x = 24$ and $x = 3$. There are 24 girls and $3x = 3(3) = 9$ boys, for a total of $24 + 9 = 33$ team members.

10. **35** If the ratio of blue marbles to red ones in a certain jar is 7:5, then the number of blue marbles can be represented by $7x$ and the number of red marbles can be represented by $5x$. The total $7x + 5x = 60$, so $12x = 60$ and $x = 5$. Blue marbles account for $7x = 7(5) = 35$.

F. Decimals

1. Place Value

Decimals are, in truth, *decimal fractions,* fractions that use powers of ten as their denominators. Because they're based on powers of ten, they can conveniently be written in an extension of the place value system we use for whole numbers, so their denominators seem to disappear. Those denominators are still there, of course, and you hear them if you give the decimal its proper name. Many people will pronounce .375 as "point 375," its technical name is "375 thousandths." The 375 names the numerator and the thousandths names the denominator.

In our decimal system of numbers, each place to the left of the decimal point represents a larger power of ten. In a similar fashion, each place to the right of the decimal point represents a smaller power of ten. In the number 6923.8471, here's what each number is:

6	9	2	3	.	8	4	7	1
Thousands	Hundreds	Tens	Ones		Tenths	Hundredths	Thousandths	Ten-thousandths

2. Comparing Decimals

When asked to compare decimals, arrange the numbers with the decimal points aligned one under another. Add zeros to the end of numbers until all the numbers have the same number of digits after the decimal point. Then forget the decimal points are there; the largest number (without the decimal points) is the largest number (with the decimal points.)

EXAMPLE:

Which of the following is largest?

A. 0.043
B. 0.43
C. 0.403
D. 0.4003
E. 0.0043

To find the answer, write the numbers with the decimal points aligned (as they are in the answer choices above). Then add one zero to the end of Choice A, two zeros to the end of Choice B, and one zero to the end of Choice C—this makes all five answer choices have the same number of digits (four after the decimal point). Finally, ignore the decimal points, and just look at the numbers you have left: 0430, 4300, 4030, 4003, and 0043. You can see that 4,300 is the largest number, so 0.4300, or 0.43, is the largest decimal.

3. Addition and Subtraction

To add or subtract decimals, arrange the numbers with the decimal points aligned one under another. This assures that you're adding the digits with the same place value. Add or subtract as you would if the decimal points were not there, doing any carrying or borrowing just as you would for whole numbers. Add a decimal point to your answer directly under the decimal points in the problem.

EXAMPLE:

Add 34.82 + 9.7.

To find the answer, align the decimal points. (Add zeros if you like.) Add normally and bring the decimal point straight down.

$$
\begin{array}{r}
34.82 \\
+9.70 \\
\hline
44.52
\end{array}
$$

4. Multiplication

Multiplying decimals requires a slightly more complicated algorithm. You perform the actual multiplication as though the decimal points were not present. If you were multiplying 3.1×2, you would first think of it as 31×2, and if you were multiplying 3.1×0.002, you would also think of that as 31×2 to begin. The difference comes in placing the decimal point.

To place the decimal point in the product, first count the number of digits to the right of the decimal point in each of the factors. Add these up to find the number of decimal places in the product. Start from the far right end of the answer and count that many places to the left to place your decimal point. If you run out of digits, add zeros to the left end of the number until you have enough places.

EXAMPLE:

Multiply 3.1×2.

To find the answer, first think of the problem as $31 \times 2 = 62$. Then count the decimal places. There is one digit after the decimal point in 3.1. There are no digits after the decimal point in 2, so the answer must have one digit after the decimal point. Place the decimal between the 6 and the 2 for an answer of 6.2.

EXAMPLE:

Multiply 3.1×0.002.

To find the answer, first think of the problem as $31 \times 2 = 62$. Then count the decimal places. There is one digit after the decimal point in 3.1. There are three digits after the decimal point in 0.002, so the answer must have a total of four digits after the decimal point. Start from the right side and count to the left. The 2 in 62 is one digit, the 6 is a second, but there must be four digits to the right of the decimal point, so place zeros for the third and fourth, giving an answer of 0.0061.

Estimation skills are useful in placing decimal points. For example, 3.1×2 should be approximately $3 \times 2 = 6$, but 3.1×0.002 should give a much smaller result.

5. Division

To divide a decimal fraction by a whole number, divide normally and bring the decimal point straight up into your quotient.

To divide a decimal by another decimal you probably learned a process that involved moving decimal points. You never actually divide by a decimal. You change the appearance of the problem so that its divisor is a whole number. This is the same process as changing the appearance of a fraction. The task of dividing 502.5 by 0.25 can be thought of as simplifying a fraction with 502.5 in the numerator and 0.25 in the denominator. Multiplying both the numerator and denominator by 100 makes the fraction 50,250 divided by 25. That is still a bit of work, but at least the divisor is now a whole number.

To divide decimals, move the decimal point in the divisor to the right until the divisor is a whole number. Move the decimal point in the dividend the same number of places to the right. Divide normally and bring the decimal point straight up into the quotient.

EXAMPLE:

Divide 17.835 by 2.05.

Move the decimal point in the divisor two places right so that 2.05 becomes 205. Move the decimal point in 17.835 two places to the right as well, making it 1,783.5:

$$\begin{array}{r} 8.7 \\ 205\overline{)1783.5} \\ \underline{1640} \\ 1435 \\ \underline{1435} \\ 0 \end{array}$$

Divide normally, and let the decimal point in the dividend (between 3 and 5) move straight up into the quotient, for a result of 8.7.

6. Scientific Notation

Scientific notation is a method of representing very large or very small numbers as the product of a number greater than or equal to 1 and less than 10 times a power of 10. A large number would be represented as a number between one and ten times a positive power of ten, whereas a small number (a fraction or decimal) would be some number times a negative power of ten. You can think of the sign of the exponent as an indicator of which way to move the decimal point: Positive exponents tell you to move the decimal to the right; negative exponents tell you to move to the left. The number 5,400,000 can be represented as 5.4×10^6. The number 0.00071 is 7.1×10^{-4}.

To change a number from standard form to scientific notation, place a decimal point after the first nonzero digit. Drop leading or trailing zeros. This will give you the number between one and ten. To find the appropriate power of ten, count the number of places from where you placed the decimal to where it actually should appear. If you must count to the right, the exponent will be positive. If you count to the left, the exponent will be negative.

$$\underset{\text{7 places right}}{58,400,000} = 5.84 \times 10^7$$

$$\underset{\text{10 places left}}{0.000000000693} = 6.93 \times 10^{-10}$$

To multiply numbers in scientific notation, multiply the front numbers normally, and multiply the powers of ten by adding the exponents: $(5 \times 10^3)(7 \times 10^9) = 35 \times 10^{12}$. Because the front number is now greater than ten, rewrite $35 \times 10^{12} = 3.5 \times 10 \times 10^{12} = 3.5 \times 10^{13}$.

To divide numbers in scientific notation, divide the front numbers normally, and divide the powers of ten by subtracting the exponents. Remember to adjust so that the answer is in correct scientific notation:

$$\frac{4.8 \times 10^{12}}{1.2 \times 10^{8}} = 4 \times 10^{12-8} = 4 \times 10^{4}$$

$$\frac{1.2 \times 10^{8}}{4.8 \times 10^{12}} = 0.25 \times 10^{8-12} = 0.25 \times 10^{-4} = 2.5 \times 10^{-1} \times 10^{-4} = 2.5 \times 10^{-5}$$

Practice

Directions (1–4): You are given two quantities, one in Column A and one in Column B. You are to compare the two quantities and choose:

A if the quantity in Column A is greater
B if the quantity in Column B is greater
C if the two quantities are equal
D if the relationship cannot be determined from the information given

	Column A	Column B
1.	0.05003	0.0503

	Column A	Column B
2.	$\dfrac{13}{17}$	0.76

	Column A	Column B
3.	0.000037	3.7×10^{-6}

	Column A	Column B
4.	0.001 + 0.1	0.01 + 0.101

Directions (5–8): You are given five answer choices. Select the best choice.

5. 46.25 + 9.107 + 108.6 =

   A. 163.957
   B. 148.18
   C. 56.443
   D. 122.332
   E. 245.92

6. $0.2 + 11.002 - 4.37 =$

    A.   15.572

    B.   6.832

    C.   8.632

    D.   6.652

    E.   10.765

7. $(4.8 \times 10^{-3}) \div (1.2 \times 10^{-5}) =$

    A. 4.0×10^{-8}

    B. 5.76×10^{-8}

    C.   400

    D.   576

    E.   360

8. If the speed of sound is slightly more than 900 feet/second, how fast would you be traveling if you reached Mach 4, or four times the speed of sound?

    A. 3.6×10^{2}

    B. 3.6×10^{3}

    C. 3.6×10^{4}

    D. 9×10^{4}

    E. 9×10^{8}

Directions (9–10): Give your answer as a number.

9. $0.0009 \times 500 \times 0.04 \times 20 =$

10. Calculate $4.65 \div 9.3 \times 4.8$ to the nearest tenth.

Answers

1. B To compare 0.05003 and 0.0503, align the decimal points and add a zero to 0.0503 to make both numbers the same length. Then ignore decimal points and leading zeros: $\dfrac{0.05003}{0.05030} \Rightarrow \dfrac{005003}{005030} \Rightarrow \dfrac{5003}{5030}$. Because the number 5,030 is larger than 5,003, 0.0503 is larger than 0.05003.

2. A Change $\dfrac{13}{17}$ to a decimal by dividing 13 by 17. Because there is still a remainder when the quotient has reached 0.76, division can continue by adding zeros:

$$
\begin{array}{r}
0.764 \\
17\overline{)13.000} \\
\underline{119} \\
110 \\
\underline{102} \\
80 \\
\underline{68} \\
12
\end{array}
$$

The decimal equivalent of $\dfrac{13}{17}$ is greater than 0.76.

3. **A** $3.7 \times 10^{-6} = 3.\underset{1}{7} \times 0.\underset{6}{000001}$, so the product has $1 + 6 = 7$ digits to the right of the decimal point. So $3.7 \times 10^{-6} = 0.\underset{7}{0000037}$. Think of moving the decimal point in 3.7 to the left (because the exponent is negative) six places: $3.7 \times 10^{-6} = 0.\underset{6\text{ to the left}}{000003}.7$. Compare 0.000037 to 0.0000037 by aligning the decimal points: $\begin{matrix} 0.000037 \\ 0.0000037 \end{matrix} \Rightarrow \begin{matrix} 370 \\ 37 \end{matrix}$ and conclude that $0.000037 > 0.0000037$.

4. **B** Add the decimals by aligning decimal points:

$$\begin{array}{r} 0.001 \\ + \ 0.100 \\ \hline 0.101 \end{array} \qquad \begin{array}{r} 0.010 \\ + \ 0.101 \\ \hline 0.111 \end{array}$$

5. **A** Add the decimals by aligning decimal points:

$$\begin{array}{r} 46.250 \\ + \quad 9.107 \\ + \ 108.600 \\ \hline 163.957 \end{array}$$

6. **B** To find the answer, do the addition first:

$$\begin{array}{r} 0.200 \\ + \ 11.002 \\ \hline 11.202 \end{array}$$

Then subtract:

$$\begin{array}{r} 11.202 \\ - \ 4.370 \\ \end{array}$$

Regrouping will be necessary:

$$\begin{array}{r} 1^0\,\cancel{1}.\,^{11}\cancel{2}\,^1 02 \\ - \ 4.\ 3\ \ \ 70 \\ \hline 6.\ \ 8\ \ \ 32 \end{array}$$

7. **C** Divide 4.8 by 1.2 and use rules for exponents to divide 10^{-3} by 10^{-5}. Keep the base of 10 and subtract the exponents: $-3 - -5 = -3 + 5 = 2$.

$$\left(4.8 \times 10^{-3}\right) \div \left(1.2 \times 10^{-5}\right) = \left(4.8 \div 1.2\right) \times \left(10^{-3} \div 10^{-5}\right)$$
$$= 4 \times 10^{-3--5} = 4 \times 10^{2} = 4 \times 100 = 400$$

8. **B** If you reached Mach 4, you would be traveling at over $4 \times 900 = 3,600$ feet/second. Because the choices are in scientific notation, convert 3,600 to a number between one and ten, 3.6, times a power of ten, 10^3.

9. **0.003600 or 0. 0036** Multiply the nonzero digits, $9 \times 5 \times 4 \times 2 = 9 \times 4 \times 5 \times 2 = 36 \times 10 = 3,600$. Then count the digits to the right of the decimal point in each of the factors. There are four digits to the right of the decimal point in 0.0009 and two in 0.04, so the product should have $4 + 2 = 6$ decimal places: $0.\underset{6\text{ places}}{003600}$. The trailing zeros can be dropped.

10. **2.4** To perform the division $4.65 \div 9.3$, move the decimal point in each number one place to the right. Dividing 46.5 by 93 is equivalent to $4.65 \div 9.3$. Use estimation to help with the calculation. If you were dividing 465 by 93, you could estimate the quotient by noting that $5 \times 90 = 450$.

$$9.\underline{3.)}\overline{4.\underline{6}.5}^{0.5}$$

Then multiply 0.5×4.8, a task that becomes easier if you recognize that this is half of 4.8, or 2.4.

G. Percent

1. Meaning of Percent

Ratios can be hard to compare if they are "out of" different numbers. Which is larger: 4 out of 9 or 5 out of 12? If you compare them as fractions, $\frac{4}{9}$ and $\frac{5}{12}$, it might help to change to a common denominator.

Changing ratios to percents is like changing to a common denominator. Percent makes it easier to compare, because everything is out of 100. Percent means "out of 100."

2. Using Proportions to Change a Ratio to a Percent

The basic rule to remember is $\frac{\text{part}}{\text{whole}} = \frac{\%}{100}$. This proportion can be used to solve most percent problems.

EXAMPLE:

The by-laws of the town council require that a candidate receive at least 51% of the vote to be elected council president. If the council membership is 1,288, what is the minimum number of votes a candidate must receive to be elected president?

Start with $\frac{\text{part}}{\text{whole}} = \frac{\%}{100}$ or $\frac{p}{1,288} = \frac{51}{100}$. Cross-multiplying, $100p = 1,288 \times 51$. Then $100p = 63,188$, and $p = 631.88$. Because no one can cast a fraction of a vote, round this to 632 votes.

When you use the $\frac{\text{part}}{\text{whole}} = \frac{\%}{100}$ rule, the only trick is determining which number is the part and which is the whole. Certain words in the problem can signal this for you. The word *of* usually precedes the whole amount, and the word *is* can generally be found near the part.

EXAMPLE:

What percent of 58 is 22?

Look for *of,* and you find that 58 is the whole. Look for *is,* and you find that 22 is the part.

$$\frac{\text{part}}{\text{whole}} = \frac{\%}{100}$$
$$\frac{22}{58} = \frac{x}{100}$$
$$58x = 2,200$$
$$x \approx 37.9$$

EXAMPLE:

46 is 27% of what number?

Look for *of,* and you find that the whole is "what number," which means it is unknown. Look for *is,* and you find that 46 is the part. Both 46 and 27 are near the *is,* but 27 has the % sign, so you know it's the percent.

$$\frac{\text{part}}{\text{whole}} = \frac{\%}{100}$$

$$\frac{46}{x} = \frac{27}{100}$$

$$27x = 4,600$$

$$x \approx 170.4$$

EXAMPLE:

What is 83% of 112?

Look for *of,* and you find that 112 is the whole. Look for *is,* and you find that the part is "what," which means the part is unknown.

$$\frac{\text{part}}{\text{whole}} = \frac{\%}{100}$$

$$\frac{x}{112} = \frac{83}{100}$$

$$100x = 112 \cdot 83$$

$$100x = 9,296$$

$$x = 92.96$$

3. Percent Increase or Decrease

Some problems ask you to compute the percent increase or percent decrease. Percent increase and percent decrease—or, in general, percent change—problems compare the change in a quantity, whether increase or decrease, to the original amount. The original amount is the whole, and the change is the part.

Identify the original amount. Calculate increase or decrease, and then use $\frac{\text{change}}{\text{original}} = \frac{\%}{100}$ to calculate the percent.

EXAMPLE:

Allison invests $857 in a stock she researched. After a year, her investment is worth $911. What is the percent increase in the value of her investment?

The original investment is $857 and it increases $911 – $857 = $54.

$$\frac{change}{original} = \frac{\%}{100}$$

$$\frac{54}{857} = \frac{x}{100}$$

$$857x = 5,400$$

$$x \approx 6.3$$

The percent increase was approximately 6.3%.

EXAMPLE:

Melissa buys $320 worth of collectibles at a flea market and tucks them away, hoping they'll increase in value. Unfortunately, when she tries to sell them, she finds that they're only worth $275. What is the percent decrease in the value of her investment?

The original cost was $320, but decreased $320 – $275 = $45.

$$\frac{change}{original} = \frac{\%}{100}$$

$$\frac{45}{320} = \frac{x}{100}$$

$$320x = 4,500$$

$$x \approx 14$$

Her investment decreased approximately 14%.

4. Changing to a Decimal

Percent problems can also be solved by using decimal equivalents. To change a percent to a decimal, drop the percent sign and move the decimal point two places to the left: 14.5% = 0.145 and 8% = 0.08. To change a decimal to a percent, move the decimal point two places to the right and add a percent sign. Leading zeros can be dropped: 0.497 = 49.7% and 5.983 = 598.3%.

When solving percent problems using decimal equivalents, remember that *of* generally signals multiplication. So, 15% of 300 becomes 0.15 × 300. In the terminology used earlier, percent × whole = part.

Practice

Directions (1–2): You are given two quantities, one in Column A and one in Column B. You are to compare the two quantities and choose:

A if the quantity in Column A is greater
B if the quantity in Column B is greater
C if the two quantities are equal
D if the relationship cannot be determined from the information given

	Column A		Column B
1.	20% of 40		40% of 20

20% of x is 25.

	Column A		Column B
2.	105% of x		105

Directions (3–8): You are given five answer choices. Select the best choice.

3. Jason paid for his new DVD player in installments. All together, he paid $408.98, which included a 5% service charge. What was the price of the DVD player alone, without the service charge?

   A. $408.93
   B. $403.98
   C. $389.50
   D. $388.53
   E. $20.45

4. Find 30% of 40% of 500.

   A. 12
   B. 20
   C. 60
   D. 150
   E. 200

5. Magdalena bought several shares of stock in a small company for $350. She held the stock for a year and then sold it for $910. What was the percent increase in Magdalena's investment?

   A. 2.6%
   B. 26%
   C. 38%
   D. 160%
   E. 260%

6. When Laura bought a new DVD player, the player was marked at 45% off the list price. Because she had a coupon for a special sale, she then received an additional 15% off the marked price. If the original list price of the DVD player was $148, what did Laura actually pay?

   A. $88
   B. $69.19
   C. $56.61
   D. $12.21
   E. $9.99

7. The constitution of a town requires that 60% of the residents vote in favor of a proposal before it can become law in the town. Maya's initiative to ban smoking in all town restaurants did not pass in the last election. If there are 9,670 residents in the town, what is the minimum number of residents who voted against Maya's proposal?

   A. 5,802
   B. 4,835
   C. 3,869
   D. 3,868
   E. 3,481

8. In a recent survey, voters in our town were asked what political party they voted for most often, and 368 people indicated they voted Republican. If this represents about 46% of the town's voters, how many voters are there in the town?

   A. 169
   B. 537
   C. 800
   D. 1,168
   E. 16,928

Directions (9–10): Give your answer as a number.

9. A pair of boots originally priced at $100 went on sale at 20% off. Later in the season, there was an additional markdown of 15% off the current (already reduced) price. If you buy the boots at the end of the season, what percent of the original price have you saved?

10. Glen finds a $40 sweater on sale for 15% off, but he must pay 5% sales tax. If he hands the cashier $40, how much change will he receive?

Answers

1. **C** To find the answer, figure 20% of 40 = 0.2 × 40 = 8 and 40% of 20 = 0.4 × 20 = 8.

2. **A** If 20% of x is 25, then $x = 5 × 25 = 125$. You know that 105% of x is more than 125, which means it's greater than 105. (You don't have to figure out 105% of x to know the answer.)

3. **C** The total payment of $408.98 was 105% of the price of the player. If x is the price of the player, $1.05x = 408.98$. Solve for x by dividing $408.98 ÷ 1.05:

$$
\begin{array}{r}
389.50 \\
1.05\overline{)408.98.00} \\
315 \\
\overline{939} \\
840 \\
\overline{998} \\
945 \\
\overline{530} \\
525 \\
\overline{50} \\
0
\end{array}
$$

4. **C** Mental math is helpful here: 10% of 500 is 50, so 40% of 500 is 4 × 50 = 200 and 30% of 200 is 3 × 20 = 60. You could also find it this way: 30% of 40% of 500 = 0.3 × 0.4 × 500 = 60.

5. **D** Magdalena's original investment of $350 increased by $910 – $350 = $560.

$$\frac{change}{original} = \frac{\%}{100}$$

$$\frac{560}{350} = \frac{x}{100}$$

$$350x = 560 \cdot 100$$

$$x = \frac{\overset{8}{560} \cdot 100}{\underset{5}{350}} = \frac{800}{5} = 160$$

Her investment increased 160%.

6. **B** List price was $148, and 45% of $148 is 0.45 × 148 = $66.60, so the marked price was $148 – $66.60 = $81.40. The additional 15% off would be 0.15 × $81.40 = $12.21, making her cost $81.40 – $12.21 = $69.19.

7. **D** To pass, Maya's proposal would have needed 60% of the 9,670 votes, or 5,802 votes. That would leave 9,670 – 5,802 = 3,868 votes against the proposal. Because the proposal did not pass, there must have been at least one more vote against, so a minimum of 3,869 residents voted against Maya's proposal.

8. **C** If the 368 people who said they voted Republican are 46% of the town's voters, and x represents the number of voters, then 368 is the part, x is the whole, and 46 is the percent.

$$\frac{part}{whole} = \frac{\%}{100}$$

$$\frac{368}{x} = \frac{46}{100}$$

$$46x = 368 \cdot 100$$

$$x = \frac{\overset{184}{\cancel{368}} \cdot 100}{\cancel{46}_{23}} = \frac{\overset{8}{\cancel{184}} \cdot 100}{\cancel{23}_{1}} = 800$$

9. **32%** Because 20% of $100 is $20, the first markdown of 20% off reduces the price from $100 to $80. The additional discount is 15% of $80.

$$\frac{part}{whole} = \frac{\%}{100}$$

$$\frac{x}{80} = \frac{15}{100}$$

$$100x = 80 \cdot 15$$

$$x = \frac{\overset{4}{\cancel{80}} \cdot 15}{\cancel{100}_{5}} = \frac{4 \cdot \overset{3}{\cancel{15}}}{\cancel{5}_{1}} = 12$$

This means that you pay $80 − $12 = $68. You've saved $32 off the original price, or 32%.

10. **$4.30** 10% of $40 is $4, so 15% will be $4 + $2 = $6. Glen will pay $40 − $6 = $34 plus 5% sales tax.

$$\frac{part}{whole} = \frac{\%}{100}$$

$$\frac{x}{34} = \frac{5}{100}$$

$$100x = 5 \cdot 34 = 170$$

$$x = \frac{170}{100} = 1.70$$

His total cost is $34 + $1.70 = $35.70. If he hands over $40, he'll receive $40 − $35.70 = $4.30.

H. Exponents

Exponents are symbols for repeated multiplication. When you write bn you say that you want to use b as a factor n times. The number b is the base, n is the exponent, and bn is the power. The expression 5^3, for example, means $5 \times 5 \times 5$.

You should remember some special exponents:

$$a^0 = 1 \ \left(\text{provided } a \neq 0 \right)$$

$$a^1 = a$$

$$a^{-1} = \frac{1}{a} \ \left(\text{NOT } -a \right)$$

$$a^{-n} = \frac{1}{a^n}$$

People are sometimes confused about exactly what the base is when they look at expressions like $(3x)^2$ or $3x^2$. Looking at what is immediately left of the exponent will help sort that out. The expression $(3x)^2 = (3x)(3x)$ because the parenthesis is immediately left of the exponent, and so the whole quantity in the parentheses is squared, but $3x^2 = 3 \times x \times x$ because only the x is immediately left of the exponent.

Avoid the common error that occurs when working with powers of signed numbers. Remember that to multiply -5 by -5, you must write $(-5)^2$ with parentheses. If you write -5^2 without parentheses, the exponent only touches the 5 and you get $-(5 \times 5)$.

1. Multiplication

When you multiply powers of the same base, keep the base and add the exponents.

EXAMPLE:

Simplify $x^7 \cdot y^3 \cdot x^5$.

You can use the rules for exponents on powers of the same base. Rearrange $x^7 \cdot y^3 \cdot x^5 = x^7 \cdot x^5 \cdot y^3$ and multiply the powers of x by keeping the base and adding the exponents: $x^7 \cdot x^5 \cdot y^3 = x^{12} \cdot y^3$. You cannot apply the rule to different bases, so it isn't possible to simplify any further.

EXAMPLE:

Which of the following is equivalent to $2^3 \times 3^2 \times 2^2 \times 3^1$?

   A. 2^8
   B. 3^8
   C. 6^8
   D. $2^5 \times 3^3$
   E. $4^5 \times 9^3$

Rearrange to group powers with the same base: $2^3 \times 3^2 \times 2^2 \times 3^1 = 2^3 \times 2^2 \times 3^2 \times 3^1$. Multiply the powers of 2 by keeping the base of 2 and adding the exponents: $2^3 \times 2^2 \times 3^2 \times 3^1 = 2^5 \times 3^2 \times 3^1$. Multiply the powers of 3 by keeping the base of 3 and adding the exponents: $2^5 \times 3^2 \times 3^1 = 2^5 \times 3^3$. The correct answer is D.

The most common errors with exponents are made by students who only learn half the rule. The active part of the rule, add the exponents, is what most people remember, but the other part, keep the base, is just as important. Asked to multiply $2^3 \times 2^4$ many people will try to add the exponents *and* multiply the 2s, giving an answer of 4^7 instead of 2^7. *Keep the base and add the exponents.*

2. Division

When you divide powers of the same base, keep the base and subtract the exponents.

EXAMPLE:

Which of the following is another way to write $\dfrac{7^{10} \cdot 5^{12}}{7^{6} \cdot 5^{4}}$?

   A. $7^{\frac{5}{3}} \cdot 5^{3}$

   B. $\dfrac{35^{22}}{35^{10}}$

   C. $7^{4} \times 5^{8}$

   D. $1^{4} \times 1^{8}$

   E. 35^{12}

The rules for exponents only work for powers of the same base, so there is nothing that can conveniently be done to $7^{10} \times 5^{12}$ or $7^{6} \times 5^{4}$. Instead, divide 7^{10} by 7^{6}, keeping the base of 7 and subtracting the exponent of the denominator from the exponent in the numerator: $7^{10} \div 7^{6} = 7^{(10-6)} = 7^{4}$. Then divide 512 by 54, keeping the base of 5 and subtracting the exponents: $5^{12} \div 5^{4} = 5^{(12-4)} = 5^{8}$. The best answer is $7^{4} \times 5^{8}$.

3. Powers

When you raise a power to a power, keep the base and multiply the exponents.

EXAMPLE:

Which of the following is *not* equivalent to 5^{24}?

   A. $(125)^{8}$

   B. $(5^{12})^{2}$

   C. $(5^{6})^{4}$

   D. $(5^{20})^{4}$

   E. $(25)^{12}$

Consider the answer choices that are conveniently written as powers of powers first. Raising a power to a power means keeping the base and multiplying the exponents, so $(5^{12})^{2} = 5^{12 \times 2} = 5^{24}$ and $(5^{6})^{4} = 5^{6 \times 4} = 5^{24}$, but $(5^{20})^{4} = 5^{20 \times 4} = 5^{80}$. Choice D is not equal to 5^{24}. If it had become necessary to test the other options, 125 could be rewritten as 5^{3} and 25 rewritten as 5^{2}.

4. Power of a Product

When a product is raised to a power, each factor is raised to that power.

EXAMPLE:

Simplify $(5a^{3}b^{2}c^{4})^{3}$.

$(5a^{3}b^{2}c^{4})^{3} = 5^{3} (a^{3})^{3} \times (b^{2})^{3} \times (c^{4})^{3}$. Then apply the power of a power rule, and you have $5^{3} (a^{3})^{3} \times (b^{2})^{3} \times (c^{4})^{3} = 125a^{9}b^{6}c^{12}$.

5. Power of a Quotient

When a quotient is raised to a power, both the numerator and the denominator are raised to that power.

EXAMPLE:

Simplify $\left(\dfrac{7x^2y^{-3}z^4}{2x^{-1}y^2z^5}\right)^2$.

First apply the power of a quotient rule:

$$\left(\frac{7x^2y^{-3}z^4}{2x^{-1}y^2z^5}\right)^2 = \frac{\left(7x^2y^{-3}z^4\right)^2}{\left(2x^{-1}y^2z^5\right)^2}$$

Then apply the power of a product rule, first to the numerator and then to the denominator:

$$\frac{\left(7x^2y^{-3}z^4\right)^2}{\left(2x^{-1}y^2z^5\right)^2} = \frac{7^2 \cdot \left(x^2\right)^2 \cdot \left(y^{-3}\right)^2 \cdot \left(z^4\right)^2}{2^2 \cdot \left(x^{-1}\right)^2 \cdot \left(y^2\right)^2 \cdot \left(z^5\right)^2}$$

Simplify both the numerator and the denominator:

$$\frac{7^2 \cdot \left(x^2\right)^2 \cdot \left(y^{-3}\right)^2 \cdot \left(z^4\right)^2}{2^2 \cdot \left(x^{-1}\right)^2 \cdot \left(y^2\right)^2 \cdot \left(z^5\right)^2} = \frac{49x^4y^{-6}z^8}{4x^{-2}y^4z^{10}}$$

Finally divide powers of the same base by keeping the base and subtracting the exponents:

$$\frac{49x^4y^{-6}z^8}{4x^{-2}y^4z^{10}} = \frac{49}{4}x^{(4--2)}y^{(-6-4)}z^{(8-10)} = \frac{49}{4}x^6y^{-10}z^{-2}$$

Remember that this answer could also be expressed without negative exponents:

$$\frac{49}{4}x^6y^{-10}z^{-2} = \frac{49}{4}x^6 \cdot \frac{1}{y^{10}} \cdot \frac{1}{z^2} = \frac{49x^6}{4y^{10}z^2}$$

Practice

Directions (1–4): You are given two quantities, one in Column A and one in Column B. You are to compare the two quantities and choose:

A if the quantity in Column A is greater
B if the quantity in Column B is greater
C if the two quantities are equal
D if the relationship cannot be determined from the information given

	Column A	Column B
1.	5^2	2^5

	Column A	Column B
2.	$(-3)^2$	-3^2

	Column A	Column B
3.	$(2^2 - 5)x$	$(5 - 2^2)x$

	Column A	Column B
4.	$3^7 \times 5^7$	15^7

Directions (5–8): You are given five answer choices. Select the best choice.

5. $(-7x^3y^5)(2xy^2)=$

   A. $-5x^3y^{10}$
   B. $-5x^4y^7$
   C. $-14x^4y^7$
   D. $-14x^3y^{10}$
   E. Cannot be simplified

6. $(-3a^7b^5)^2 =$

   A. $9a^{14}b^{10}$
   B. $-9a^{14}b^{10}$
   C. $-3a^{14}b^{10}$
   D. $9a^9b^7$
   E. $-9a^9b^7$

7. $\dfrac{18xy^2z^5}{6x^3y^2z^2} =$

   A. $3x^2z^3$

   B. $12x^2z^3$

   C. $\dfrac{3z^3}{x^2}$

   D. $\dfrac{12z^3}{x^2}$

   E. $\dfrac{3y^4z^3}{x^2}$

8. $-\left(\dfrac{r^4t}{5rt^3}\right)^2 =$

   A. $\dfrac{-r^4}{5t^2}$

   B. $\dfrac{r^6}{5t^4}$

   C. $\dfrac{-r^6}{5t^4}$

   D. $\dfrac{r^6}{25t^4}$

   E. $\dfrac{-r^6}{25t^4}$

Directions (9–10): Give your answer as a number.

9. $\left(\dfrac{7^0 \cdot (-4)^2}{2^3}\right)^5 =$

10. The quotient of 27 squared and 15 squared is the square of what number?

Answers

1. **B** $5^2 = 5 \times 5 = 25$, but $2^5 = 2 \times 2 \times 2 \times 2 \times 2 = 32$.

2. **A** Because $(-3)^2 = (-3)(-3)$, the quantity in Column A is $+9$. But $-3^2 = -(3 \times 3)$, so Column B is -9.

3. **D** The two expressions being raised to the x power differ in sign: $2^2 - 5 = -1$ and $5 - 2^2 = 1$. If x is an even number, the quantity in Column A will equal that in Column B; if x is odd, however, they will have opposite signs. Because you can't know whether x is odd or even, you can't determine which expression is larger.

4. **C** Don't spend time evaluating seventh powers. Just note that $15^7 = (3 \times 5)^7 = 3^7 \times 5^7$.

5. **C** $(-7x^3y^5)(2xy^2) = -7 \times 2 \times x^3 \times x \times y^5 \times y^2 = -14x^4y^7$.

6. **A** $(-3a^7b^5)^2 = (-3)^2(a^7)^2(b^5)^2 = 9a^{14}b^{10}$.

7. **C** $\dfrac{18xy^2z^5}{6x^3y^2z^2} = \dfrac{18}{6} \cdot \dfrac{x}{x^3} \cdot \dfrac{y^2}{y^2} \cdot \dfrac{z^5}{z^2} = 3 \cdot \dfrac{1}{x^2} \cdot 1 \cdot \dfrac{z^3}{1} = \dfrac{3z^3}{x^2}$.

8. **E** $-\left(\dfrac{r^4t}{5rt^3}\right)^2 = -\left(\dfrac{r^3t}{5t^3}\right)^2 = -\left(\dfrac{r^3}{5t^2}\right)^2 = -\left(\dfrac{r^6}{25t^4}\right) = \dfrac{-r^6}{25t^4}$.

9. **32** $\left(\dfrac{7^0 \cdot (-4)^2}{2^3}\right)^5 = \left(\dfrac{1 \cdot 16}{8}\right)^5 = \left(\dfrac{16}{8}\right)^5 = 2^5 = 32$.

10. **$\dfrac{9}{5}$** The quotient of 27 squared and 15 squared can be written as $\dfrac{27^2}{15^2} = \left(\dfrac{27}{15}\right)^2 = \left(\dfrac{9}{5}\right)^2$.

I. Roots

Exponents talk about repeated multiplication; roots take you in the other direction. A number, r, is called the nth root of a number, x, if $rn = x$. The number 5 is the third root, or cube root, of 125 because $5^3 = 125$. The square root of 49 is 7 because $7^2 = 49$.

The symbol for the nth root of x is $\sqrt[n]{x}$. The sign is called a *radical.* The small number in the crook of the sign is called the *index,* and the index tells what power of the root produces x. If no index is shown, it's a square root.

Positive real numbers have two square roots: a positive root and a negative root. Both 7^2 and $(-7)^2$ will produce 49, so both 7 and -7 are square roots of 49. When you see the symbol $\sqrt{49}$, however, you may assume it means the principal, or positive, square root, so $\sqrt{49} = 7$. Remember that $\left(\sqrt{x}\right)^2 = \sqrt{x} \cdot \sqrt{x} = x$ and that roots can be written as fractional exponents: $\sqrt{x} = x^{\frac{1}{2}}$. Only non-negative numbers have square roots in the real number system, so $\sqrt{x}$ and $x^{\frac{1}{2}}$ only make sense if $x \geq 0$.

1. Simplifying Radicals

Most positive real numbers have square roots that are *irrational numbers,* numbers that cannot be expressed as fractions. Such numbers would be non-terminating, non-repeating decimals, and could only be written in approximate form. So it is often simpler and more useful to leave the numbers in simplest radical form. *Simplest radical form* means no radicals in the denominator and the smallest possible number under the radical sign.

To simplify a radical:

1. **Express the number under the radical as the product of a perfect square and some other factor.**
2. **Give each factor its own radical.**
3. **Take the known square root.**

EXAMPLE:

Which of the following is the simplest radical form of $\sqrt{128}$?

   A. $2\sqrt{32}$
   B. $4\sqrt{8}$
   C. $32\sqrt{2}$
   D. $8\sqrt{4}$
   E. $8\sqrt{2}$

The number 128 could be factored as 4×32, 16×8, or 64×2, but because you want the smallest number left under the radical, you should choose the largest perfect square factor: $\sqrt{128} = \sqrt{64 \cdot 2} = \sqrt{64} \cdot \sqrt{2} = 8\sqrt{2}$.

2. Rationalizing Denominators

Eliminating a radical from the denominator is essentially the same process as finding an equivalent fraction with a different denominator. You change the appearance of the fraction without changing its value by multiplying by a disguised form of 1. If the denominator is a single term, multiply the numerator and denominator by the radical in the denominator.

EXAMPLE:

Which of the following is equivalent to $\dfrac{5}{3\sqrt{7}}$?

   A. $\dfrac{5\sqrt{7}}{21}$

   B. $\dfrac{35}{21}$

   C. $\dfrac{5}{21}$

   D. $\dfrac{5\sqrt{7}}{147}$

   E. $\dfrac{5 - \sqrt{7}}{3}$

Multiply both the numerator and the denominator by $\sqrt{7}$: $\dfrac{5}{3\sqrt{7}} \cdot \dfrac{\sqrt{7}}{\sqrt{7}} = \dfrac{5\sqrt{7}}{3 \cdot 7} = \dfrac{5\sqrt{7}}{21}$.

If the denominator has two terms, and one or both of them are radicals, multiply the numerator and denominator by the conjugate of the denominator. The *conjugate* is the same two terms connected by the opposite sign. The conjugate of $3 + \sqrt{5}$ is $3 - \sqrt{5}$. The conjugate of $\sqrt{2} - \sqrt{3}$ is $\sqrt{2} + \sqrt{3}$. The conjugate of $-7 + \sqrt{23}$ is $-7 - \sqrt{23}$.

EXAMPLE:

Which of these is equivalent to $\dfrac{5}{3+\sqrt{2}}$?

A. $\sqrt{2}$

B. $\dfrac{15-5\sqrt{2}}{7}$

C. $\dfrac{15+5\sqrt{2}}{13}$

D. $\dfrac{15+5\sqrt{2}}{11}$

E. $\dfrac{15-5\sqrt{2}}{11}$

Multiply the numerator and denominator by the conjugate of $3+\sqrt{2}$:

$$\frac{5}{3+\sqrt{2}}\cdot\frac{3-\sqrt{2}}{3-\sqrt{2}}=\frac{5\left(3-\sqrt{2}\right)}{\left(3+\sqrt{2}\right)\left(3-\sqrt{2}\right)}$$

Multiplying out the numerator and denominator produces the following:

$$\frac{5\left(3-\sqrt{2}\right)}{\left(3+\sqrt{2}\right)\left(3-\sqrt{2}\right)}=\frac{5\cdot3-5\sqrt{2}}{3\cdot3-3\sqrt{2}+3\sqrt{2}-\sqrt{2}\cdot\sqrt{2}}=\frac{15-5\sqrt{2}}{9-2}=\frac{15-5\sqrt{2}}{7}$$

3. Adding and Subtracting

When adding (or subtracting) variable terms, you add only like terms, and then you add the numerical coefficient and keep the same variable. When adding (or subtracting) radicals, add only like radicals, and do so by adding the coefficient and keeping the radical.

$4x + 5y + 3x = 7x + 5y$

$4\sqrt{3} + 5\sqrt{2} + 3\sqrt{3} = 7\sqrt{3} + 5\sqrt{2}$

When multiplying or dividing radicals, remember that radicals can be re-expressed as powers, and the rules for exponents apply.

$5x \times 3y = 15xy \qquad 5\sqrt{2} \cdot 3\sqrt{3} = 15\sqrt{6}$

$4x \times 5x = 20x^2 \qquad 4\sqrt{3} \cdot 5\sqrt{3} = 20\left(\sqrt{3}\right)^2 = 20\cdot3 = 60$

$\left(\dfrac{2x}{3y}\right)^2 = \dfrac{\left(2x\right)^2}{\left(3y\right)^2} = \dfrac{4x^2}{9y^2} \qquad \left(\dfrac{2\sqrt{5}}{3\sqrt{2}}\right)^2 = \dfrac{\left(2\sqrt{5}\right)^2}{\left(3\sqrt{2}\right)^2} = \dfrac{4\cdot5}{9\cdot2} = \dfrac{20}{18}$

Practice

Directions (1–2): You are given two quantities, one in Column A and one in Column B. You are to compare the two quantities and choose:

A if the quantity in Column A is greater
B if the quantity in Column B is greater
C if the two quantities are equal
D if the relationship cannot be determined from the information given

	Column A	Column B
1.	$\sqrt{72}$	$12\sqrt{6}$

	Column A	Column B
2.	$20\sqrt{5}$	$2\sqrt{50}$

Directions (3–8): You are given five answer choices. Select the best choice.

3. Simplify $\sqrt{125} - \sqrt{5}$.

   A. $2\sqrt{30}$
   B. 5
   C. $4\sqrt{5}$
   D. $\sqrt{5}$
   E. Cannot be simplified

4. Which of the following is equivalent to $\dfrac{\sqrt{162}}{\sqrt{72}}$?

   A. $3\sqrt{10}$

   B. $\dfrac{3}{2}\sqrt{2}$

   C. $\dfrac{3}{2}$

   D. $3\sqrt{2}$

   E. 3

5. Simplify $\sqrt{8} - \sqrt{9} + \sqrt{16} - \sqrt{18}$.

   A. $2\sqrt{3}$

   B. $2\sqrt{6} - 3\sqrt{3}$

   C. $1 - \sqrt{2}$

   D. $\sqrt{2} - 1$

   E. Cannot be simplified

6. Express in simplest form: $\dfrac{-2}{\sqrt{12}}$.

   A. $\dfrac{-1}{6}$

   B. -2

   C. $\dfrac{-\sqrt{3}}{3}$

   D. $\sqrt{3}$

   E. $\dfrac{-1}{\sqrt{6}}$

7. Express in simplest form: $\dfrac{5}{\sqrt{3} + 2}$.

   A. $5\sqrt{3} - 10$

   B. $10 - 5\sqrt{3}$

   C. $2 - \sqrt{3}$

   D. $-2 + \sqrt{3}$

   E. Cannot be simplified

8. Express in simplest form: $\dfrac{5 - \sqrt{6}}{5 + \sqrt{6}}$.

   A. $\dfrac{-1}{11}$

   B. -1

   C. 1

   D. $\dfrac{31 - 10\sqrt{6}}{19}$

   E. $\dfrac{10\sqrt{6} - 31}{11}$

Directions (9–10): Give your answer as a number.

9. Simplify: $\left(\dfrac{-2\sqrt{2}}{\sqrt{5}}\right)^2$.

10. Express in simplest form: $\dfrac{3\sqrt{2}}{\sqrt{27}} - \dfrac{2\sqrt{2}}{\sqrt{12}}$.

Answers

1. **B** The correct answer is B, because $\sqrt{72} = \sqrt{36 \cdot 2} = \sqrt{36}\sqrt{2} = 6\sqrt{2}$, which is less than $12\sqrt{6}$.

2. **A** Reverse the process of simplifying to make these easier to compare:
   $20\sqrt{5} = \sqrt{20^2}\sqrt{5} = \sqrt{400}\sqrt{5} = \sqrt{400 \cdot 5} = \sqrt{2000}$, but $2\sqrt{50} = \sqrt{2^2}\sqrt{50} = \sqrt{4}\sqrt{50} = \sqrt{4 \cdot 50} = \sqrt{200}$.
   Alternately, use estimation: $\sqrt{5}$ is between 2 and 3, so $20\sqrt{5}$ is between 40 and 60. $\sqrt{50}$ is between 7 and 8, so $2\sqrt{50}$ is between 14 and 16.

3. **C** Unlike radicals cannot be combined, so start by simplifying $\sqrt{125}$: $\sqrt{125} = \sqrt{25}\sqrt{5} = 5\sqrt{5}$. Then $\sqrt{125} - \sqrt{5} = 5\sqrt{5} - \sqrt{5} = 4\sqrt{5}$.

4. **C** Do not rationalize the denominator until you've tried simplifying the radicals:
   $$\frac{\sqrt{162}}{\sqrt{72}} = \frac{\sqrt{81}\sqrt{2}}{\sqrt{36}\sqrt{2}} = \frac{9\sqrt{2}}{6\sqrt{2}} = \frac{9}{6} = \frac{3}{2}.$$

5. **C** Simplify radicals, and then combine like terms:
   $$\sqrt{8} - \sqrt{9} + \sqrt{16} - \sqrt{18} = \sqrt{4}\sqrt{2} - 3 + 4 - \sqrt{9}\sqrt{2} = 2\sqrt{2} + 1 - 3\sqrt{2} = 1 - \sqrt{2}.$$

6. **C** Expressing $\dfrac{-2}{\sqrt{12}}$ in simplest form calls for rationalizing the denominator, as well as simplifying radicals: $\dfrac{-2}{\sqrt{12}} \cdot \dfrac{\sqrt{12}}{\sqrt{12}} = \dfrac{-2\sqrt{12}}{12} = \dfrac{-\sqrt{12}}{6} = \dfrac{-\sqrt{4}\sqrt{3}}{6} = \dfrac{-2\sqrt{3}}{6} = \dfrac{-\sqrt{3}}{3}$.

7. **B** Rationalize the denominator of $\dfrac{5}{\sqrt{3}+2}$ by multiplying both the numerator and the denominator by the conjugate of the denominator, $\sqrt{3} - 2$:
   $$\frac{5}{\sqrt{3}+2} \cdot \frac{\sqrt{3}-2}{\sqrt{3}-2} = \frac{5(\sqrt{3}-2)}{3+2\sqrt{3}-2\sqrt{3}-4} = \frac{5(\sqrt{3}-2)}{-1} = -5(\sqrt{3}-2) = -5\sqrt{3}+10 = 10 - 5\sqrt{3}.$$

8. **D** Multiply the numerator and the denominator by the conjugate of the denominator:
   $$\frac{(5-\sqrt{6})}{(5+\sqrt{6})} \cdot \frac{(5-\sqrt{6})}{(5-\sqrt{6})} = \frac{25-5\sqrt{6}-5\sqrt{6}+6}{25-5\sqrt{6}+5\sqrt{6}-6} = \frac{31-10\sqrt{6}}{19}.$$ Do not allow yourself to be distracted by the similarity of the numerator and denominator.

9. $\dfrac{8}{5}\left(\dfrac{-2\sqrt{2}}{\sqrt{5}}\right)^2 = \dfrac{(-2)^2\left(\sqrt{2}\right)^2}{\left(\sqrt{5}\right)^2} = \dfrac{4\cdot 2}{5} = \dfrac{8}{5}.$

10. 0 Simplify the radicals in the denominators, and reduce each fraction to lowest terms:

$$\dfrac{3\sqrt{2}}{\sqrt{27}} - \dfrac{2\sqrt{2}}{\sqrt{12}} = \dfrac{3\sqrt{2}}{\sqrt{9}\sqrt{3}} - \dfrac{2\sqrt{2}}{\sqrt{4}\sqrt{3}} = \dfrac{\cancel{3}\sqrt{2}}{\cancel{3}\sqrt{3}} - \dfrac{\cancel{2}\sqrt{2}}{\cancel{2}\sqrt{3}} = \dfrac{\sqrt{2}}{\sqrt{3}} - \dfrac{\sqrt{2}}{\sqrt{3}} = 0.$$

XI. Algebra

A. Linear Equations and Inequalities

Linear equations and inequalities are mathematical sentences that contain variables and constants. Variables are letters or other symbols that take the place of numbers, because the value of the number is unknown, or because a pattern is being represented in which different values are possible. Constants are numbers; their value is fixed.

The verb in an equation is the equal sign; in an inequality, it is the less than (<) or greater than (>) symbol. Linear equations and inequalities take their name from the fact that their graphs are lines.

1. Distributing

Before you begin the actual work of solving an equation, you'll want to make the equation as simple as possible. Focus on one side of the equation at a time, and if parentheses or other grouping symbols are present, remove them. You may do this by simplifying the expression inside the parentheses, by using the distributive property, or, occasionally, by deciding that the parentheses are not necessary and just removing them.

Focus on the left side of the equation.	$5(x + 3) = 4 - (5 - x)$
Multiply 5 times $x + 3$.	$5x + 15 = 4 - (5 - x)$
Focus on the right side of the equation.	$5x + 15 = 4 - (5 - x)$
Change signs of terms in the parentheses.	$5x + 15 = 4 - 5 + x$

The parentheses in this equation help to organize your thinking, but serve no other mathematical purpose.
$x + (x + 1) + (x + 2) = 18$

Remove the parentheses. $x + x + 1 + x + 2 = 18$

2. Combining Like Terms

After parentheses have been cleared, take the time to combine like terms (and *only* like terms) before you begin solving. Each side of the equation should have no more than one variable term and one constant term when you begin to solve.

On the right side, combine $4 - 5$.	$5x + 15 = 4 - 5 + x$
	$5x + 15 = -1 + x$
	$x + x + 1 + x + 2 = 18$
Combine the x terms, and add $1 + 2$.	$x + x + x + 1 + 2 = 18$
	$3x + 3 = 18$

3. Solving Equations

In solving an equation, your job is to undo the arithmetic that has been performed and get the variable alone, or isolated, on one side of the equation. Since you're undoing, you do the opposite of what has been done. To keep the equation balanced, you perform the same operation on both sides of the equation.

If there are variable terms on both sides of the equation, add or subtract to eliminate one of them. Next, add or subtract to eliminate the constant term that is on the same side as the variable term. You want to have one variable term equal to one constant term. Finally, divide both sides by the coefficient of the variable term.

Variables appear on both sides. $\qquad$ $5x + 15 = -1 + x$

Subtract x from both sides. Constants appear on both sides. $\qquad$ $4x + 15 = -1$

Subtract 15 from both sides. A single variable term equals a single constant term. $\qquad$ $4x = -16$

Divide both sides by 4. $\qquad$ $\dfrac{4x}{4} = \dfrac{-16}{4}$

$$x = -4$$

4. Identities and Other Oddities

Sometimes when you try to isolate the variable, all the variable terms disappear. There are two reasons why this may happen. If all the variables disappear and what is left is *true,* you have an identity, an equation which is true for all real numbers. It has infinitely many solutions.

EXAMPLE:

Solve $5x + 3 - x = 1 + 4x + 2$.

Combine like terms. $\qquad$ $4x + 3 = 4x + 3$

Subtract $4x$ from both sides. $\qquad$ $3 = 3$

What is left is true, so the solution set is all real numbers.

If all the variables disappear and what is left is false, the equation has no solution.

EXAMPLE:

Solve $5x + 3 - x = 1 + 4x$.

Combine like terms. $\qquad$ $4x + 3 = 4x + 1$

Subtract $4x$ from both sides. $\qquad$ $3 = 1$

What is left is false, so there is no solution.

5. Absolute Value

Equations that involve the absolute value of a variable expression generally have two solutions. Use simplifying and solving techniques to isolate the absolute value, and then consider that the expression between the absolute value signs might be a positive number or a negative number. Each possibility will produce a different solution.

EXAMPLE:

Solve $-3\,|4-5x|+12=6$.

First isolate the absolute value by subtracting 12 from both sides and dividing both sides by -3:

$$-3|4-5x|+12=6$$
$$-3|4-5x|=-6$$
$$|4-5x|=2$$

If $4-5x$ is equal to 2, its absolute value will be 2, but the absolute value will also be 2 if $4-5x$ is equal to -2, so consider both possibilities:

$$4-5x=2 \qquad\qquad 4-5x=-2$$
$$-5x=-2 \qquad\qquad -5x=-6$$
$$x=\frac{2}{5} \qquad\qquad x=\frac{6}{5}$$

6. Simple Inequalities

The rules for solving inequalities are the same as those for solving equations, except at the last step. When you divide both sides of an inequality by the coefficient of the variable term, you have to make a decision about the inequality sign.

If you divide both sides of an inequality by a positive number, leave the inequality sign as is. If you divide both sides of an inequality by a negative number, reverse the inequality sign.

$$5x-7>2x+5$$

Subtract $2x$ from both sides. $\qquad 3x-7>5$

Add 7 to both sides. $\qquad\qquad 3x>12$

Divide both sides by positive 3. $\qquad \dfrac{3x}{3}\,?\,\dfrac{12}{3}$

Inequality sign stays as is. $\qquad\qquad x>4$

$$5t-9\leq 8t+15$$

Subtract $8t$ from both sides. $\qquad -3t-9\leq 15$

Add 9 to both sides. $\qquad\qquad -3t\leq 24$

Divide both sides by –3.

$$\frac{-3t}{-3} \; ? \; \frac{24}{-3}$$

Dividing by a negative reverses the direction of the inequality sign.

$$t \geq -8$$

7. Compound Inequalities

Statements that condense two inequalities into a single statement are referred to as *compound inequalities.* Generally, these compound inequalities set upper and lower boundaries on the value of an expression. If it is known that the expression $5x + 4$ is between –1 and 19, inclusive, that information can be expressed by the inequality $-1 \leq 5x + 4 \leq 19$. This compound inequality condenses two statements: $5x + 4 \geq -1$ (or $-1 \leq 5x + 4$) and $5x + 4 \leq 19$.

Solving a compound inequality requires solving each of the inequalities it contains.

EXAMPLE:

Solve $-1 \leq 5x + 4 \leq 19$.

See the compound inequality as two simple inequalities: $-1 \leq 5x + 4$ and $5x + 4 \leq 19$. Solve each inequality.

$$
\begin{array}{ll}
-1 \leq 5x + 4 & 5x + 4 \leq 19 \\
-5 \leq 5x & 5x \leq 15 \\
-1 \leq x & x \leq 3
\end{array}
$$

If desired, the two solutions can be condensed into a compound inequality: $-1 \leq x \leq 3$.

8. Absolute Value Inequalities

When an equation contains an absolute value expression, two cases must be considered. The same is true of inequalities containing absolute value expressions, and since each case becomes an inequality, the direction of the inequality must be considered carefully.

It's important to isolate the absolute value first, as with equations, and then translate the absolute value inequality into a compound inequality. If the absolute value of the expression is less than a constant, the value of the expression is bounded by that constant and its opposite. For example, if $|3x - 7| < 4$, then $-4 < 3x - 7 < 4$. If the absolute value of an expression is greater than a constant, as in $|8 - 2x| > 9$, then the expression itself is either greater than that constant or less than its opposite. $|8 - 2x| > 9$ translates to $8 - 2x > 9$ or $8 - 2x < -9$.

EXAMPLE:

Solve $4 + 9 \, |3 - 5x| \leq 22$.

Isolate the absolute value by subtracting 4 and dividing by 9. The resulting inequality, $|3 - 5x| \leq 2$, translates into the compound inequality $-2 \leq 3 - 5x \leq 2$. Solve each of the inequalities contained in the compound inequality.

$$-2 \leq 3 - 5x \qquad \text{and} \qquad 3 - 5x \leq 2$$
$$-5 \leq -5x \qquad\qquad\qquad -5x \leq -1$$
$$1 \geq x \qquad\qquad\qquad x \geq \frac{1}{5}$$

$$1 \geq x \geq \frac{1}{5}$$

EXAMPLE:

Solve $|8x + 9| \geq 1$.

Since the absolute value is greater than 1, the expression $8x + 9$ is either greater than 1 or less than its opposite so $8x + 9 \geq 1$ or $8x + 0 \leq -1$.

$$8x + 9 \leq -1$$
$$8x + 9 \geq 1 \qquad\qquad 8x \leq -10$$
$$8x \geq -8$$
$$x \geq -1 \qquad \text{or} \qquad x \leq \frac{-5}{4}$$

Practice

Directions (1–10): You are given five answer choices. Select the best choice.

1. Solve $-2(5t - 7) + 3(4 + 2t) = 38$.

   A. $t = -3$

   B. $t = 3$

   C. $t = -\dfrac{3}{4}$

   D. $t = \dfrac{3}{4}$

   E. $t = -9$

2. Solve $(9 + 5a) - (3 - 6a) = 28$.

   A. $a = -22$

   B. $a = 22$

   C. $a = -2$

   D. $a = 2$

   E. $a = \dfrac{34}{11}$

3. Solve $2x - 5 + 3x = 7 - 4x + 78$.

   A. $x = 41.5$

   B. $x = 30$

   C. $x = 10$

   D. $x = -10$

   E. $x = -30$

4. Solve $2(-7z - 5) = -3(4z + 6)$.

   A. $z = -4$

   B. $z = -14$

   C. $z = 4$

   D. $z = 14$

   E. $z = 28$

5. Solve $1 - (2y - 1) = -4(y - 3)$.

   A. $y = 6$

   B. $y = 5$

   C. $y = 2$

   D. $y = -5$

   E. $y = -6$

6. Solve $ad - bc = x$ for d.

   A. $d = \dfrac{x + bc}{a}$

   B. $d = x + bc - a$

   C. $d = \dfrac{x - a}{bc}$

   D. $d = \dfrac{x}{a} + bc$

   E. $d = \dfrac{x}{a} - bc$

7. Solve $-5p + 12 \geq -p + 8$.

   A. $p \leq 1$

   B. $p \geq 1$

   C. $p \leq -1$

   D. $p \geq -1$

   E. $p \geq \dfrac{2}{3}$

8. Solve $15 - 8y \leq 3y + 4$.

   A. $y \leq 1$

   B. $y \geq 1$

   C. $y \leq \dfrac{11}{5}$

   D. $y \leq -1$

   E. $y \geq -1$

9. Solve $4|9 - 2x| - 7 \leq -1$.

   A. $\dfrac{15}{4} \leq x \leq \dfrac{21}{4}$

   B. $x \leq \dfrac{7}{2}$ or $x \geq \dfrac{21}{4}$

   C. $\dfrac{7}{2} \leq x \leq \dfrac{15}{4}$

   D. $x \leq \dfrac{7}{2}$ or $x \geq \dfrac{21}{4}$

   E. $\dfrac{7}{2} \leq x \leq \dfrac{21}{4}$

10. Solve $2|3x - 7| + 5 \geq 37$.

   A. $x \leq -3$ or $x \geq \dfrac{23}{3}$

   B. $-3 \leq x \leq \dfrac{23}{3}$

   C. $x \geq \dfrac{23}{3}$ or $x \leq \dfrac{-14}{3}$

   D. $\dfrac{-14}{3} \leq x \leq \dfrac{23}{3}$

   E. $-3 \leq x \leq \dfrac{-14}{3}$

Answers

1. **A** Remove parentheses by applying the distributive property, and combine like terms on the left side: $-2(5t - 7) + 3(4 + 2t) = -10t + 14 + 12 + 6t = -4t + 26$. Subtract 26 from both sides and divide by -4:

$$-4t + 26 = 38$$
$$-4t = 12$$
$$t = \dfrac{12}{-4} = -3$$

2. **D** The first set of parentheses has no real purpose, but the second set indicates that the minus sign applies to the entire quantity, so remove the parentheses by "distributing the minus"—multiplying the quantity by –1.

$$\left(9+5a\right)-\left(3-6a\right)=28$$
$$9+5a-3+6a=28$$

Combine like terms on the left side. Subtract 6 from both sides and divide by 11.

$$6+11a=28$$
$$11a=22$$
$$a=2$$

3. **C** Combine like terms on each side of the equation to simplify before beginning to solve.

$$2x-5+3x=7-4x+78$$
$$5x-5=-4x+85$$

Eliminate one of the variable terms; then eliminate a constant term so that the variable is on one side of the equation and the constant is on the other. In this example, add $4x$ to both sides, and then add 5 to both sides. Then divide both sides by 9.

$$5x-5=-4x+85$$
$$9x-5=85$$
$$9x=90$$
$$x=10$$

4. **C** Remove the parentheses by distributing.

$$2\left(-7z-5\right)=-3\left(4z+6\right)$$
$$-14z-10=-3\left(4z+6\right)$$
$$-14z-10=-12z-18$$

Add $12z$ to both sides to eliminate a variable term, and then add 10 to both sides to eliminate a constant term. Finally, divide both sides by –2.

$$-14z-10+12z=-18$$
$$-2z-10=-18$$
$$-2z=-8$$
$$z=4$$

5. **B** On the left side, "distribute the negative"—that is, multiply by –1—and combine like terms. On the right side, distribute the –4.

$$1-\left(2y-1\right)=-4\left(y-3\right)$$
$$1-2y+1=-4\left(y-3\right)$$
$$2-2y=-4\left(y-3\right)$$
$$2-2y=-4y+12$$

Add $4y$ to both sides, then subtract 2 from both sides, and finally divide both sides by 2.

$$2-2y+4y=12$$
$$2+2y=12$$
$$2y=10$$
$$y=5$$

6. **A** Don't be distracted by the use of letters rather than numbers. Your task is to solve for d, so treat that as the variable, and treat everything else as numbers. If it helps you, make up numbers for the other parameters and think about what steps you would take to solve. Follow those steps here as well. To get the d term by itself, add bc to both sides.

$$ad-bc=x \text{ for } d$$
$$ad=x+bc$$

Then divide both sides by a.

$$d=\frac{x+bc}{a}$$

7. **A** Solve inequalities just as you solve equations, except if it becomes necessary to divide both sides by a negative number. Add p to both sides, and then subtract 12 from both sides.

$$-5p+12\geq -p+8$$
$$-5p+12+p\geq 8$$
$$-4p+12\geq 8$$
$$-4p\geq -4$$

Since you now need to divide both sides by –4, you must reverse the direction of the inequality sign.

$$\frac{-4p}{-4}\leq \frac{-4}{-4}$$
$$p\leq 1$$

8. **B** Add $8y$ to both sides, and then subtract 4 from both sides. Divide both sides by 11. Since you're dividing by a positive number, there is no change in the inequality sign.

$$15-8y\leq 3y+4$$
$$15\leq 3y+4+8y$$
$$15\leq 11y+4$$
$$11\leq 11y$$
$$1\leq y$$

9. **A** Begin by isolating the absolute value. Add 7 to both sides, and divide both sides by 4.

$$4\left|9-2x\right|-7\leq -1$$
$$4\left|9-2x\right|\leq 6$$
$$\left|9-2x\right|\leq \frac{3}{2}$$

Since the absolute value is less than $\frac{3}{2}$, the expression between the absolute value signs is between $\frac{3}{2}$ and $-\frac{3}{2}$—that is, greater than $-\frac{3}{2}$ and less than $\frac{3}{2}$.

$$-\frac{3}{2} \leq 9 - 2x \text{ and } 9 - 2x \leq \frac{3}{2}$$

Solve each inequality by subtracting 9 from both sides and dividing by –2. Remember that dividing by a negative number will reverse the direction of the inequality.

$$-\frac{3}{2} - 9 \leq -2x \text{ and } -2x \leq \frac{3}{2} - 9$$

$$-\frac{3}{2} - \frac{18}{2} \leq -2x \text{ and } -2x \leq \frac{3}{2} - \frac{18}{2}$$

$$-\frac{21}{2} \leq -2x \text{ and } -2x \leq -\frac{15}{2}$$

$$\frac{21}{4} \geq x \text{ and } x \geq \frac{15}{4}$$

$$\frac{21}{4} \geq x \geq \frac{15}{4}$$

10. **A** Isolate the absolute value by subtracting 5 from both sides and dividing both sides by 2.

$$2|3x - 7| + 5 \geq 37$$

$$2|3x - 7| \geq 32$$

$$|3x - 7| \geq 16$$

Since the absolute value is greater than or equal to 16, the expression in the absolute value signs must be either greater than 16 or less than –16. Solve both inequalities by adding 7 to both sides and dividing by 3.

$$-16 \geq 3x - 7 \text{ or } 3x - 7 \geq 16$$

$$-9 \geq 3x \text{ or } 3x \geq 23$$

$$-3 \geq x \text{ or } x \geq \frac{23}{3}$$

B. Simultaneous Equations

A system of equations is a set of two equations with two variables. The solution of a system of equations is a pair of values that makes both equations true. A system of equations may have one solution, no solution, or infinitely many solutions.

It is not possible to solve for the values of two variables in the same equation. So solving a system of equations requires that you eliminate one variable and solve for the variable remaining. Once you've found the value of one variable, you can substitute to find the other.

1. Substitution

To solve a system by substitution, choose one equation and isolate one variable. When you have one variable expressed in terms of the other, go to the other equation and replace the variable with the equivalent expression. You should have an equation involving only one variable, which you can solve. When you know the value of one variable, choose an equation, replace the known variable by its value, and solve for the variable remaining:

$$\text{Solve: } \begin{cases} 3x - y = -15 \\ 5x + 2y = -14 \end{cases}$$

Choose one equation and isolate a variable.

Isolate y in the first equation:

$$3x - y = -15$$
$$3x = -15 + y$$
$$3x + 15 = y$$

Use this expression for y to eliminate y in the second equation. Substitute $3x + 15$ for y in the second equation. Clear parentheses and combine like terms. Solve for x:

$$5x + 2y = {}^{-}14$$
$$5x + 2(3x + 15) = {}^{-}14$$
$$5x + 6x + 30 = {}^{-}14$$
$$11x + 30 = {}^{-}14$$
$$11x = {}^{-}44$$
$$x = {}^{-}4$$

Substitute the value found into one of the original equations. Substitute –4 for x in the first equation. Solve for y:

$$3x - y = -15$$
$$3(-4) - y = -15$$
$$-12 - y = -15$$
$$-y = -3$$
$$y = 3$$

2. Combination

The elimination method uses addition or subtraction to eliminate one of the variables. If the coefficient of one variable is the same in both equations, subtracting one equation from the other will eliminate that variable. If the coefficients are opposites, adding will eliminate the variable. When you've eliminated one variable, solve and then use substitution to find the value of the other variable.

EXAMPLE:

$$\text{Solve: } \begin{cases} 8a - 2b = 18 \\ 3a + 2b = -7 \end{cases}$$

Adding the equations eliminates b.

$$8a - 2b = 18$$
$$\underline{3a + 2b = -7}$$
$$11a = 11$$

Solve for a.

$$\frac{11a}{11} = \frac{11}{11}$$
$$a = 1$$

Substitute 1 for a in the second equation.

$$3a + 2b = -7$$
$$3(1) + 2b = -7$$
$$3 + 2b = -7$$

Solve for b.

$$2b = -10$$
$$b = -5$$

EXAMPLE:

Solve: $\begin{cases} -5p + 4t = -21 \\ 3p + 4t = 19 \end{cases}$

Subtracting the equations eliminates t.

$$-5p + 4t = -21$$
$$\underline{3p + 4t = 19}$$
$$-8p = -40$$

Solve for p.

$$p = \frac{-40}{-8}$$
$$p = 5$$

$$3p + 4t = 19$$
$$3(5) + 4t = 19$$

Substitute 5 for p in the second equation.

$$15 + 4t = 19$$

$$4t = 4$$

Solve for t.

$$t = 1$$

3. Combination with Multiplication

If neither adding nor subtracting will eliminate a variable (because the coefficients don't match), it's still possible to use the elimination method. First, you must multiply each equation by a constant to produce more agreeable coefficients. The fastest way to do this is generally to choose the variable you want to eliminate, and then multiply each equation by the coefficient of that variable from the other equation:

Solve: $\begin{cases} 3x + 4y = -34 \\ 2x - 5y = 31 \end{cases}$

In order to eliminate y, multiply the first equation by 5 and the second equation by 4:

$$5(3x + 4y = -34)$$
$$4(2x - 5y = 31)$$

$$15x + 20y = -170$$
$$8x - 20y = 124$$

Adding the equations eliminates y.

$$23x = -46$$

Solve for x.

$$x = -2$$

$$3x + 4y = -34$$

$$3(-2) + 4y = -34$$

Substitute -2 for x in the first equation.

$$-6 + 4y = -34$$

$$4y = -28$$

Solve for y.

$$y = -7$$

Practice

Directions (1–4): You are given two quantities, one in Column A and one in Column B. You are to compare the two quantities and choose:

A if the quantity in Column A is greater
B if the quantity in Column B is greater
C if the two quantities are equal
D if the relationship cannot be determined from the information given

$$-x + 2y = {}^-5$$
$$7x - 3y = 2$$

	Column A	**Column B**
1.	x	y

$$\frac{1}{2}x - \frac{1}{3}y = 14$$
$$\frac{1}{5}x + \frac{3}{4}y = -5$$

	Column A	**Column B**
2.	$-3x$	$-5y$

$$1.5x - 3.75y = 15$$
$$2.5x + 7.5y = 35$$

	Column A	**Column B**
3.	$x - y$	$y - x$

$$3x - 5y = -4$$
$$7x + 2y = 18$$

Column A	**Column B**

4. x y

Directions (5–8): You are given five answer choices. Select the best choice.

5. Solve: $\begin{cases} x + 2y = 7 \\ 3x - y = 14 \end{cases}$

    A. (5,1)
    B. (1,5)
    C. (–5,1)
    D. (1,–5)
    E. (–1,5)

6. Solve: $\begin{cases} x - 9y = 34 \\ 2x - 3y = 23 \end{cases}$

    A. (7,3)
    B. (3,7)
    C. (–7,3)
    D. (7,–3)
    E. (–3,7)

7. Solve: $\begin{cases} x + y = -8 \\ x - y = 8 \end{cases}$

    A. (0,8)
    B. (0,–8)
    C. (–8,0)
    D. (8,0)
    E. (–8,8)

8. Solve: $\begin{cases} 5x + 2y = -14 \\ 8x - 9y = -59 \end{cases}$

    A. (–3,4)
    B. (3,–4)
    C. (–4,3)
    D. (4,–3)
    E. (–4,–3)

Directions (9–10): Give your answer as a number.

9. Find the value of y: $\begin{cases} y = 2x - 17 \\ x - y = 4 \end{cases}$

10. Find the value of x: $\begin{array}{c} x + 5y = 27 \\ 9y - 2x = 3 \end{array}$

Answers

1. **A** Multiply the first equation by 7 and add to eliminate the x terms.

$$\begin{array}{l} -x + 2y = -5 \\ 7x - 3y = 2 \end{array} \Rightarrow \begin{array}{l} 7(-x + 2y = -5) \\ 7x - 3y = 2 \end{array} \Rightarrow \begin{array}{l} -7x + 14y = -35 \\ 7x - 3y = 2 \\ \hline 11y = -33 \end{array}$$

Divide both sides by 11 to solve for y.

$$11y = -33$$
$$y = -3$$

Choose one of the original equations and replace y with -3, and solve for x.

$$-x + 2y = -5$$
$$-x + 2(-3) = -5$$
$$-x - 6 = -5$$
$$-x = 1$$
$$x = -1$$

2. **B** It may be helpful to clear the fractions before attempting to solve. For each equation, find the common denominator of the fractions, and multiply through by that number.

$$\begin{array}{l} \dfrac{1}{2}x - \dfrac{1}{3}y = 14 \\ \dfrac{1}{5}x + \dfrac{3}{4}y = -5 \end{array} \Rightarrow \begin{array}{l} 6\left(\dfrac{1}{2}x - \dfrac{1}{3}y = 14\right) \\ 20\left(\dfrac{1}{5}x + \dfrac{3}{4}y = -5\right) \end{array} \Rightarrow \begin{array}{l} 3x - 2y = 84 \\ 4x + 15y = -100 \end{array}$$

Multiply the top equation by 15 and the bottom equation by 2; then add to eliminate the y terms. Divide by 53 to solve for x.

$$\begin{array}{l} 15(3x - 2y = 84) \\ 2(4x + 15y = -100) \end{array} \Rightarrow \begin{array}{l} 45x - 30y = 1260 \\ 8x + 30y = -200 \\ \hline 53x = 1060 \\ x = 20 \end{array}$$

Choose one of the original equations, replace x with 20, and solve for y.

$$\frac{1}{2}x - \frac{1}{3}y = 14$$

$$\frac{1}{2}(20) - \frac{1}{3}y = 14$$

$$10 - \frac{1}{3}y = 14$$

$$-\frac{1}{3}y = 4$$

$$y = 4 \div -\frac{1}{3} = \frac{4}{1} \cdot \frac{-3}{1} = -12$$

Since $x = 30$ and $y = -12$, $-3x = -60$ and $-5y = 60$, so $-5y > -3x$.

3. **A** If the decimals make the problem seem difficult, multiply both equations by 100 to move the decimal points two places right and eliminate the decimals.

$$\begin{array}{l} 1.5x - 3.75y = 15 \\ -2.5x + 7.5y = 35 \end{array} \Rightarrow \begin{array}{l} 150x - 375y = 1{,}500 \\ -250x + 750y = 3{,}500 \end{array}$$

Multiply the top equation by 2, then add to eliminate the y terms, and solve for x by dividing by 50.

$$\begin{array}{l} 150x - 375y = 1{,}500 \\ -250x + 750y = 3{,}500 \end{array} \Rightarrow \begin{array}{l} 2(150x - 375y = 1{,}500) \\ -250x + 750y = 3{,}500 \end{array} \Rightarrow \begin{array}{l} 300x - 750y = 3{,}000 \\ -250x + 750y = 3{,}500 \end{array}$$

$$\overline{50x = 6{,}500}$$

$$x = \frac{6{,}500}{50} = 130$$

Replace x with 130 in one of the original equations, and solve for y.

$$1.5x - 3.75y = 15$$

$$1.5(130) - 3.75y = 15$$

$$195 - 3.75y = 15$$

$$-3.75y = 15 - 195$$

$$-3.75y = -180$$

$$y = \frac{-180}{-3.75} = \frac{18{,}000}{375} = \frac{25 \cdot 3 \cdot 5 \cdot 48}{25 \cdot 3 \cdot 5} = 48$$

Then realize that $x - y = -1(y - x)$, so evaluate $x - y = 130 - 48 > 0$. Since $x - y$ is positive, $y - x$ will be negative, and $x - y$ is larger.

4. **C** To eliminate the y terms, multiply the top equation by 2 and the bottom equation by 5, and then add. Divide both sides by 41 to solve for x.

$$\begin{array}{l} 3x - 5y = -4 \\ 7x + 2y = 18 \end{array} \Rightarrow \begin{array}{l} 2(3x - 5y = -4) \\ 5(7x + 2y = 18) \end{array} \Rightarrow \begin{array}{l} 6x - 10y = -8 \\ 35x + 10y = 90 \end{array}$$

$$\overline{41x = 82}$$

$$x = 2$$

To find the value of y, choose one of the original equations, replace x with 2, and solve for y.

$3x - 5y = -4$

$3(2) - 5y = -4$

$6 - 5y = -4$

$-5y = -10$

$y = 2$

5. **A** The first equation can easily be solved for x: $x + 2y = 7 \rightarrow x = 7 - 2y$. Replace x in the second equation with the expression $7 - 2y$, and solve for y.

$3x - y = 14$

$3(7 - 2y) - y = 14$

$21 - 6y - y = 14$

$21 - 7y = 14$

$-7y = 14 - 21 = -7$

$y = 1$

Once the value of y is known, substitute for y in one of the original equations, and solve for x.

$x + 2y = 7$

$x + 2(1) = 7$

$x + 2 = 7$

$x = 5$

6. **D** Solve the first equation for x, and substitute this expression into the second equation.

$x - 9y = 34 \Rightarrow x = 34 + 9y$

$2x - 3y = 23$

$2(34 + 9y) - 3y = 23$

$68 + 18y - 3y = 23$

$68 + 15y = 23$

Solve the equation to find the value of y.

$68 + 15y = 23$

$15y = 23 - 68$

$15y = -45$

$y = -3$

Substitute -3 for y in one of the original equations and solve for x.

$x - 9y = 34$

$x - 9(-3) = 34$

$x + 27 = 34$

$x = 34 - 27 = 7$

7. **B** Add the two equations to eliminate y. The value of x can be found by dividing.

$$x + y = -8$$
$$\underline{x - y = 8}$$
$$2x = 0$$
$$x = 0$$

Substitute 0 for x in one of the original equations, and the value of y becomes clear: $y = -8$.

8. **C** Multiply the first equation by 9, multiply the second equation by 2, and then add to eliminate the y terms. Divide by 61 to solve for x.

$$\begin{array}{l} 5x + 2y = -14 \\ 8x - 9y = -59 \end{array} \Rightarrow \begin{array}{l} 9(5x + 2y = -14) \\ 2(8x - 9y = -59) \end{array} \Rightarrow \begin{array}{l} 45x + 18y = -126 \\ \underline{16x - 18y = -118} \\ 61x = -244 \\ x = -4 \end{array}$$

Replace x with –4 in one of the original equations, and solve for y.

$$5x + 2y = -14$$
$$5(-4) + 2y = -14$$
$$-20 + 2y = -14$$
$$2y = 6$$
$$y = 3$$

9. **9** The first equation gives an expression for y that can be substituted into the other equation. Solve for y.

$$y = 2x - 17$$
$$x - y = 4$$
$$x - (2x - 17) = 4$$
$$x - 2x + 17 = 4$$
$$-x + 17 = 4$$
$$-x = -13$$
$$x = 13$$

Substitute 13 for x in the first equation to find that y is 9.

$$y = 2x - 17$$
$$y = 2(13) - 17$$
$$y = 26 - 17 = 9$$

10. 12 Solve the first equation for x, and substitute the resulting expression into the second equation. Solve for y.

$$x + 5y = 27$$
$$x = 27 - 5y$$
$$9y - 2x = 3$$
$$9y - 2(27 - 5y) = 3$$
$$9y - 54 + 10y = 3$$
$$19y - 54 = 3$$
$$19y = 57$$
$$y = \frac{57}{19} = 3$$

Return to the original equation and replace y with 3. Solve for x.

$$x + 5y = 27$$
$$x + 5(3) = 27$$
$$x + 15 = 27$$
$$x = 12$$

C. Multiplying and Factoring

Just as two numbers can be multiplied and a single number can be expressed as a product of factors, polynomials can be multiplied and factored as well.

1. Distributive Property

To multiply a single term times a sum or difference, distribute the multiplication to each term of the sum or difference.

EXAMPLE:

Simplify $-7x^2(5x^3 - 4x^2 + 8x - 1)$.

The term $-7x^2$ must be multiplied by each of the four terms in the parentheses: $-7x^2(5x^3 - 4x^2 + 8x - 1) = (-7x^2 \times 5x^3) - (-7x^2 \times 4x^2) + (-7x^2 \times 8x) - (-7x^2 \times 1)$. Simplify each term, paying careful attention to signs: $(-7x^2 \times 5x^3) - (-7x^2 \times 4x^2) + (-7x^2 \times 8x) - (-7x^2 \times 1) = -35x^5 + 28x^4 - 56x^3 + 7x^2$.

2. Greatest Common Factor

Expressing a polynomial as the product of a single term and a simpler polynomial requires using the distributive property in reverse. You know the answer to the multiplication problem and you're trying to re-create the question.

To factor out a greatest common monomial factor:

1. **Determine the largest number that will divide the numerical coefficient of every term.**
2. **Determine the highest power of each variable that is common to all terms.**

139

3. **Place the common factor outside the parentheses.**

4. **Inside the parentheses, create a new polynomial by dividing each term of the original by the common factor.**

EXAMPLE:

Factor $6x^5y^2 - 9x^4y^4 + 27x^3y^7$.

The largest number that divides 6, 9, and 27 is 3; the largest power of x common to all terms is x^3; and the largest power of y common to all terms is y^2. So the greatest common factor is $3x^3y^2$.

$$\frac{6x^5y^2}{3x^3y^2} = 2x^2 \qquad \frac{-9x^4y^4}{3x^3y^2} = -3xy^2 \qquad \frac{27x^3y^7}{3x^3y^2} = 9y^5$$

Place the common factor outside the parentheses, and the simpler polynomial inside: $6x^5y^2 - 9x^4y^4 + 27x^3y^7 = 3x^3y^2(2x^2 - 3xy^2 + 9y^5)$.

3. FOIL

The FOIL rule is a memory device to help you multiply two binomials. The letters in FOIL stand for:

First $(x+5)(x-3) \Rightarrow x \cdot x$

Outer $(x+5)(x-3) \Rightarrow x \cdot -3$

Inner $(x+5)(x-3) \Rightarrow 5 \cdot x$

Last $(x+5)(x-3) \Rightarrow 5 \cdot -3$

To multiply binomials, multiply the first terms of the binomials, multiply the outer terms, multiply the inner terms, and multiply the last terms of the binomials. Combine like terms (usually the inner and the outer).

EXAMPLE:

Multiply $(2x - 7)(3x + 4)$.

First: $2x \times 3x$. Outer: $2x \times 4$. Inner: $-7 \times 3x$. Last: -7×4.

$$(2x - 7)(3x + 4) = (2x \cdot 3x) + (4 \cdot 2x) + (-7 \cdot 3x) + (-7 \cdot 4)$$
$$= 6x^2 + 8x - 21x - 28$$
$$= 6x^2 - 13x - 28$$

4. Factoring

To factor a trinomial into the product of two binomials, begin by putting the trinomial in standard form $(ax^2 + bx + c)$. List the factors of the squared term and the factors of the constant term. Try different arrangements of these factors, checking to see if the inner and outer products can combine to produce the desired middle term. When you've found the correct combination, place signs. If the constant term is positive, both signs will be the same as the sign of the middle term. If the constant term is negative, one factor should have a plus and the other a minus. Place the signs so that the larger of the inner and the outer has the sign of the middle term.

EXAMPLE:

Factor $6x^2 + 5x - 56$.

Possible factors for $6x^2$ are $3x \times 2x$ or $6x \times x$. The possible factors of 56 are 1×56, 2×28, 4×14, or 7×8. There are many possible arrangements but the fact that the middle term is small is a hint that you want factors that are close together, so start with $3x \times 2x$ and 7×8.

$(3x \_ 7)(2x \_ 8)$ produces an outer of $24x$ and an inner of $14x$. $24x$ and $14x$ could add to $38x$ or subtract to $10x$, but they cannot produce a middle term of $5x$, so switch the 7 and the 8.

$(3x \_ 8)(2x \_ 7)$ produces an outer of $21x$ and an inner of $16x$, which will subtract to $5x$.

The constant term is negative, -56, so place one $-$ and one $+$. The middle term, $5x$, is positive, so the larger of the inner and the outer must be positive. $21x$ is larger than $16x$, so you want $+21x$ and $-16x$, which means the factors are $(3x - 8)(2x + 7)$.

5. Special Factoring Patterns

There are certain patterns of multiplication that should be committed to memory, either because they give surprising results or because they appear frequently. The most important is the difference of squares.

$(a + b)(a - b) = a^2 - b^2$

This form is surprising, since the product of two binomials usually produces a trinomial, but here the inner and the outer add to zero, leaving only two terms. It is also a common form, used, for example, when rationalizing denominators requires multiplying by the conjugate.

EXAMPLE:

Multiply $(5x + 4)(5x - 4)$.

Since the two factors are the sum and difference of the same two terms, the difference of squares rule applies: $(5x + 4)(5x - 4) = (5x)^2 - 4^2 = 25x^2 - 16$.

EXAMPLE:

Factor $(3x - 7)^2 - 36$.

Don't let the extra quantity intimidate you—this is a difference of squares: The quantity $(3x - 7)^2$ minus 6^2. So $a = 3x - 7$ and $b = 6$. Then the factors are $(a + b)(a - b)$ or $[(3x - 7) + 6] \times [(3x - 7) - 6]$. Simplifying each factor gives you $(3x - 1)(3x - 13)$.

Another form commonly encountered is the perfect square trinomial. Of course, you can always square a binomial by using the FOIL rule, and you can factor a perfect square trinomial by trial and error, but recognizing the form will help you get through problems faster.

$(a + b)^2 = a^2 + 2ab + b^2$
$(a - b)^2 = a^2 - 2ab + b^2$

Notice that the first and last terms are squares and the middle term is twice the product of the terms of the binomial. The sign of the middle term matches the sign connecting the terms of the binomial.

EXAMPLE:

$(8x - 9)^2 =$

 A. $8x^2 - 81$
 B. $8x^2 + 81$
 C. $64x^2 - 81$
 D. $64x^2 + 144x - 81$
 E. $64x^2 - 144x + 81$

The first term must be $(8x)^2$ or $64x^2$ so choices A and B can be eliminated immediately. Squaring a binomial produces a trinomial, not a binomial so eliminate Choice C. In choosing between D and E, check the signs. The last term of a square trinomial should always be positive, and the middle term should match the connecting sign of the binomial. Therefore, $(8x - 9)^2 = 64x^2 - 144x + 81$.

You may also want to know the forms of the sum and difference of cubes.

$$a^3 + b^3 = (a + b)(a^2 - ab + b^2)$$
$$a^3 - b^3 = (a - b)(a^2 + ab + b^2)$$

The rules are similar, which means less to memorize but trouble keeping them straight. Remember that the binomial factor gets the same sign as the original expression. Each rule is entitled to one minus sign, so the sum of cubes must use its minus sign in the trinomial.

EXAMPLE:

$(3t + 5p)(9t^2 - 15tp + 25p^2) =$

 A. $3t^3 + 5p^3$
 B. $3t^3 - 5p^3$
 C. $27t^3 + 125p^3$
 D. $27t^3 - 125p^3$
 E. $27t^3 + 5p^3$

If you multiply $(3t + 5p)(9t^2 - 15tp + 25p^2)$, you'll invest far too much time and risk making mistakes. Instead, recognize the form. The trinomial has squares as its first and last term, and the middle term is the product of their square roots. This will be either a sum or a difference of squares, and the answer choices confirm that analysis. The binomial terms are connecting by a plus, so it is a sum of cubes, eliminating choices B and D. The first term must be $(3t)^3$, or $27t^3$, and a quick look at the problem, which would require you to begin by multiplying $3t$ by $9t^2$, will remind you of this. Eliminate Choice A, and carefully compare choices C and E. The numerical coefficient of p^3 is wrong in Choice E, so the correct answer is C.

Many complicated-looking expressions can be factored by applying the special forms. The expression $(3x-1)^2 - \frac{4x^2}{9y^2}$ might look impossible at first glance, but the first term is a square, and so is the second—it can be rewritten as $\left(\frac{2x}{3y}\right)^2$. The whole expression is a difference of squares with $a = 3x - 1$ and $b = \frac{2x}{3y}$. The factors are $\left[(3x-1)+\frac{2x}{3y}\right]\cdot\left[(3x-1)-\frac{2x}{3y}\right]$. Learning to look for patterns will help you solve many problems.

Practice

Directions (1–2): You are given two quantities, one in Column A and one in Column B. You are to compare the two quantities and choose:

A if the quantity in Column A is greater
B if the quantity in Column B is greater
C if the two quantities are equal
D if the relationship cannot be determined from the information given

$$24x^5 - 32x^8 = ax^5(b - cx^3)$$

Column A	Column B
$c - b$	$c - a$

1.

$$(-2x - 3)(2x + 5) = ax^2 + bx + c$$

Column A	Column B
b	c

2.

Directions (3–8): You are given five answer choices. Select the best choice.

3. $-3t^3(2t - 1) =$

    A. $-6t^4 - 1$
    B. $-6t^4 - 3t^3$
    C. $-6t^4 + 3t^3$
    D. $-t^4 + 3t^3$
    E. $-5t^4 - 3t^3$

4. $(5x + 3)(2x – 1) =$

    A. $10x^2 + x – 3$
    B. $10x^2 – 3$
    C. $10x^2 + 11x – 3$
    D. $10x^2 – 11x – 3$
    E. $7x^2 – 3$

5. $\left(\frac{1}{2}t + 12\right)\left(\frac{1}{2}t – 12\right)$

    A. $\frac{1}{2}t^2 + 144$

    B. $\frac{1}{2}t^2 – 144$

    C. $t^2 – 144$

    D. $\frac{1}{4}t^2 – 144$

    E. $\frac{1}{4}t^2 – 144$

6. Which of the following is *not* a possible factorization of $48x^2 – 1{,}200y^2$?

    A. $3(4x + 20y)(4x – 20y)$
    B. $12(2x + 10y)(2x – 10y)$
    C. $48(x + 5y)(x – 5y)$
    D. $6(4x + 100y)(4x – 100y)$
    E. All are correct.

7. Which of the following is the correct factorization for $32x^2 – 72$?

    A. $(16x – 36)^2$
    B. $(16x + 36)^2$
    C. $(16x + 36)(16x – 36)$
    D. $8(2x – 3)(2x + 3)$
    E. $(8x + 3)(4x – 3)$

8. Which of the following is the best factorization for $9x^2 – 30x + 25$?

    A. $(3x + 5)^2$
    B. $(3x – 5)^2$
    C. $(3x + 5)(3x – 5)$
    D. $3x(3x – 10) + 25$
    E. $(x + 3)(9x + 5)$

Directions (9–10): Give your answer as a number.

9. $2x^2 - 11x - 21 = (x + a)(2x + b)$. Find $b - a$.

10. Find the coefficient of x when the product $(4x - 7)(2x + 5)$ is expressed in $ax^2 + bx + c$ form.

Answers

1. **A** $24x^5 - 32x^8 = 8x^5(3 - 4x^3)$, so $c - b = 4 - 3 = 1$ and $c - a = 4 - 8 = -4$.

2. **B** $(-2x - 3)(2x + 5) = -4x^2 - 10x - 6x - 15 = -4x^2 - 16x - 15$, so $b = -16$ and $c = -15$.

3. **C** $-3t^3(2t - 1) = (-3t^3)(2t) - (-3t^3)(1) = -6t^4 + 3t^3$.

4. **A** $(5x + 3)(2x - 1) = (5x)(2x) + (5x)(-1) + 3(2x) + 3(-1) = 10x^2 - 5x + 6x - 3 = 10x^2 + x - 3$.

5. **D** Recognize this as the sum and difference of the same two terms, and, therefore, equal to the difference of squares: $\left(\dfrac{1}{2}t + 12\right)\left(\dfrac{1}{2}t - 12\right) = \left(\dfrac{1}{2}t\right)^2 - (12)^2 = \dfrac{1}{4}t^2 - 144$.

6. **D** Look first at the common factors in the various choices and verify that any one of them is a factor of $48x^2 - 1,200y^2$. Then factor (or if you prefer, multiply out the choices).

   $48x^2 - 1,200y^2 = 3(16x^2 - 400y^2) = 3(4x + 20y)(4x + 20y)$

   $48x^2 - 1,200y^2 = 12(4x^2 - 100y^2) = 12(2x + 10y)(2x + 10y)$

   $48x^2 - 1,200y^2 = 48(x^2 - 25y^2) = 48(x + 5y)(x + 5y)$

   $48x^2 - 1,200y^2 = 6(8x^2 - 200y^2)$

   This last option does not involve a difference of squares, so it cannot factor as shown in Choice D.

7. **D** Look at the answer choices and apply what you know about factoring patterns. The square of a binomial will always have an x term, and $32x^2 - 72$ does not, so choices A and B can be eliminated. Choice C would be equal to $(16x)^2 - (36)^2$, and 36 squared is far larger than 72. Since $32x^2 - 72 = 8(4x^2 - 9) = 8(2x + 3)(2x - 3)$, you can choose D, but you can also verify that Choice E will have an x term.

8. **B** Recognize that $9x^2 - 30x + 25$ is a perfect square trinomial, and choices C, D, and E can be eliminated. In order for the x term to have a minus sign, choose B.

9. **10** $2x^2 - 11x - 21 = (x - 7)(2x + 3) = (x + a)(2x + b)$ so $a = -7$ and $b = 3$. Therefore $b - a = 3 - -7 = 3 + 7 = 10$.

10. **6** $(4x - 7)(2x + 5) = 8x^2 + 20x - 14x - 35 = 8x^2 + 6x - 35$.

D. Applications of Factoring

1. Quadratic Equations

Equations of the form $ax^2 + bx + x = 0$ are called *quadratic equations.* You may encounter quadratic equations that are not perfectly aligned to this definition, so it's good to develop the habit of immediately transforming the equation to this form when you see an x^2 term.

a. Taking the Root of Both Sides

Quadratic equations that consist only of a variable expression squared and a constant term can be solved by taking the square root of both sides. If you can transform the equation so that you have a square on one side equal to a constant on the other, you can take the square root of both sides. This may give you an irrational result; if so, you can leave it in simplest radical form, or use your calculator for an approximation.

EXAMPLE:

Solve $3(x + 1)^2 - 48 = 0$.

While you could FOIL out $(x + 1)^2$, simplify, and solve the simplified version of the equation, taking the root of both sides may be easier. Add 48 to both sides, and divide both sides by 3.

$$3(x + 1)^2 - 48 = 0$$
$$3(x + 1)^2 = 48$$
$$(x + 1)^2 = 16$$

Take the square root of both sides. $x + 1 = \pm 4$. This produces two solutions. $x + 1 = 4$ gives $x = 3$ and $x + 1 = -4$ gives $x = -5$.

b. Solving by Factoring

The zero product property says something you know almost instinctively. If the product of two factors is zero, then one or both factors will be zero. Transform a quadratic equation so that one side of the equation is zero, and see if you can factor the other side. If you can, use the zero product property to create two simple equations, each of which produces one of the solutions of your quadratic equation.

EXAMPLE:

Solve $3x^2 + 2x - 6 = 50 - 3x - 3x^2$.

First bring all the terms to one side, equal to zero.

$$3x^2 + 2x - 6 = 50 - 3x - 3x^2$$
$$6x^2 + 2x - 6 = 50 - 3x$$
$$6x^2 + 5x - 6 = 50$$
$$6x^2 + 5x - 56 = 0$$

Factor the polynomial $(3x - 8)(2x + 7) = 0$ and set each factor equal to zero.

$$(3x - 8) = 0 \quad (2x + 7) = 0$$
$$3x = 8 \quad\quad 2x = -7$$
$$x = \frac{8}{3} \quad\quad x = \frac{-7}{2}$$

EXAMPLE:

If the product of two positive integers is 54 and their sum is 15, find the larger number.

If you write a system of equations, using x for the larger number and y for the smaller one, you get

$$\begin{cases} xy = 54 \\ x + y = 15 \end{cases}$$

The second equation is linear, but the first is not. Don't let that stop you. Solve the second equation for y, and use the fact that $y = 15 - x$ to substitute into the first equation. The first equation becomes $x(15 - x) = 54$, which can be simplified to $0 = x^2 - 15x + 54$ and solved by factoring to give you $(x - 6)(x - 9) = 0$ and $x = 6$ or $x = 9$. Therefore, the larger number is 9.

2. Rational Expressions

Factoring is an important tool in working with rational expressions, sometimes called *algebraic fractions*.

a. Simplifying Rational Expressions

To reduce an algebraic fraction to lowest terms, factor the numerator and the denominator and cancel any factors that appear in both.

EXAMPLE:

Which of the following is NOT equal to $\frac{x+1}{x+2}$?

A. $\dfrac{3x+3}{3x+6}$

B. $\dfrac{x^2+x}{x^2+2x}$

C. $\dfrac{x^2-1}{x^2+x-2}$

D. $\dfrac{x^2-x-2}{x^2-4}$

E. $\dfrac{x^2+x+1}{x^2+x+2}$

Factor the numerator and denominator of each fraction, if possible.

- **Choice A:** $\dfrac{3x+3}{3x+6} = \dfrac{3(x+1)}{3(x+2)}$

- **Choice B:** $\dfrac{x^2+x}{x^2+2x} = \dfrac{x(x+1)}{x(x+2)}$

- **Choice C:** $\dfrac{x^2-1}{x^2+x-2} = \dfrac{(x+1)(x-1)}{(x+2)(x-1)}$

- **Choice D:** $\dfrac{x^2-x-2}{x^2-4} = \dfrac{(x+1)(x-2)}{(x+2)(x-2)}$

All of these fractions can be reduced to $\dfrac{x+1}{x+2}$, but Choice E is a fraction in which neither the numerator nor the denominator can be factored, so it cannot be reduced to $\dfrac{x+1}{x+2}$.

b. Multiplying and Dividing Rational Expressions

To multiply rational expressions, factor all numerators and denominators, cancel any factor that appear in both a numerator and a denominator, and multiply numerator times numerator and denominator times denominator. To divide rational expressions, invert the divisor and multiply.

EXAMPLE:

Express in simplest form: $\dfrac{x^2-25}{x^2+8x+15} \div \dfrac{3x+15}{x^2+6x+9}$.

Invert the divisor and multiply.

$$\dfrac{x^2-25}{x^2+8x+15} \cdot \dfrac{x^2+6x+9}{3x+15}$$

Factor all numerators and denominators.

$$\dfrac{(x+5)(x-5)}{(x+3)(x+5)} \cdot \dfrac{(x+3)(x+3)}{3(x+5)}$$

Cancel and multiply.

$$\dfrac{(x+5)(x-5)}{(x+3)(x+5)} \cdot \dfrac{(x+3)(x+3)}{3(x+5)} = \dfrac{(x-5)(x+3)}{3(x+5)}$$

c. Adding and Subtracting Rational Expressions

Adding and subtracting algebraic fractions calls upon the same skills as adding and subtracting numeric fractions. If the fractions have different denominators, they must be transformed to have a common denominator. Once the denominators are the same, add or subtract the numerators, and reduce if possible. Because the numerators and denominators are polynomials, factoring is essential to the process.

If the fractions have different denominators:

1. **Factor the denominators.**
2. **Identify any factors common to both denominators.**

   The lowest common denominator is the product of each factor that is common, used once, and any remaining factors of either denominator.

3. **Transform each fraction by multiplying the numerator and denominator by the same quantity.**

When the fractions have common denominators, add or subtract the numerators. For subtraction, use parentheses around the second numerator to avoid sign errors. Finally, factor the numerator and denominator and reduce if possible.

EXAMPLE:

Express in simplest form: $\dfrac{5x}{3x-3} - \dfrac{2}{3x}$.

Factor each denominator: $3x - 3 = 3(x - 1)$ and $3x = 3 \times x$. The denominators have the factor 3 in common.

The lowest common denominator is $3(x - 1) \times x$ or $3x(x - 1)$. Transform each fraction:

$\dfrac{5x}{3(x-1)} \cdot \dfrac{x}{x} = \dfrac{5x^2}{3x(x-1)}$ and $\dfrac{2}{3x} \cdot \dfrac{(x-1)}{(x-1)} = \dfrac{2x-2}{3x(x-1)}$. The problem now becomes $\dfrac{5x}{3x-3} - \dfrac{2}{3x} =$

$\dfrac{5x^2}{3x(x-1)} - \dfrac{2x-2}{3x(x-1)}$. Put parentheses around the second numerator, as a reminder to change all the signs:

$\dfrac{5x^2 - (2x - 2)}{3x(x-1)} = \dfrac{5x^2 - 2x + 2}{3x(x-1)}$.

Practice

Directions (1–2): You are given two quantities, one in Column A and one in Column B. You are to compare the two quantities and choose:

A if the quantity in Column A is greater
B if the quantity in Column B is greater
C if the two quantities are equal
D if the relationship cannot be determined from the information given

$$5x^2 + 20x + 20 = 0$$

	Column A	**Column B**
1.	The sum of the solutions	The product of the solutions

$$x^2 + 18x + 81 = 0$$

	Column A	**Column B**
2.	x	9

Directions (3–8): You are given five answer choices. Select the best choice.

3. The solutions of the equation $3x^2 - 5x + 4 = 6$ are

   A. $x = \dfrac{-4}{3}, x = 2$

   B. $x = 2, x = \dfrac{-1}{3}$

   C. $x = -4, x = -6$

   D. $x = 4, x = -3$

   E. $x = -4, x = 3$

4. $\dfrac{x^2 - 1}{x^2 - 8x + 16} \cdot \dfrac{x^2 + 3x - 4}{x^2 - 16} =$

   A. $\dfrac{(x+1)(x-1)^2}{(x-4)^3}$

   B. $\dfrac{(x-1)(x+1)^2}{(x+4)(x-4)^2}$

   C. $\dfrac{x-4}{x+1}$

   D. -4

   E. $\dfrac{(x-1)(x+4)}{(x-4)^2}$

5. $\dfrac{x^2 - 1}{x^2 + 11x + 28} \div \dfrac{x^2 + 6x - 7}{x^2 + 5x + 4} =$

   A. $\left(\dfrac{x-1}{x+4}\right)^2$

   B. $\left(\dfrac{x+1}{x+7}\right)^2$

   C. 1

   D. $\dfrac{-1(5x+4)}{(11x+28)(6x-7)}$

   E. $\dfrac{-1(6x-7)}{(11x+28)(5x+4)}$

6. $\dfrac{x}{3a} - \dfrac{y}{5a} =$

   A. $\dfrac{x-y}{8a}$

   B. $\dfrac{x-y}{15a}$

   C. $\dfrac{5x-3y}{15a}$

   D. $\dfrac{5x-3y}{8a}$

   E. $\dfrac{x-y}{-2a}$

7. An object is dropped from the top of a 64-foot tower. Its height after t seconds is given by the formula $h = -16t^2 + 64$. After how many seconds will the object hit the ground?

   A. 1.0
   B. 1.5
   C. 1.7
   D. 2.0
   E. 2.5

8. The product of two consecutive positive odd numbers is one less than nine times their sum. Find the smaller of the two numbers.

   A. 15
   B. 16
   C. 17
   D. 18
   E. 19

Directions (9–10): Give your answer as a number.

9. Find the largest of three consecutive positive odd numbers for which the product of the smallest and the largest is 117.

10. Three less than the square of a positive number is five more than twice the number. Find the number.

Answers

1. **B**

$$5x^2 + 20x + 20 = 0$$

$$5(x^2 + 4x + 4) = 0$$

$$5(x + 2)^2 = 0$$

$$x + 2 = 0$$

$$x = -2$$

Since the two solutions are identical, the sum of the solutions is $-2 + -2 = -4$, and the product of the solutions is $(-2)(-2) = 4$.

2. **B** The polynomial $x^2 + 18x + 81$ is a perfect square trinomial, so its two factors will be identical $(x + 9)^2 = 0$, and produce only one solution, $x = -9$. Therefore $x < 9$.

3. **B**

$$3x^2 - 5x + 4 = 6$$

$$3x^2 - 5x - 2 = 0$$

$$(3x + 1)(x - 2) = 0$$

$$3x + 1 = 0 \qquad x - 2 = 0$$

$$3x = -1 \qquad x = 2$$

$$x = \frac{-1}{3}$$

4. **C** Before multiplying, factor all the numerators and denominators to locate opportunities for cancellation.

$$\frac{x^2 - 16}{x^2 - 8x + 16} \cdot \frac{x^2 + 3x - 4}{x^2 - 1} = \frac{(x+4)(x-4)}{(x-4)(x+4)} \cdot \frac{(x+4)(x-1)}{(x+1)(x-1)} = \frac{x-4}{x+1}$$

5. **B** To divide, multiply by the reciprocal, and factor all the numerators and denominators to locate opportunities for cancellation.

$$\frac{x^2 - 1}{x^2 + 11x + 28} \div \frac{x^2 + 6x - 7}{x^2 + 5x + 4} = \frac{x^2 - 1}{x^2 + 11x + 28} \cdot \frac{x^2 + 5x + 4}{x^2 + 6x - 7}$$

$$= \frac{(x+1)(x-1)}{(x+4)(x+7)} \cdot \frac{(x+4)(x+1)}{(x+7)(x-1)}$$

$$= \frac{(x+1)^2}{(x+7)^2} = \left(\frac{x+1}{x+7}\right)^2$$

6. **C** In order to subtract, you'll need a common denominator. Multiply the first fraction by $\frac{3}{3}$ and the second by $\frac{5}{5}$: $\frac{x}{3a} - \frac{y}{5a} = \frac{5x}{5(3a)} - \frac{3y}{3(5a)} = \frac{5x - 3y}{15a}$.

7. **D** When the object hits the ground, its height is zero. So solve $0 = -16t^2 + 64$ for t. Add $16t^2$ to both sides, divide by 16, and take the square root:

$$0 = -16t^2 + 64$$
$$16t^2 = 64$$
$$t^2 = \frac{64}{16} = 4$$
$$t = \pm 2$$

8. **C** Let the two numbers be x and $x + 2$. Then the product is one less than nine times their sum becomes

$$x(x+2) = 9(x+x+2) - 1$$
$$x^2 + 2x = 9(2x+2) - 1$$
$$x^2 + 2x = 18x + 18 - 1$$
$$x^2 + 2x = 18x + 17$$
$$x^2 - 16x - 17 = 0$$
$$(x-17)(x+1) = 0$$
$$x - 17 = 0 \quad x + 1 = 0$$
$$x = 17 \quad\quad x = -1$$

The numbers are 17 and 19.

9. **13** Call the three consecutive odd numbers x, $x + 2$, and $x + 4$. The product of the smallest and the largest is 117 becomes

$$x(x + 4) = 117$$
$$x^2 + 4x = 117$$
$$x^2 + 4x - 117 = 0$$

This will factor as $(x + 13)(x - 9) = 0$ giving solutions of $x = -13$ or $x = 9$. Since the consecutive odd numbers are positive, the numbers are 9, 11, and 13.

10. **4** Three less than the square of a positive number is five more than twice the number can be written as

$$x^2 - 3 = 5 + 2x$$
$$x^2 - 2x - 3 - 5 = 0$$
$$x^2 - 2x - 8 = 0$$
$$(x-4)(x+2) = 0$$
$$x - 4 = 0 \quad x + 2 = 0$$
$$x = 4 \quad\quad x = -2$$

XII. Geometry

A. Lines, Rays, Segments, and Angles

One of the fundamental concepts in geometry is a line. A *line* has infinite length, but no width or thickness. The term *straight line* is redundant, because all lines are straight. A *ray,* sometimes called a *half-line,* has one endpoint, but continues forever in the other direction; it resembles an arrow. A *line segment* is a portion of a line between two endpoints. Most work in geometry deals with line segments.

1. Length

It isn't possible to assign lengths to lines or rays because they go on forever, but it is possible to talk about the length of a line segment. That length is the distance between its endpoints. What we call a ruler is simply a way of assigning numbers to points on a line segment, so that the distance between two points can be found by subtracting the numbers assigned to those points. Distance and length are always positive numbers. Two segments that have the same length are *congruent segments*.

2. Angle Measurement and Classification

In geometry, angles are measured in degrees. A full rotation is 360°. Half of this, or 180°, is the measure of a straight angle. The straight angle takes its name from the fact that it looks like a straight line.

An angle of 90°, or a quarter rotation, is called a *right angle*.

Angles between 0° and 90° are called *acute angles*. (One definition of acute is "sharp." Acute angles have a sharp point.)

Angles with measurements greater than 90° but less that 180° are *obtuse angles*. ("Thick" is a synonym for obtuse. Obtuse angles are thick.)

3. Midpoints and Segment Bisectors

The *midpoint* of a segment is the point on the segment that is equidistant from the endpoints. It sits exactly at the middle of the segment and divides the segment into two congruent segments. Each of the two congruent segments is half as long as the original segment.

A *segment bisector* is a line, ray, or segment that passes through the midpoint. A bisector divides the segment into two congruent segments, each half as long as the original. If a bisector intersects the segment to form 90-degree angles, it is called a *perpendicular bisector*. Note that not all bisectors are perpendicular.

4. Angle Bisectors

An *angle bisector* is a line, ray, or segment that divides an angle into two congruent angles. Each of those congruent angles is half the size of the original angle.

EXAMPLE:

$\overline{BD}$ bisects $\angle ABC$ and $m\angle ABD = 44°$. Find the measure of $\angle ABC$.

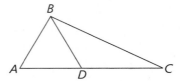

Because $\overline{BD}$ bisects $\angle ABC$, $\angle ABD \cong \angle CBD$, so each is 44°. That measurement is half of the measure of $\angle ABC$, so $\angle ABC$ measures 88°.

Be careful not to assign other jobs to an angle bisector. It bisects the angle, but it does not necessarily bisect the opposite side of the triangle, for example.

5. Angle Pair Relationships

When two lines intersect, four angles are formed. Each pair of angles across the X from one another is a pair of vertical angles. Vertical angles are congruent.

Two angles whose measurements total 90° are called *complementary angles*. If two angles are complementary, each is the *complement* of the other.

Two angles whose measurements total 180° are called *supplementary angles*. If two angles are supplementary, each is the *supplement* of the other.

EXAMPLE:

Find the complement of an angle of 25°.

To find the complement, subtract the known angle from 90°: 90° – 25° = 65°.

EXAMPLE:

Find the supplement of an angle of 132°.

To find the supplement, subtract the known angle from 180°: 180° – 132° = 48°.

6. Parallel Lines

Lines that are always the same distance apart and, therefore, never intersect are called *parallel lines*. When a pair of parallel lines is cut by another line, called a *transversal,* eight angles are formed. Different pairs from this group of eight are classified in different ways.

As the transversal crosses the top line, it creates a cluster of four angles, here labeled $\angle 1$, $\angle 2$, $\angle 3$, and $\angle 4$. As it crosses the lower line, it creates another cluster of four angles, labeled $\angle 5$, $\angle 6$, $\angle 7$, and $\angle 8$. In each cluster, there is an angle in the upper-left position ($\angle 1$ from the top cluster or $\angle 5$ from the bottom cluster).

There are also angles in the upper-right, lower-left, and lower-right positions. The angle from the upper cluster and the angle from the lower cluster that are in the same position are called *corresponding angles*.

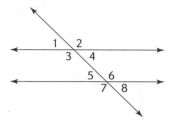

When parallel lines are cut by a transversal, corresponding angles are congruent. They have the same measurements. $\angle 1 \cong \angle 5$, $\angle 2 \cong \angle 6$, $\angle 3 \cong \angle 7$, and $\angle 4 \cong \angle 8$.

Consider only the angles that are between the parallel lines: $\angle 3$, $\angle 4$, $\angle 5$, and $\angle 6$. These are called *interior angles*. Choose one from the top cluster (say, $\angle 3$) and one from the bottom cluster on the other side of the transversal (in this case, $\angle 6$), and you have a pair of alternate interior angles.

When parallel lines are cut by a transversal, alternate interior angles are congruent. They have the same measurements: $\angle 3 \cong \angle 6$ and $\angle 4 \cong \angle 5$. Alternate interior angles are easy to spot because they form a Z (or a backward Z).

When parallel lines are cut by a transversal, alternate exterior angles are congruent: $\angle 1 \cong \angle 8$ and $\angle 2 \cong \angle 7$.

Using these facts, and the fact that vertical angles are congruent, you can quickly deduce that $\angle 1 \cong \angle 4 \cong \angle 5 \cong \angle 8$ and $\angle 2 \cong \angle 3 \cong \angle 6 \cong \angle 7$. Add the fact that $\angle 1$ and $\angle 2$ are supplementary, and it becomes possible to assign each of the angles one of two measurements: $m\angle 1 = m\angle 4 = m\angle 5 = m\angle 8 = n°$ and $m\angle 2 = m\angle 3 = m\angle 6 = m\angle 7 = (180 - n)°$.

EXAMPLE:

Transversal $\overrightarrow{PQ}$ intersects $\overrightarrow{AB}$ at point M and intersects $\overrightarrow{CD}$ at point N. If $\overrightarrow{AB} \parallel \overrightarrow{CD}$, and $m\angle PMB = 35°$, find the measure of $\angle MNC$.

Draw a diagram to show the situation, and mark the congruent angles: $\angle PMB$ and $\angle MNC$ are not congruent, so they must be supplementary. Therefore, $m\angle MNC = 180° - m\angle PMB = 180° - 35° = 145°$.

7. Perpendicular Lines

Perpendicular lines are lines that intersect at right angles. The symbol for "is perpendicular to" is $\perp$. Remember that all right angles are congruent, because all right angles measure 90°. When a line segment is drawn from a vertex of a triangle perpendicular to the opposite side, that segment is called an *altitude* of the triangle.

If a line is perpendicular to one of two parallel lines, it is perpendicular to the other.

If a line is parallel to one of two perpendicular lines, it is perpendicular to the other.

EXAMPLE:

$\overleftrightarrow{AB} \perp \overleftrightarrow{CD}$ at point N. Line $\overleftrightarrow{PQ}$ intersects $\overleftrightarrow{AB}$ at P and $\overleftrightarrow{CD}$ at Q. What is $m\angle NPQ + m\angle NQP$?

A. 45°
B. 60°
C. 90°
D. 180°
E. Cannot be determined

Draw the diagram to help you see the situation. The perpendicular lines form right angles at N, so $\triangle PNQ$ is a right triangle. Since $\angle N$ is 90°, the other two angles in the triangle make up the rest of the 180°, so $m\angle NPQ + m\angle NQP = 90°$.

Practice

Use the following diagram for questions 1–3. Line m is parallel to line n. The figure is not drawn to scale.

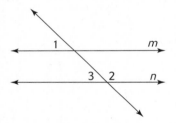

Directions (1–2): You are given two quantities, one in Column A and one in Column B. You are to compare the two quantities and choose:

A if the quantity in Column A is greater
B if the quantity in Column B is greater
C if the two quantities are equal
D if the relationship cannot be determined from the information given

	Column A	Column B
1.	$m\angle 1$	$m\angle 3$

	Column A	Column B
2.	$m\angle 1$	$m\angle 2$

Directions (3–8): You are given five answer choices. Select the best choice.

3. If line m is parallel to line n, which of the following must be true?

   I. $\angle 1 \cong \angle 2$

  II. $\angle 1 \cong \angle 3$

 III. $\angle 2 \cong \angle 3$

   A. I only

   B. II only

   C. III only

   D. I and II

   E. II and III

4. If $\overleftrightarrow{XY}$ is parallel to $\overrightarrow{RS}$ and $\angle XMP$ measures 24° find the measure of $\angle RPM$.

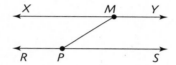

   A. 24°

   B. 48°

   C. 66°

   D. 156°

   E. 336°

5. If $\overleftrightarrow{XY} \perp \overrightarrow{RT}$, which of the following is not true?

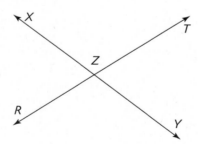

   A. $\angle YZT$ is supplementary to $\angle XZR$.

   B. $\angle XZR$ is complementary to $\angle RZY$.

   C. $\angle XZT \cong \angle RZY$.

   D. $\angle XZR$ is a right angle.

   E. $\angle XZY$ is a straight angle.

6. $m\angle A = 89°$. Which of the following is the measure of the supplement of $\angle A$?

    A. 189°
    B. 91°
    C. 89°
    D. 44.5°
    E. 1°

7. Find the complement of an angle of 9°.

    A. 9°
    B. 18°
    C. 81°
    D. 171°
    E. 351°

8. $\angle V$ and $\angle W$ are complementary. Which of the following best describes $\angle W$?

    A. acute
    B. right
    C. obtuse
    D. reflex
    E. straight

Directions (9–10): Give your answer as a number.

---

9. $\triangle XYZ$ is drawn with $\angle X \cong \angle Z$. If the measure of $\angle X$ is 40°, find the measure, in degrees, of $\angle Y$.

10. $\triangle ABC$ has a right angle at B and $\angle C$ measures 15°. Find the measure, in degrees, of $\angle A$.

Answers

1. C When parallel lines are cut by a transversal, corresponding angles are congruent. $\angle 1$ and $\angle 3$ are corresponding angles, so $m\angle 1 = m\angle 3$.

2. D Because $\angle 2$ and $\angle 3$ are a linear pair, they're supplementary, and because $\angle 1$ and $\angle 3$ are congruent, you can show by substitution that $\angle 1$ and $\angle 2$ are supplementary. But without knowing the measure of any of the angles, you can't determine which is larger.

3. B When parallel lines are cut by a transversal, corresponding angles are congruent, so $\angle 1 \cong \angle 3$. $\angle 2$ and $\angle 3$ are supplementary, but they would only be congruent if the transversal were perpendicular to the parallel lines.

4. D $\angle XMP$ and $\angle RPM$ are supplementary, so $m\angle RPM = 180° - 24° = 156°$.

5. B If $\overleftrightarrow{XY} \perp \overleftrightarrow{RT}$, all four angles are right angles. Complementary angles total 90°, so it is impossible for two right angles to be complementary.

6. B The measure of the supplement of $\angle A$ is $180° - 89° = 91°$.

7. **C** The complement of an angle of 9° is 90° – 9° = 81°.

8. **A** If $\angle V$ and $\angle W$ are complementary, their measurements total 90°, so each must be less than 90°.

9. **100°** If $\angle X \cong \angle Z$ and the measure of $\angle X$ is 40°, then the measure of $\angle Z$ is also 40°. That leaves 180° – (40° + 40°) = 180° – 80° = 100° for the measure of $\angle Y$.

10. **75°** The three angles of the triangle total 180°. $m\angle B + m\angle C$ = 90° + 15° = 105°, leaving 180° – 105° = 75° for $\angle A$.

B. Triangles

1. Classifying Triangles

Right triangles are triangles that contain one right angle. *Obtuse triangles* contain one obtuse angle, and *acute triangles* contain three acute angles.

Isosceles triangles are triangles with two congruent sides. The angles opposite the congruent sides, often called the *base angles,* are congruent to each other. In an isosceles triangle, the altitude drawn from the vertex to the base bisects the base and the vertex angle.

An *equilateral triangle* is one in which all three sides are the same lengths. Each of its angles measures 60°. Any altitude bisects the side to which it is drawn and the angle from which it is drawn.

EXAMPLE:

In $\triangle$ABC, $\overline{AB} \cong \overline{BC}$ and $\overline{BD}$ is an altitude.

Column A	Column B
$m\angle ABD$	$m\angle CBD$

Draw the triangle. The angles being compared make up the vertex angle. Because we know that an altitude from the vertex of an isosceles triangle bisects the vertex angle, the two angles are equal.

2. Angles in Triangles

a. Sum of the Angles of a Triangle

In any triangle, the sum of the measures of the three angles is 180°. In a right triangle, the two acute angles are complementary.

b. Exterior Angles

An *exterior angle* of a triangle is formed by extending one side of the triangle. The exterior angle is supplementary to the interior angle adjacent to it. Because the three interior angles of the triangle add up to 180°, it's easy to show that the measure of an exterior angle of a triangle is equal to the sum of the two remote interior angles.

$$m\angle 1 + m\angle 2 + m\angle 3 = 180°$$
$$m\angle 1 + m\angle 4 = 180°$$
$$m\angle 1 + m\angle 2 + m\angle 3 = m\angle 1 + m\angle 4$$
$$m\angle 2 + m\angle 3 = m\angle 4$$

EXAMPLE:

In $\triangle ABC$, $m\angle A = 43°$ and $m\angle B = 28°$. What is the measure of the exterior angle of the triangle at C?

Sketch the triangle. The exterior angle is equal to the sum of the two remote interior angles, so $m\angle BCD = 43° + 28° = 71°$.

Alternatively, you could calculate the measure of $\angle BCA$ (180° – 43° – 28° = 109°) and, because $\angle BCD$ is supplementary to $\angle BCA$, it will be 180° – 109° = 71°.

3. Triangle Inequality

In any triangle, the sum of the lengths of any two sides will be greater than the length of the third. Put another way, the length of any side of a triangle is less than the sum of the other two sides but more than the difference between them.

EXAMPLE:

Gretchen lives 5 miles from the library and 2 miles from school. Which of the following cannot be the distance from the library to school?

A. 4
B. 5
C. 6
D. 7
E. 8

If Gretchen's house, the library, and the school are the vertices of a triangle, then the distance from the library to school must be greater than 5 – 2 and less than 5 + 2. So the distance is between 3 and 7 miles. Choice E, 8 miles, would not be possible. It's wise to consider the possibility that Gretchen's house, the library, and the school lie in a straight line, but even if that were the case, the maximum distance from the library to the school would be 7 miles.

4. Pythagorean Theorem

The Pythagorean theorem is a statement about the relationship among the sides of a right triangle. A *right triangle* is one that contains one right angle; the side opposite the right angle is called the *hypotenuse*. The other two sides, which form the right angle, are called *legs*. The Pythagorean theorem states that in any right triangle, the square of the hypotenuse is equal to the sum of the squares of the other two sides. Most people remember it in symbolic form, though.

If the legs of the right triangle are a and b and the hypotenuse is c, then $a^2 + b^2 = c^2$.

EXAMPLE:

> Dorothy walks to school every morning and, on sunny days, she cuts through a vacant lot. On snowy days, she must go around the block. One side of the rectangular lot measures 5 meters and the other measures 12 meters. How much shorter is Dorothy's walk on sunny days?

The path through the lot is the hypotenuse of a right triangle, so its length can be found using the Pythagorean theorem: $5^2 + 12^2 = c^2$, so $c^2 = 25 + 144 = 169$, and $c = 13$ yards. On sunny days, she takes the path through the lot, which is 13 yards, but on snowy days, she must walk around the legs of the triangle, a total of 17 yards. On sunny days, her walk is 4 yards shorter.

5. Special Right Triangles

When an altitude is drawn in an equilateral triangle, it divides the triangle into two congruent right triangles. Each of these smaller triangles has an angle of 60° and an angle of 30° in addition to the right angle. The hypotenuse of the 30°-60°-90° triangle is the side of the original equilateral triangle. The side opposite the 30° angle is half as large. Using the Pythagorean theorem, you can determine that the side opposite the 60° angle must be half the hypotenuse times the square root of 3. If s is the side of the equilateral triangle,

$$a^2 + b^2 = c^2$$

$$\left(\frac{1}{2}s\right)^2 + b^2 = s^2$$

$$\frac{1}{4}s^2 + b^2 = s^2$$

$$b^2 = \frac{3}{4}s^2$$

$$b = \sqrt{\frac{3}{4}s^2}$$

$$b = \frac{\sqrt{3}s}{2} = \frac{1}{2}s\sqrt{3}$$

In an isosceles right triangle, the two legs are of equal length. Apply the Pythagorean theorem and you can see that the hypotenuse must be equal to the side times the square root of 2. If s is the side of the isosceles right triangle,

$$a^2 + b^2 = c^2$$
$$s^2 + s^2 = c^2$$
$$2s^2 = c^2$$
$$\sqrt{2s^2} = c$$
$$s\sqrt{2} = c$$

EXAMPLE:

Find the area of a square whose diagonal is $15\sqrt{2}$.

The diagonal of a square divides it into two isosceles right triangles, and the diagonal is the hypotenuse of each. If the hypotenuse is $15\sqrt{2}$, the sides must be 15, so the area is 225 square units.

EXAMPLE:

The altitude of an equilateral triangle is 7 cm. Find the perimeter of the triangle.

The altitude divides the equilateral triangle into two 30°-60°-90° triangles. The altitude is the side opposite the 60° angle, so its length is $\frac{1}{2}h\sqrt{3}$, where h is the length of a side of the triangle.

$$\frac{1}{2}h\sqrt{3} = 7$$
$$h\sqrt{3} = 14$$
$$h = \frac{14}{\sqrt{3}} = \frac{14\sqrt{3}}{3}$$

Be sure to answer the question asked. The perimeter of the triangle is $3 \cdot \frac{14\sqrt{3}}{3} = 14\sqrt{3}$.

6. Congruence and Similarity

a. Congruence

Triangles are *congruent* if they are the same shape and the same size. Because the size of the angles controls the shape of the triangle, in a pair of congruent triangles, corresponding angles are congruent. Because the length of sides controls size, corresponding sides are of equal length.

To conclude that triangles are congruent, you must have evidence that certain combinations of sides and angles of one triangle are congruent to the corresponding parts of the other triangle. Here are the minimums required to prove that triangles are congruent:

- **Three sides:** SSS
- **Two sides and the included angle:** SAS
- **Two angles and the included side:** ASA
- **Two angles and the non-included side:** AAS

b. Similarity

Triangles are similar if they are the same shape, but not necessarily the same size. Corresponding angles are congruent and corresponding sides are in proportion.

To conclude that triangles are similar you must know that two angles of one triangle are congruent to the corresponding angles of the other (AA).

EXAMPLE:

Given that $\angle A \cong \angle BXC$, $\angle BCA \cong \angle XYC$, and $\overline{BX} \parallel \overline{AY}$, which of the following is true?

A. $\triangle CXY$ is isosceles
B. $\triangle XCB$ is isosceles
C. $\triangle ABC$ is equilateral
D. $\triangle ABC$ is isosceles
E. $\triangle ABC \sim \triangle CXY$

Mark the diagram to show the given information. Because $\overline{BX} \parallel \overline{AY}$, it is possible to conclude that $\angle BCA \cong \angle CBX$ and $\angle BXC \cong \angle XCY$. Therefore, (E) is true by AA.

7. Area

The area of a triangle is equal to half the product of the length of the base and the height. Any side may be considered the base, but the height must be drawn from the opposite vertex, perpendicular to the base. This can sometimes cause the altitude to fall outside the triangle.

EXAMPLE:

$\triangle PQR$ has an area of 24 square units. If the lengths of its sides are 3cm, 6cm, and 8cm, find the length of the longest altitude.

The area of the triangle will be the same no matter which side is called the base, provided that the altitude is drawn correctly. If we say the base is the side of length 3, then $A = \frac{1}{2}bh$ becomes $24 = \frac{1}{2} \cdot 3 \cdot h$ and $h = 16$. Logically, the longest altitude will be drawn to the shortest side, but repeating the calculation with other sides as bases will show that the altitude drawn to the 6cm side is 8cm long, and the altitude to the longest side is 6cm long. The longest altitude is 16cm.

Practice

Use the following diagram for questions 1–2. $\overline{RS} \parallel \overline{TU}$ *The figure is not drawn to scale.*

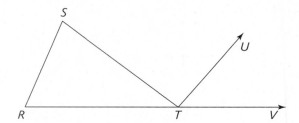

Directions (1–2): You are given two quantities, one in Column A and one in Column B. You are to compare the two quantities and choose:

A if the quantity in Column A is greater
B if the quantity in Column B is greater
C if the two quantities are equal
D if the relationship cannot be determined from the information given

	Column A	**Column B**
1.	$m\angle SRT$	$m\angle UTV$

	Column A	**Column B**
2.	$m\angle STV$	$m\angle S$

Directions (3–8): You are given five answer choices. Select the best choice.

3. $\triangle CDE$ is an isosceles triangle in which $CD = DE$ and side $\overline{CE}$ is extended through E to F, forming exterior $\angle DEF$. Which of the following must be true?

   I. $m\angle DEF > m\angle CDE$
   II. $\angle DEF$ and $\angle DEC$ are supplementary
   III. $\angle DEC$ and $\angle DCE$ are congruent

   A. I only
   B. I and II
   C. I and III
   D. II and III
   E. I, II, and III

4. $\triangle RST \sim \triangle MNP$. $RS = 12$ and $ST = 18$. Find the length of $\overline{MN}$ if $NP = 6$.

   A. 4
   B. 9
   C. 12
   D. 24
   E. 48

5. If $\triangle PQR \cong \triangle MNO$ and both are isosceles triangles, which of the following is not necessarily true?

   A. $PQ = MN$
   B. $PQ = NO$
   C. $NO = QR$
   D. $\angle M \cong \angle P$
   E. $\angle Q \cong \angle N$

6. The town of Treadway is 40 miles north of Centerville and 30 miles east of Dodge. Which of the following is the best estimate of the distance from Centerville to Dodge?

   A. 10 miles
   B. 30 miles
   C. 40 miles
   D. 50 miles
   E. 70 miles

7. $\triangle RST$ is a scalene triangle. If $RS = 7$ and $RT = 4$, which of the following is not true?

   A. $TS > 3$
   B. $TS < 11$
   C. $TS \neq 7$
   D. $TS \neq 4$
   E. $TS = \sqrt{65}$

8. The area of a square is 100 square meters. Find the length of its diagonal.

   A. 10m
   B. 15m
   C. $10\sqrt{2}$m
   D. $5\sqrt{3}$m
   E. 20m

Directions (9–10): Give your answer as a number.

9. $\triangle RST \cong \triangle MNP$. If $RS = 12$ and $ST = 18$, find the length of $\overline{MN}$.

10. $\triangle PRT$ is a right triangle with $\overline{PR} \perp \overline{RT}$. Side $\overline{RT}$ is extended through R to S. Find the measure of $\angle PRS$.

Answers

1. **C** $\angle SRT$ and $\angle UTV$ are corresponding angles. When parallel lines are cut by a transversal, corresponding angles are congruent.

2. **A** $m\angle STV = m\angle STU + m\angle UTV$ and $m\angle S = m\angle STU$ because they are alternate interior angles. Since the whole is greater than the part, $m\angle STV > m\angle S$.

3. **E** $m\angle DEF > m\angle CDE$ because the measure of an exterior angle of a triangle is greater than the measure of either remote interior angle. $\angle DEF$ and $\angle DEC$ are supplementary because they're a linear pair. $\angle DEC$ and $\angle DCE$ are congruent because base angles of an isosceles triangle are congruent.

4. **C** $\triangle RST \sim \triangle MNP$ implies $RS = MN$. Therefore, $MN = 12$, and the additional information is unnecessary.

5. **B** If $\triangle PQR \cong \triangle MNO$, the correspondence described by that statement tells us that choices A, C, D, and E must be true. Choice B may also be true, if $MN = NO$, but that information is not available.

6. **D** The distance from Centerville to Dodge is the third side of a triangle, so its length is more than $40 - 30 = 10$ miles and less than $40 + 30 = 70$ miles. The description suggests that the triangle is a right triangle, so by the Pythagorean theorem, $30^2 + 40^2 = 900 + 1,600 = 2,500$ and $\sqrt{2,500} = 50$ miles.

7. **E** If $RS = 7$ and $RT = 4$, the length of the third side is greater than the difference of the two known sides but less than their sum, so choices A and B are true. Because the triangle is scalene, side ST cannot be the same length as RS or RT, so choices C and D are true. Choice E would be true only if TS were the hypotenuse of a right triangle, which we know is not true.

8. **C** The area of a square is the square of the length of its side, so if the area is 100 square meters, the side is 10 meters long. Use the Pythagorean theorem to find the length of its diagonal:

$$a^2 + b^2 = c^2$$
$$10^2 + 10^2 = c^2$$
$$200 = c^2$$
$$\sqrt{200} = 10\sqrt{2} = c$$

9. 12 Since $\triangle RST \cong \triangle MNP$, $\overline{MN} \cong \overline{RS}$ so $MN = RS = 12$.

10. 90° $\angle PRS$ is an exterior angle of $\triangle PRT$ and is adjacent to the right angle at R. The measure of $\angle PRS$ is 90°.

C. Quadrilaterals

The term *quadrilateral* denotes any four-sided polygon, but most of the attention falls on the members of the parallelogram family.

1. Parallelograms

A parallelogram is a quadrilateral with two pairs of opposite sides parallel and congruent. In any parallelogram, consecutive angles are supplementary and opposite angles are congruent. Drawing one diagonal in a parallelogram divides it into two congruent triangles. When both diagonals are drawn in the parallelogram, the diagonals bisect each other.

EXAMPLE:

$ABDE$ and $BCDE$ are parallelograms with $BD = BE$. Which of the following are true?

   I. $\angle A \cong \angle C$

  II. $AE = CD$

 III. $\triangle AEB \cong \triangle CDB$

A. I only
B. II only
C. III only
D. I and II
E. I, II, and III

Since $BD = BE$, $\triangle EBD$ is isosceles, and $\angle DEB \cong \angle EDB$. Because opposite angles of a parallelogram are congruent, $\angle A \cong \angle EDB \cong \angle DEB \cong \angle C$, so I is true. Because opposite sides of a parallelogram are congruent, $AE = BE = BD = CD$, so II is true. Because $\triangle AEB$, $\triangle EBD$, and $\triangle BDC$ are all isosceles triangles, $\angle A \cong \angle EBA \cong \angle DBC \cong \angle C$, and $\triangle AEB \cong \triangle CDB$ by AAS. Therefore, III is also true and the answer is E.

a. Area

The area of a parallelogram is found by multiplying the base times the height: $A = bh$. Remember that the height must be measured as the perpendicular distance between the bases. Do not confuse the side with the height.

EXAMPLE:

Find the area of parallelogram $ABCD$ if $AB = 13$, $BC = 10$, and $BX = 12$.

BX is the height and BC is the base, so the area is $12 \times 10 = 120$ square units.

2. Rhombuses

A rhombus is a parallelogram with four sides of the same length. Because the rhombus is a parallelogram, it has all the properties of a parallelogram. The diagonals of a rhombus are perpendicular to one another.

a. Area

Because the diagonals are perpendicular bisectors of one another, they divide the rhombus into four congruent right triangles. The area of each right triangle can be easily found. The legs of the right triangle are $\frac{1}{2}d_1$ and $\frac{1}{2}d_2$, so the area of each right triangle is $\frac{1}{2} \cdot \frac{1}{2}d_1 \cdot \frac{1}{2}d_2 = \frac{1}{8}d_1 d_2$. Because there are four triangles making up the rhombus, the area of the rhombus is $4 \cdot \frac{1}{8}d_1 \cdot d_2 = \frac{1}{2}d_1 \cdot d_2$. The area of a rhombus is one-half the product of the diagonals.

EXAMPLE:

Find the area of a rhombus whose diagonals are 12cm and 20cm.

The area of the rhombus is $\frac{1}{2} \cdot 12 \cdot 20 = 120\text{cm}^2$.

3. Rectangles and Squares

A rectangle is a parallelogram with four right angles. Because the rectangle is a parallelogram, it has all the properties of a parallelogram. The perimeter of any figure is the sum of the lengths of its sides. Because opposite sides of a rectangle are congruent, this can be expressed as $P = 2l + 2w$.

A square is a parallelogram that is both a rhombus and a rectangle. Squares have four right angles and four equal sides.

EXAMPLE:

Marianna wants to build a fence around her vegetable garden. If the garden is a rectangle 30 feet long and 15 feet wide, and fencing costs $1.25 per foot, how much will it cost to fence the garden?

The perimeter of a rectangle $= 2l + 2w$, so she'll need $(2 \times 30) + (2 \times 15) = 60 + 30 = 90$ feet of fencing. You're asked the cost of the fencing, however, not how much fencing is needed. So 90 feet of fencing at $1.25 per foot will cost $90 \times 1.25 = \$112.50$.

The diagonals of a rectangle are congruent, and because the rectangle is a parallelogram, the diagonals bisect each other.

EXAMPLE:

In rectangle $ABCD$, the diagonals intersect at E. If $BE = 8$, find AE.

Because the diagonals are congruent and bisect each other, $AE = EC = BE = ED$. So $AE = 8$.

a. Area

Since the rectangle is a parallelogram, its area is base times height. But because the adjacent sides of the rectangle are perpendicular, the length and width are the base and the height, so $A = lw$.

EXAMPLE:

What is the area in square yards of Marianna's garden if the garden plot is 30 feet long and 15 feet wide?

The dimensions of the garden are given in feet, but the answer must be in square yards. While you can convert to square yards at the end, it may be simpler to convert the length and width to yards before finding the area. Because there are 3 feet in a yard, 30 feet = 10 yards and 15 feet = 5 yards. The area is $10 \times 5 = 50$ square yards.

Alternatively, you can find the area as $30 \times 15 = 450$ square feet. There are 9 square feet in one square yard, so $450 \div 9 = 50$ square yards.

4. Trapezoids

A *trapezoid* is a quadrilateral with one pair of parallel sides and one nonparallel pair. If the nonparallel sides are congruent, the trapezoid is an *isosceles trapezoid*. Base angles of an isosceles trapezoid are congruent. Consecutive angles of a trapezoid are supplementary. In an isosceles trapezoid, diagonals are congruent. Diagonals of other trapezoids are not congruent. Diagonals of a trapezoid do not necessarily bisect one another.

The line segment joining the midpoints of the nonparallel sides is called the *median* of the trapezoid. The median is parallel to the bases. Its length is the average of the bases.

a. Area

If you cut the top off a trapezoid by cutting along the median, and flip the top piece over and set it next to the bottom piece, you create a parallelogram. The height of the parallelogram is half the height of the trapezoid. The base of the parallelogram is the sum of the length of the long and the short base of the trapezoid. So the area of a trapezoid is equal to half the height times the sum of the bases. Some people remember this formula as the average of the bases times the height, or the length of the median times the height.

EXAMPLE:

The area of a trapezoid is 40 square centimeters. If the bases are 3cm and 5cm, how high is the trapezoid?

$A = \frac{1}{2}h\left(b_1 + b_2\right)$ and you know the bases are 3 and 5, so:

$$40 = \frac{1}{2}h\left(3 + 5\right)$$
$$40 = \frac{1}{2}h \cdot 8$$
$$40 = 4h$$
$$h = 10$$

Practice

Directions (1–9): You are given five answer choices. Select the best choice.

1. *RSTU* is a rhombus. *UV* = 4 and *RV* = 6. Find the area of the rhombus.

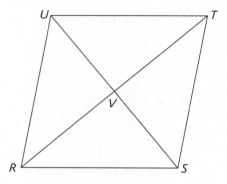

    A.   12
    B.   24
    C.   36
    D.   48
    E.   60

2. In rectangle *ABCD*, all of the following must be true EXCEPT

    A. $AD = BC$
    B. $\angle ABC$ is a right angle
    C. $\overline{CD} \perp \overline{DA}$
    D. $AB = AE$
    E. $\angle EAB \cong \angle EBA$

3. Find the perimeter of rectangle *ABCD* if *BC* = 30, and *AC* = 50.

    A.   70
    B.   80
    C.   140
    D.   160
    E.   240

4. *ABCD* is a trapezoid with $\overline{BC} \parallel \overline{AD}$. *BC* = 8 and *AD* = 22. If the area of the trapezoid is 150 square units, find the height.

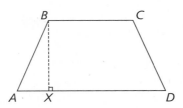

   A. 5
   B. 10
   C. 15
   D. 20
   E. 25

5. Find the perimeter of isosceles trapezoid *ABCD* if the median is 18 units long and each of the nonparallel sides is 6 units long.

   A. 24
   B. 30
   C. 42
   D. 48
   E. 108

6. A parallelogram has a base of 12m and a height of 8. Find its area.

   A. 20
   B. 40
   C. 48
   D. 96
   E. 100

7. The diagonal of a square is $9\sqrt{2}$cm. If another square is drawn with one vertex at a vertex of the large square and the opposite vertex on the diagonal as shown, find the perimeter of the smaller square.

   A. 18cm
   B. $18\sqrt{2}$cm
   C. 36cm
   D. $36\sqrt{2}$cm
   E. 72cm

8. Find the area of trapezoid *ABCD* if the median = 18 and height *BX* = 6.

   A. 6
   B. 18
   C. 27
   D. 54
   E. 108

9. A parallelogram has a base equal in length to its shorter diagonal. If the angle formed by that base and the shorter diagonal is 40°, which of the following could be the measure of an angle of the parallelogram?

   A. 40
   B. 70
   C. 80
   D. 100
   E. 140

Directions (10): Give your answer as a number.

10. A rhombus has diagonals of 8cm and 6cm. Find the side of the rhombus, in centimeters.

Answers

1. **D**   The area of a rhombus is equal to half the product of the lengths of the diagonals. Because the rhombus is a parallelogram, the diagonals bisect each other, so we can conclude from the given information that the lengths of the diagonals are 8 and 12. Then the area is $\frac{1}{2}(8)(12) = 48$.

2. **D**   Choice A is true because *AD* and *BC* are opposite sides of the rectangle, so *AD* = *BC*. Because any pair of adjacent sides of a rectangle meet at right angles, both choices B and C are true. $\angle EAB \cong \angle EBA$ because the diagonals of a rectangle are congruent and bisect each other, so $\triangle AEB$ is isosceles with *AE* = *BE*, and the angles opposite those sides congruent. However, *AB* will be equal to *AE* only if $\triangle AEB$ is equilateral, and there is not sufficient information to know if that is true.

3. **C**   Use the Pythagorean theorem to find *AB*.

$$(AB)^2 + (BC)^2 = (AC)^2$$
$$(AB)^2 + 30^2 = 50^2$$
$$(AB)^2 + 900 = 2,500$$
$$(AB)^2 = 1,600$$
$$AB = 40$$

Then the perimeter is 2(30) + 2(40) = 60 + 80 = 140.

4. **B**   The area of the trapezoid is $\frac{1}{2}(b_1 + b_2)h$. The bases are 8 and 22 units long, and the area is 150 square units.

$$A = \frac{1}{2}(b_1 + b_2)h$$
$$150 = \frac{1}{2}(8 + 22)h$$
$$150 = \frac{1}{2}(30)h$$
$$150 = 15h$$
$$10 = h$$

5. **D**   The length of the median is half the sum of the two bases, so if the median is 18, the sum of the two bases is 36. Add to that the two nonparallel sides, each 6, to find the perimeter: 36 + 2(6) = 48.

6. **D**   The area of the parallelogram is equal to the product of the base and the height, so $12 \times 8 = 96m^2$.

7. **A**   The diagonal of the square is $9\sqrt{2}$cm, so the side of the larger square is 9. The smaller square has a side half as long as the larger square, so its perimeter is 4(4.5) = 18cm.

8. **E**   The length of the median is equal to half the sum of the bases, so the area of the trapezoid is equal to $18 \times 6 = 108$ square units.

9. **B**   The shorter diagonal divides the parallelogram into two triangles and because the shorter diagonal is congruent to the base, the triangle is isosceles. The angle formed by the two congruent line segments is the vertex angle of the isosceles triangle, so the two congruent base angles of the isosceles triangle total 140°. This means that each of those angles is 70°, and one of them is an angle of the parallelogram. The angles of the parallelogram are 70° and 110°.

10. **5 centimeters**   The diagonals of a rhombus are perpendicular and bisect each other; therefore they create four congruent right triangles, each with legs of 3cm and 4cm. Using the Pythagorean theorem, or Pythagorean triples, those triangles would be 3-4-5 right triangles, so each side of the rhombus will be 5cm long.

D. Other Polygons

1. Names

Polygons are named according to the number of sides. Triangles have three sides, and quadrilaterals four. A polygon with five sides is a pentagon, and one with six sides is a hexagon. Octagons have eight sides, and decagons have ten.

2. Diagonals

The number of diagonals that can be drawn in a polygon with n sides is $n(n - 3) \div 2$. That formula comes from the realization that there are n vertices, and from each of them there are $n - 3$ vertices to which you can draw. It is not possible to draw a diagonal to the vertex you start from, nor to either of the adjacent vertices, since those would be sides, not diagonals. The reason for dividing by 2 is to eliminate repetition, such as counting both the diagonal from A to E and the diagonal from E to A.

3. Angles

The sum of the interior angles of any polygon can be found with the formula $s = 180°(n-2)$, where n is the number of sides. If the polygon is divided into triangles by drawing all the possible diagonals from a single vertex, there are $n-2$ triangles, each with angles totaling 180°.

If the polygon is regular—that is, all sides are congruent and all angles are congruent—then the measure of any interior angle can be found by dividing the total by the number of angles. The sum of the exterior angles of any polygon is 360°.

EXAMPLE:

Find the measure of the interior angle of a regular pentagon.

The total of the measures of the five angles of a pentagon is $180(5-2) = 180(3) = 540°$. The pentagon is regular so all the angles are the same size. Divide 540° by 5 to find that each angle is 108°.

4. Area

You'll sometimes be asked to find the area of polygons for which you have not learned a specific formula. Use a diagram to try to divide the figure into sections whose areas you *do* know how to calculate.

EXAMPLE:

Find the area of quadrilateral $ABCD$ if $AB = AD = 6$cm, $\overline{EF}$ is the perpendicular bisector of $\overline{AD}$, and $\triangle BEC$ is equilateral.

Break the polygon into two triangles and a rectangle. The area of the rectangle is $6 \cdot 3 = 18$. $\triangle DFE$ is a right triangle with legs of 6 and 3, so its area is $\frac{1}{2} \cdot 6 \cdot 3 = 9$. Triangle BEC is equilateral with a base of 3 and a height of $\frac{3}{2}\sqrt{3}$, so its area is $\frac{1}{2} \cdot 3 \cdot \frac{3}{2}\sqrt{3} = \frac{9}{4}\sqrt{3}$. The total area is $18 + 9 + \frac{9}{4}\sqrt{3} = 27 + \frac{9}{4}\sqrt{3} \approx 30.9$.

In regular polygons, you can easily divide the figure into congruent triangles. Find the area of one triangle and multiply by the number of triangles present. If the regular polygon is divided as shown, the height of each little triangle is called the *apothem* of the polygon. The area of each little triangle is half the apothem times a side of the polygon. The area of a regular polygon is half the product of the apothem and the perimeter.

Practice

Directions (1–2): You are given two quantities, one in Column A and one in Column B. You are to compare the two quantities and choose:

A if the quantity in Column A is greater
B if the quantity in Column B is greater
C if the two quantities are equal
D if the relationship cannot be determined from the information given

Column A	Column B
1. The sum of the interior angles of a triangle	The sum of the exterior angles of a triangle

Column A	Column B
2. The sum of the interior angles of a pentagon	The sum of the exterior angles of a pentagon

Directions (3–8): You are given five answer choices. Select the best choice.

3. Find the sum of the measures of the interior angles of an octagon.

    A.   180°
    B.   360°
    C.   720°
    D.   1080°
    E.   1800°

4. Find the measure of an interior angle of a regular pentagon.

    A.   18°
    B.   36°
    C.   72°
    D.   108°
    E.   540°

5. The number of sides in a decagon minus the number of sides in a hexagon equals

    A.   the number of sides in an octagon
    B.   the number of sides in a pentagon
    C.   the number of sides in a quadrilateral
    D.   the number of diagonals in a rectangle
    E.   the number of diagonals in a hexagon

6. Find the number of diagonals in a polygon of 20 sides

   A. 400
   B. 360
   C. 340
   D. 180
   E. 170

7. Find the perimeter of a regular pentagon if its area is 50 square meters and the length of the *apothem* (distance from center to edge) is 5 meters.

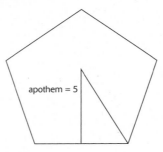

apothem = 5

   A. 4 meters
   B. 5 meters
   C. 10 meters
   D. 20 meters
   E. 50 meters

8. Find the area of a regular hexagon 4 inches on each side.

   A. 16
   B. 24
   C. 36
   D. $16\sqrt{3}$
   E. $24\sqrt{3}$

Directions (9): Give your answer as a number.

9. The length of each outer wall of the Pentagon in Washington, D.C., is 921 feet, and the structure, including its inner courtyard, covers an area of 1,481,000 square feet. Find the length of the apothem to the nearest foot.

Answers

1. **B**   The sum of the interior angles of a triangle is 180°. The sum of the exterior angles of a triangle is 360°.

2. **A**   The sum of the interior angles of a pentagon is $(5 - 2) \times 180° = 540°$. The sum of the exterior angles of a pentagon—the sum of the exterior angles of any polygon—is 360°.

3. **D**   The sum of the measures of the interior angles of an octagon is $(8 - 2) \times 180° = 1,080°$.

4. **D**   The sum of the interior angles of a pentagon is $(5 - 2) \times 180° = 540°$. Since the pentagon is regular, all the interior angles are equal, and you can divide $540° \div 5 = 108°$.

5. **C**   The number of sides in a decagon is 10 and the number of sides in a hexagon is 6, so the difference is 4.

6. **E**   From each of the vertices of a polygon, you can draw a number of diagonals that is three fewer than the number of vertices. So from each of the 20 vertices you can draw 17 diagonals. At first glance, the answer would seem to be $20 \times 17 = 340$. But that counts each diagonal twice—once from one end and again from the other team. To eliminate the duplication, divide $340 \div 2 = 170$.

7. **D**   The area of the hexagon is half the product of the apothem and the perimeter, so if the area is 50, the apothem times the perimeter equals 100. Since the apothem is 5, the perimeter is 20.

8. **E**   A regular hexagon can be divided into six identical equilateral triangles by drawing diagonals. Each of these triangles has a base of 4 inches and, by using 30-60-90 right-triangle relationships, a height of $2\sqrt{3}$. The area of each equilateral triangle is $\frac{1}{2} \cdot 4 \cdot 2\sqrt{3} = 4\sqrt{3}$ and there are six of them so the area of the hexagon is $6 \cdot 4\sqrt{3} = 24\sqrt{3}$.

9. **643 feet**   The area is made up of five triangles, so each triangle has an area of $1,481,000 \div 5 = 296,200$ square feet. Each of the triangles has a base of 921 feet and a height that is the apothem of the pentagon.

$$A = \frac{1}{2}bh$$
$$296,200 = \frac{1}{2} \cdot 921h$$
$$2(296,200) = 921h$$
$$h = \frac{2(296,200)}{921} \approx 643.2$$

E. Areas of Shaded Regions

Problems that ask you to find the area of a shaded region are a favorite of most test writers. Sometimes these areas can be found by calculating the area of the shaded region directly, and other times it's easier to calculate the area of the overall figure and then subtract the area of the unshaded region.

EXAMPLE:

The whole figure is a square with side of length 4 centimeters. The shaded center square has a side of 2 centimeters, and all the shaded regions are squares. Find the total shaded area.

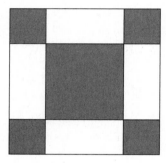

If the center square has a side of 2 centimeters, then each of the small shaded squares in the corners has a side of 1 centimeter. The shaded area is the area of the center square plus the areas of the four corner squares: $2^2 + (4 \times 1^2) = 4 + 4 = 8$ square centimeters.

EXAMPLE:

Right triangle ABC is inscribed in a circle of radius 5. If $AB = 6$, find the shaded area.

The area of the circle is πr^2 or 25π square units. When a right triangle is inscribed in a circle, the inscribed right angle intercepts a semicircle, so the hypotenuse of the triangle is a diameter. The diameter is 10 and leg AB is 6, so the remaining leg of the triangle is 8. The area of the triangle is $\frac{1}{2}bh = \frac{1}{2} \cdot 6 \cdot 8 = 24$ square units. The shaded area is the area of the circle minus the area of the triangle or $25\pi - 24$.

Practice

Directions (1–5): You are given five answer choices. Select the best choice.

1. The circles in the figure are congruent to one another, and tangent to one another and to the rectangle. If the diameter of each circle is 4 inches, find the shaded area.

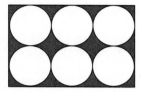

   A. $12 - 4\pi$
   B. $12 - 24\pi$
   C. 92π
   D. $96 - 4\pi$
   E. $96 - 24\pi$

2. In the figure, the large circle has a radius of 10cm. What percent of the large circle is shaded?

   A. 10%
   B. 33%
   C. 50%
   D. 66%
   E. 90%

3. If the side of the square is 4, find the area of the shaded region.

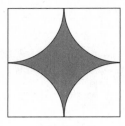

    A. $4 - \pi$
    B. $4 - 4\pi$
    C. $8 - 4\pi$
    D. $16 - 2\pi$
    E. $16 - 4\pi$

4. In the figure, the circle has a diameter of 12 inches. Which of the following is the best expression for the area of the shaded region?

    A. $144 - 1442\pi$
    B. $48 - 36\pi$
    C. $144 - 36\pi$
    D. $144 - 12\pi$
    E. $24 - 12\pi$

5. Each triangle in the figure is an isosceles right triangle. The large triangle has legs 30cm long, and the small triangles have legs 10cm long. Find the area of shaded polygon.

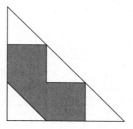

A. 100cm²
B. 150cm²
C. 200cm²
D. 250cm²
E. 300cm²

Answers

1. **E** The diameter of each circle is 4 inches, so the radius of each circle is 2 inches, and the area of each circle is $\pi r^2 = 4\pi$ square inches. The diameters of the circles also allow you to determine that the rectangle measures 12 inches by 8 inches, so it has an area of 96 square inches. The shaded region has an area equal to the area of the rectangle minus the area of the six circles. This is $96 - 6(4\pi) = 96 - 24\pi$ square inches.

2. **C** If the large circle has a radius of 10cm, then each of the small circles has a diameter of 10cm, and so a radius of 5cm. The area of the large circle is 100πcm², and the area of the two smaller circles totals $2(25\pi) = 50\pi$cm². Subtracting the combined area of the small circles from the area of the large circle leaves a shaded area of 50πcm², or half of the large circle.

3. **E** The shaded region is the area of the square minus the four quarter circles, which make one full circle. The radius of that circle is half the side of the square, or 2. The area of the square is 16 square units and the area of the circle is 4π, so the shaded area is $16 - 4\pi$.

4. **C** The side of the square is equal to the diameter of the circle, so the area of the square is $12 \times 12 = 144$ square inches. The radius of the circle is 6 inches, so the area of the circle is 36π. The shaded area is $144 - 36\pi$.

5. **D** The area of the largest triangle is $\frac{1}{2}(30)^2 = \frac{1}{2} \cdot 900 = 450$cm². The area of each of the small triangles is $\frac{1}{2}(10)^2 = \frac{1}{2} \cdot 100 = 50$. The shaded region is the area of the large triangle minus the combined area of the four small triangles, so the shaded area is $450 - 4(50) = 250$cm².

F. Circles

A circle is the set of all points in a plane at a fixed distance from a given point, called the *center*.

1. Lines and Segments

The fixed distance that determines the size of the circle is called the *radius;* all radii of a circle are the same length. A *chord* is a line segment whose endpoints lie on the circle; the longer the chord, the closer it is to the center of the circle. The *diameter* is the longest chord of a circle. It passes through the center of the circle; the diameter is twice as long as the radius. Congruent chords cut off congruent arcs. If two chords intersect in a circle, the product of the lengths of the sections of one chord is equal to the product of the lengths of the sections of the other. A *secant* is a line that contains a chord; it's a line that intersects the circle in two distinct points. A *tangent* is a line that touches the circle in exactly one point. The radius drawn to the point of tangency is perpendicular to the tangent line. Two tangent segments drawn to a circle from the same point are congruent.

EXAMPLE:

In circle O, chords $\overline{AB}$ and $\overline{CD}$ intersect at E. If $AE = 4$, $BE = 10$, and $CE = 8$, find the length of DE.

The segments of chord $\overline{AB}$ are 4 units and 10 units long. Multiplying 4×10 gives a product of 40. The known segment of $\overline{CD}$ is 8 units. If the other is x, then $8x = 40$, so $x = 5$.

2. Angles

A central angle is an angle formed by two radii. Its vertex is at the center of the circle. A measure of a central angle is equal to the measure of its intercepted arc. An *inscribed angle* is an angle whose sides are chords, and whose vertex lies on the circle. The measure of an inscribed angle is equal to one-half the measure of its intercepted arc.

EXAMPLE:

In circle O, $\overline{OA}$ and $\overline{OB}$ are radii and $\overline{AC}$ and $\overline{BC}$ are chords. If $\overset{\frown}{AB} = 50°$, find $m\angle AOB$ and $m\angle ACB$

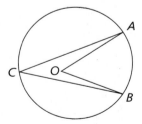

$\overset{\frown}{AB}$ is the intercepted arc for both angles. $\angle AOB$ is a central angle, so its measure is the same as the measure of the arc. $m\angle AOB = 50°$. $\angle ACB$ is an inscribed angle, so its measure is half the measure of the arc: $m\angle ACB = 25°$.

When two chords intersect within a circle, they form four angles. Vertical angles are congruent, and adjacent angles are supplementary. The measure of an angle formed by two chords (and of its vertical angle partner) is one-half the sum of the two intercepted arcs. To find the measure of an angle formed by two chords, average the arcs intercepted by the two vertical angles.

EXAMPLE:

Two chords intersect in the circle as shown. Find the value of x.

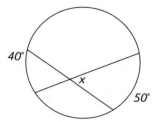

The two vertical angles whose measure is x intercept arcs of 40° and 50°. $x = \frac{1}{2}(40 + 50) = 45°$.

Angles formed by two secants, a tangent and a secant, or two tangents intercept two arcs. The arc nearer to the vertex of the angle is smaller. The measure of the angle is one-half the difference of the two arcs it intercepts.

EXAMPLE:

A secant and a tangent both drawn from point P intersect the circle as shown. Find the measure of $\angle P$.

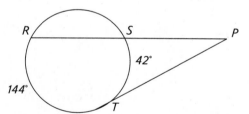

The measure of $\angle P$ is half the difference of $\widehat{RT}$ and $\widehat{ST}$. $\angle P = \frac{1}{2}\left(\widehat{RT} - \widehat{ST}\right) = \frac{1}{2}(144 - 42) = \frac{1}{2}(102) = 51°$.

3. Circumference

The circumference of a circle is the distance around the circle. The circumference of the circle is similar to the perimeter of a polygon. The formula for the circumference of a circle is $C = 2\pi r = \pi d$, where r is the radius of the circle, d is the diameter of the circle, and π is a constant approximately equal to 3.14159. For most questions, you can use 3.14 or $\frac{22}{7}$ as approximate values of π.

EXAMPLE:

If the radius of the large circle is equal to the diameter of the smaller circles, then the circumference of the large circle is equal to

A. the circumference of the small circle
B. half the circumference of the small circle
C. twice the circumference of the small circle
D. four times the circumference of the small circle
E. none of these

For convenience, make up a radius for the large circle, say 10cm. The circumference of the large circle is $2\pi \times 10 = 20\pi$. The circumference of the small circle is $\pi \times 10 = 10\pi$ so the circumference of the large circle is twice the circumference of the small circle.

4. Area

The area of a circle is the product of π and the square of the radius: $A = \pi r^2$.

EXAMPLE:

If the radius of the large circle is equal to the diameter of the smaller circles, then the area of the large circle is equal to

A. the area of the smaller circle
B. half the area of the smaller circle
C. twice the area of the smaller circle
D. four times the area of the smaller circle
E. none of these

Make up a value for the radius of the large circle—say, 10. The area of the large circle is $\pi \times 10^2 = 100\pi$. The diameter of the small circle is 10, so its radius is 5. The area of the small circle is $\pi \times 5^2 = 25\pi$. The area of the large circle is four times as large as the area of the small circle.

Practice

Directions (1–2): You are given two quantities, one in Column A and one in Column B. You are to compare the two quantities and choose:

A if the quantity in Column A is greater
B if the quantity in Column B is greater
C if the two quantities are equal
D if the relationship cannot be determined from the information given

	Column A	Column B
1.	The number of centimeters in the circumference of a circle of radius 5cm	The number of square centimeters in the area of a circle of diameter 10cm

	Column A	Column B
2.	The area of a circle whose radius is 7	The area of a rhombus whose side is 7

Directions (3–8): You are given five answer choices. Select the best choice.

Questions 3–4 refer to the following figure.

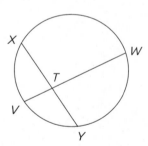

3. $\overarc{XW} = 120°$ and $\overarc{VY} = 40°$. Find $m\angle YTW - m\angle XTW$.

    A. 20°
    B. 45°
    C. 85°
    D. 100°
    E. 120°

4. In the circle, $XY = 12$, $TW = 16$, and $VT = 2$. find TX.

   A. 5
   B. 6
   C. 7
   D. 8
   E. 9

5. $\triangle ABC$ with $\overline{AC} \perp \overline{BC}$ is inscribed in the circle. Which of the following must be true statements?

   I. $\overline{AB}$ is a diameter
   II. $\triangle ACB$ is isosceles
   III. $\angle B$ is acute

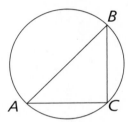

   A. I only
   B. II only
   C. III only
   D. I and II
   E. I and III

Questions 6–7 refer to the following figure.

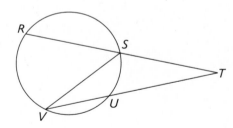

6. $\triangle STV$ is isosceles, with $ST = SV$. $\overset{\frown}{RV} = 110°$. Find the measure of $\overset{\frown}{SU}$.

   A. 35°
   B. 45°
   C. 55°
   D. 65°
   E. 105 °

7. In the circle, secant $RT = 10$ and $VT = 8$. If $ST = 6$, Find TU.

    A.   5
    B.   7.5
    C.   10
    D.   12.5
    E.   15

8. Two tangents are drawn to the circle from point P. $m\angle P = 60°$, and $m\overset{\frown}{ACB} = 240°$. Which of the following must be true?

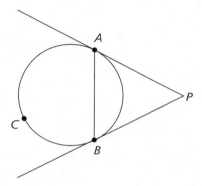

    A. $\triangle APB$ is a scalene triangle.
    B. $\triangle APB$ is a right triangle.
    C. $\triangle APB$ is a scalene triangle.
    D. $\triangle APB$ is an equilateral triangle.
    E. AB is a diameter.

Directions (9–10): Give your answer as a number.

9. The radius of a circle is $\dfrac{2}{\pi}$. Find its area.

10. A central angle and an inscribed angle both intercept an arc of 86°. Find the difference in their measures.

Answers

1. **B**   The number of centimeters in the circumference of a circle of radius 5cm is $2\pi r = 10\pi$. The number of square centimeters in the area of a circle of diameter 10cm is $\pi r^2 = 25\pi$.

2. **A**   Estimation is enough to allow you to decide. The area of a circle whose radius is 7 is 49π, and the area of a rhombus whose side is 7 is 7 times the height. The height of the rhombus will be less than or equal to the side, since the perpendicular distance between the parallel sides is the shortest distance. That means the height will be less than 7 and the area will be less than 49.

3. **D** $m\angle XTW = \frac{1}{2}\left(\widehat{XW} - \widehat{VY}\right) = \frac{1}{2}(120 - 40) = \frac{1}{2}(80) = 40°$. $\angle YTW$ and $\angle XTW$ are supplementary, so $m\angle YTW = 180° - 40° = 140°$. Then $m\angle YTW - m\angle XTW = 140° - 40° = 100°$.

4. **D** When two chords intersect within a circle, the product of the lengths of the two pieces of one chord is equal to the product of the lengths of the two pieces of the other. So $TW \times VT = TX \times TY$, and if you let x represent the length of TX, that means $16 \times 2 = x(12 - x)$. Solve the quadratic equation, to find that $x = 8$ or $x = 4$.

5. **E** An angle inscribed in a circle will intercept an arc equal to twice its measure, so a right angle will intercept a semicircle and $\overline{AB}$ will be a diameter. The other two angles of the right triangle must be acute, but it is not possible to determine whether they're equal.

6. **C** Let x represent the measure of $\widehat{SU}$. The measure of $\angle V$ is half of $\widehat{SU}$ and the measure of $\angle T$ is half the difference of $\widehat{RV}$ and $\widehat{SU}$. Since $m\angle V = m\angle T$, $\frac{1}{2}x = \frac{1}{2}(110 - x)$ and that means $x = 110 - x$, so $2x = 110$ and $x = 55°$.

7. **B** When two secants are drawn to a circle from the same point, the product of the lengths of the secant and its external segment are constant, so $RT \times ST = VT \times TU$. Substituting known values, $10 \times 6 = 8 \times TU$, or $TU = 60 \div 8 = 7.5$.

8. **D** $m\angle P = \frac{1}{2}\left(m\widehat{ACB} - m\widehat{AB}\right) = \frac{1}{2}(240 - x)$. Since $m\angle P = 60$, you have $60 = \frac{1}{2}(240 - x)$. Solving, $240 - x = 120$ and $x = 120°$. The tangent segments $\overline{PA}$ and $\overline{PB}$ will be congruent, so $m\angle PAB = m\angle PBA = \frac{1}{2}m\widehat{AB}$; therefore, both angles measure $60°$ and $\triangle APB$ is an equilateral triangle.

9. $\frac{4}{\pi}$ The area of the circle is $\pi r^2 = \pi\left(\frac{2}{\pi}\right)^2 = \pi\left(\frac{4}{\pi^2}\right) = \frac{4}{\pi}$. The radius of a circle is $\frac{2}{\pi}$. Find its area to the nearest tenth.

10. **43°** The central angle has a measure equal to its intercepted arc, $86°$, and the inscribed angle has a measure equal to half the intercepted arc, or $43°$, so the difference between them is $43°$.

G. Solids

1. Volume

Instead of memorizing a lot of different volume formulas, remember that the volume of a prism or a cylinder is equal to the area of its base times its height. $V = A(base) \times height$.

The volume of a pyramid or cone is $V = \frac{1}{3} \cdot A(base) \cdot height$.

EXAMPLE:

Find the volume of a triangular prism 4 inches high, whose base is an equilateral triangle with sides 6 inches long.

First you need to find the area of the base. Because it is an equilateral triangle, you can use the 30°-60°-90° triangle relationship to find the height. The altitude of the equilateral triangle is half the side times the square root of three, or $3\sqrt{3}$. The area of the triangle is $\frac{1}{2}bh = \frac{1}{2} \cdot 6 \cdot 3\sqrt{3} = 9\sqrt{3}$. Finally, the volume of the prism is the area of the base times the height, or $9\sqrt{3} \cdot 4 = 36\sqrt{3}$.

2. Surface Area

Questions about surface area can be answered by finding the area of each surface of the solid and adding. The surface area of a rectangular solid, for example, is $SA = 2lw + 2lh + 2wh$.

The surface area of a cylinder is the total of the areas of the two circles at the ends, plus the area of the rectangle that forms the cylindrical wall. (Think about a label on a can.) The area of each circle is πr^2. The rectangle has a height equal to the height of the cylinder and a base equal to the circumference of the circle, so its area is $2\pi rh$. The total surface area is $SA = 2\pi r^2 + 2\pi rh$.

EXAMPLE:

Column A	Column B
The surface area of a cylinder of diameter 4cm and height 4cm	The surface area of a cube of side 4cm

The diameter is 4cm, so the radius is 2, and the surface area of the cylinder is

$$SA = 2\pi r^2 + 2\pi rh$$
$$= 2 \cdot \pi \cdot 2^2 + 2 \cdot \pi \cdot 2 \cdot 4$$
$$= 8\pi + 16\pi = 24\pi \approx 75.4$$

The surface area of the cube is the total of the areas of six identical squares, each with an area of 16cm². The total surface area is $6 \times 16 = 96$ cm², so the cube has the larger surface area.

Practice

Directions (1–2): You are given two quantities, one in Column A and one in Column B. You are to compare the two quantities and choose:

A if the quantity in Column A is greater
B if the quantity in Column B is greater
C if the two quantities are equal
D if the relationship cannot be determined from the information given

<table>
<tr><td align="center">Column A</td><td align="center">Column B</td></tr>
<tr><td>1.</td><td></td></tr>
</table>

	Column A	**Column B**
1.	The surface area of a cube with an edge of 2 cm	The surface area of a cylinder with a radius of 2cm and a height of 2 cm

	Column A	**Column B**
2.	The edge of a cube whose volume is 64 cm^3	The edge of a cube whose surface area is 64 cm^2

Directions (3–4): You are given five answer choices. Select the best choice.

3. A hexagonal paving stone is made by pouring concrete into a mold. If the area of the hexagonal face is 54 square inches and the block is 2 inches thick, what volume of concrete will be needed to make 100 paving stones?

    A.   102 in.^{3}
    B.   108 in.^{3}
    C.   154 in.^{3}
    D.   1,080 in.^{3}
    E.   10,800 in.^{3}

4. A beam is formed from metal in the shape of a cross. Each "arm" of the cross is a square, as is the center section. Each of these squares has a side of 6 inches, and the beam is 6 feet long. Find the weight of the beam if the metal from which it is formed weighs 1.5 ounces per cubic inch.

    A. 54 ounces
    B. 216 ounces
    C. 1,296 ounces
    D. 10,368 ounces
    E. 19,440 ounces

Directions (5–6): Give your answer as a number.

5. Find the volume of the washer shown if the outer diameter is 10 inches, the inner diameter (the diameter of the hole) is 6 inches, and the washer is $\frac{1}{4}$ inch thick. Use $\pi \approx \frac{22}{7}$.

6. Find the surface area of the prism shown if its base is a right triangle.

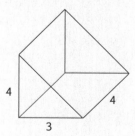

4   4

3

Answers

1. **B** The surface area of a cube with an edge of 2cm is 6(22) =24cm². The surface area of a cylinder with a radius of 2cm and a height of 2cm = $2\pi r^2 + 2\pi rh = 2\pi \times 2^2 + 2\pi \times 2 \times 2 = 8\pi + 8\pi = 16\pi$cm², which is greater than 48.

2. **A** The edge of a cube whose volume is 64cm³ is 4cm, since $4^3 = 64$. If a cube has surface area of 64cm², that represents the total area of the six faces, all identical squares. Each square would have an area of $\frac{64}{6} = 10\frac{2}{3}$cm², and so the edge would be between 3 and 4.

3. E The volume of one paving stone is the area of the base, 54 in.², times the height, 2 in., or 108 in.³. To make 100 such stones will require $100 \times 108 = 10{,}800$ in³.

4. E The face of the beam has a surface area of $5(6)^2$ in.² or 180 in.². Multiply this by the length of the beam, 6 feet or 72 inches, to find the volume of the beam: $180 \times 72 = 12{,}960$ in.³ is the volume of the beam. To find the weight of the beam, multiply the volume by 1.5 ounces per cubic inch. The weight is 12,960 in³ × 1.5 ounces per cubic inch = 19,440 ounces.

5. $\frac{88}{7} = 12\frac{4}{7}$ First, calculate the volume of the outer cylinder, and then subtract the volume of the hole in the washer. The outer cylinder has a volume of $\pi r^2 h \approx \frac{22}{7} \cdot 5^2 \cdot \frac{1}{4} = \frac{550}{28} = \frac{275}{14}$, and the hole has a volume of $\pi r^2 h \approx \frac{22}{7} \cdot 3^2 \cdot \frac{1}{4} = \frac{99}{14}$. Subtracting, $\frac{275}{14} - \frac{99}{14} = \frac{176}{14} = \frac{88}{7} = 12\frac{4}{7}$.

6. 60 square units The surface area can be broken down into the area of the two 3-4-5 right triangles plus the areas of the three rectangular faces. The area of each right triangle is $\frac{1}{2} \cdot 3 \cdot 4 = 6$, so the two right triangles have a total area of 12. The rectangular faces are 3×4, 4×4, and 5×4 and, therefore, total $12 + 16 + 20 = 48$. The total surface area is $12 + 48 = 60$ square units.

H. Coordinate Geometry

In coordinate geometry, the plane is divided into four quadrants by two perpendicular number lines called the x-axis and the y-axis. The x-axis is horizontal; the y-axis is vertical. These axes intersect at their zero points. The point (0,0) is called the *origin*. Every point in the plane can be represented by a set of numbers or coordinates (x,y). This ordered pair allows you to locate the point by counting from the origin. The x-coordinate indicates the left/right movement. The y-coordinate indicates the up/down movement.

1. Midpoints

To find the midpoint of the segment connecting two points in the plane, average the x-coordinates of the two points, and average the y-coordinates. The resulting ordered pair gives the coordinates of the midpoint. The midpoint, M, of the segment joining (x_1,y_1) with (x_2,y_2) is the point $\left(\frac{x_1 + x_2}{2}, \frac{y_1 + y_2}{2} \right)$.

EXAMPLE:

Find the midpoint of the segment that joins the points (–7,5) and (4,–6).

The midpoint is the point whose x-coordinate is midway between –7 and 4, and whose y-coordinate is the average of 5 and –6. So, $M = \left(\frac{-7+4}{2}, \frac{5+-6}{2} \right) = \left(\frac{-3}{2}, \frac{-1}{2} \right)$.

2. Distances

The formula for the distance between two points in the coordinate plane is a disguised version of the Pythagorean theorem. To find the distance between the points (x_1,y_1) and (x_2,y_2), imagine a right triangle with vertices (x_1,y_1), (x_2,y_2), and (x_2,y_1). The length of the vertical leg is $y_2 - y_1$ and the length of the horizontal leg is $x_2 - x_1$. Using the Pythagorean theorem, the distance, d, between (x_1,y_1) and (x_2,y_2) is $a^2 + b^2 = c^2$ or $(x_2 - x_1)^2 + (y_2 - y_1)^2 = d^2$.

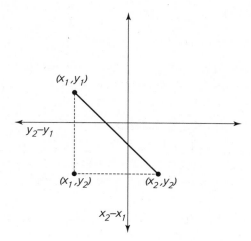

To find d, take the square root of both sides and you have the distance formula: $d = \sqrt{(x_2 - x_1)^2 + (y_2 - y_1)^2}$.

EXAMPLE:

Find the distance from the point $(-7,5)$ to the point $(4,-6)$.

Call $(-7,5)$ the first point, so $x_1 = -7$ and $y_1 = 5$. The second point is $(4,-6)$ so $x_2 = 4$ and $y_2 = -6$.
Use the distance formula $d = \sqrt{(x_2 - x_1)^2 + (y_2 - y_1)^2}$. Substitute $x_1 = -7$, $y_1 = 5$, $x_2 = 4$, and $y_2 = -6$:
$d = \sqrt{(-7 - 4)^2 + (5 - -6)^2}$. Subtract: $d = \sqrt{(-11)^2 + (11)^2}$. Square: $d = \sqrt{121 + 121}$. Add: $d = \sqrt{242}$. Take the square root: $d = 11\sqrt{2} \approx 15.56$.

3. Slope

The slope of a line is a means of talking about whether the line is rising or falling, and how quickly it is doing so. In the coordinate plane, slope can be expressed as the ratio of rise to run—that is, the amount of vertical change to the amount of horizontal change. If two points on the line are known to be (x_1,y_1) and (x_2,y_2), then the slope, m, of the line is given by the following formula:

$$m = \frac{\text{rise}}{\text{run}} = \frac{\Delta y}{\Delta x} = \frac{y_2 - y_1}{x_2 - x_1}$$

EXAMPLE:

Find the slope of the line through the points $(-4,-4)$ and $(7,3)$.

From a sketch, you can count the rise and the run. The rise is 7 and the run is 11. Or, using the formula, let $x_1 = 7$, $y_1 = 3$, $x_2 = -4$, $y_2 = -4$.

$$m = \frac{\text{rise}}{\text{run}} = \frac{\Delta y}{\Delta x} = \frac{y_2 - y_1}{x_2 - x_1}$$

$$m = \frac{3 - -4}{7 - -4} = \frac{3 + 4}{7 + 4} = \frac{7}{11}$$

A horizontal line has a rise of 0; therefore its slope is 0. A vertical line has a run of 0; because of the zero in the denominator, the slope of a vertical line is undefined. We say a vertical line has no slope.

4. Finding the Equation of a Line

The slope intercept form of a linear equation is $y = mx + b$, where m is the slope and b is the y-intercept. If the slope and y-intercept of a line are known, you can write the equation by simply putting these numbers into the correct positions. In other situations, it is more helpful to use the point-slope form, $y - y_1 = m(x - x_1)$. In this form, m is the slope and (x_1, y_1) is a point on the line.

EXAMPLE:

Find the equation of the line through the points (2,5) and (–7, 23).

First, find the slope. $m = \frac{y_2 - y_1}{x_2 - x_1} = \frac{23 - 5}{-7 - 2} = \frac{18}{-9} = -2$. Use the point-slope form with $m = -2$ and either point:

$y - y_1 = m(x - x_1)$

$y - 5 = -2(x - 2)$

$y - 5 = -2x + 4$

$y\quad = -2x + 9$

5. Parallel and Perpendicular Lines

Parallel lines have the same slope. You can decide whether two lines are parallel by finding the slope of each line. If the slopes are the same, the lines are parallel. You can use this fact to help find the equation of a line parallel to a given line. In order to be parallel the lines must have the same slope.

EXAMPLE:

Find the equation of a line through the point (–1, 3) parallel to $3x + 2y = 7$.

First find the slope of the line $3x + 2y = 7$. Rearranging into $y = mx + b$ form, you get $y = \frac{-3}{2}x + \frac{7}{2}$, so the slope is $\frac{-3}{2}$. Use point-slope form with $m = \frac{-3}{2}$ and the point $(x_1, y_1) = (-1, 3)$.

$$y - y_1 = m(x - x_1)$$

$$y - 3 = \frac{-3}{2}(x - -1)$$

$$y - 3 = \frac{-3}{2}x - \frac{3}{2}$$

$$y = \frac{-3}{2}x + \frac{3}{2}$$

If two lines are perpendicular, their slopes will be negative reciprocals. You can determine if two lines are perpendicular by looking at their slopes, or you can use the relationship between the slopes of the lines to help you find the equation of a line perpendicular to a given line.

EXAMPLE:

Find the equation of a line through the point $(-1, 3)$ perpendicular to $3x + 2y = 7$.

First find the slope of the line $3x + 2y = 7$. Rearranging into $y = mx + b$ form, you get $y = \frac{-3}{2}x + \frac{7}{2}$, so the slope is $\frac{-3}{2}$. The slope of the line perpendicular to this will be $\frac{2}{3}$. Use point-slope form with $m = \frac{2}{3}$ and the point $(x_1, y_1) = (-1,3)$.

$$y - y_1 = m(x - x_1)$$

$$y - 3 = \frac{2}{3}(x - -1)$$

$$y - 3 = \frac{2}{3}x + \frac{2}{3}$$

$$y = \frac{2}{3}x + \frac{11}{3}$$

6. Transformations

In transformational geometry, objects are moved about the plane by different methods.

a. Reflection

Anyone who has used a mirror has some experience with reflection. Reflection preserves distances, so objects stay the same size, and angle measure remains the same. Orientation changes, however, as you know if you've ever tried to do something that requires a sense of left and right while watching yourself in a mirror. The reflection of an object is congruent to the original.

On the coordinate plane, the most common reflections are reflection across the x-axis, reflection across the y-axis, and reflection across the line $y = x$. Reflection across the x-axis inverts the image. Under such a reflection, the image of the point (x,y) is the point $(x,-y)$. Reflection across the y-axis flips the image left to right. The image of the point (x,y) under a reflection across the y-axis is $(-x,y)$. Reflection across the line $y = x$ swaps the x- and y-coordinates. If the point (x,y) is reflected across the line $y = x$, its image is (y,x).

b. Translation

Translation is moving an object by sliding it across the plane. Translating a point left or right causes a change in the x-coordinate, while translating it up or down changes the y-coordinate. What appears to be a diagonal slide can be resolved into a horizontal and a vertical component. If the point (x,y) is translated h units horizontally and k units vertically, the image is $(x + h, y + k)$.

c. Rotation

Rotation is the transformation that moves an object in a circular fashion about a point. Because rotation is really a series of reflections across intersecting lines, you can predict coordinates as you did with reflections.

Rotation Counterclockwise	Image of (x,y)
90°	(–y,x)
180°	(–x,–y)
270°	(y,–x)

Practice

Directions (1–4): You are given two quantities, one in Column A and one in Column B. You are to compare the two quantities and choose:

A if the quantity in Column A is greater
B if the quantity in Column B is greater
C if the two quantities are equal
D if the relationship cannot be determined from the information given

---

A is the point (7,–3) and B is the point (–1,5).

	Column A	Column B
1.	The x-coordinate of the midpoint of $\overline{AB}$	The y-coordinate of the midpoint of $\overline{AB}$

A is the point (–3,2) and B is the point (4,7).

	Column A	Column B
2.	The distance from A to B	The distance from the origin to B

Line m has the equation $x + y = 5$.

Column A	Column B
3. The slope of a line parallel to m	The slope of a line perpendicular to m

X is the point $(-5,0)$.

Column A	Column B
4. The x–coordinate of the image of P under a rotation of 90° about the origin	The x-coordinate of the image of P under a rotation of 270° about the origin

Directions (5–10): You are given five answer choices. Select the best choice.

5. The midpoint of the segment that connects the origin with point P is $(7,-5)$. Find point P.

- **A.** $(14,-5)$
- **B.** $(7,-10)$
- **C.** $(14,-10)$
- **D.** $(3.5,-2.5)$
- **E.** $(7,-5)$

6. The line segment connecting points $(4,1)$ and $(x,-3)$ has its midpoint at $(8,-1)$. Find the value of x.

- **A.**   4
- **B.**   8
- **C.**   6
- **D.**   12
- **E.**   32

7. Find the equation of a line through the point $(0,-4)$ perpendicular to $3x - 2y = 7$.

- **A.** $y = 3x - 4$
- **B.** $y = -3x - 4$
- **C.** $y = \dfrac{-3}{2}x - 4$
- **D.** $y = \dfrac{2}{3}x - 4$
- **E.** $3y = -2x - 12$

8. $\overrightarrow{AB}$ is parallel to the line $5x - 4y = 20$. The slope of $\overrightarrow{AB}$ is

   A. $\dfrac{5}{4}$

   B. $\dfrac{4}{5}$

   C. $\dfrac{-5}{4}$

   D. $\dfrac{-4}{5}$

   E. -5

9. A line passing through the point $(0,-5)$ has a slope of 4. Which of the following could not be a point on that line?

   A. $(1,-1)$
   B. $(12,43)$
   C. $(-1,-9)$
   D. $(-5,-5)$
   E. $(3,7)$

10. The image of the point $(6,-3)$ under translation 4 units left and 5 units up is the point

    A. $(10,2)$
    B. $(11,1)$
    C. $(2,2)$
    D. $(2,-8)$
    E. $(1,-7)$

Answers

1. **A** If A is the point $(7,-3)$ and B is the point $(-1,5)$, the midpoint is $\left(\dfrac{7+-1}{2}, \dfrac{-3+5}{2}\right) = \left(\dfrac{6}{2}, \dfrac{2}{2}\right) = (3,1)$.

2. **A** The distance from A to B is $\sqrt{(-3-4)^2 + (2-7)^2} = \sqrt{49+25} = \sqrt{74}$. The distance from the origin to B is $\sqrt{(0-4)^2 + (0-7)^2} = \sqrt{16+49} = \sqrt{65}$.

3. **B** Line m has the equation $x + y = 5$ or $y = -x + 5$ and, therefore, a slope of -1. The slope of a line parallel to m is -1 and the slope of a line perpendicular to m is 1.

4. **C** The image of P under a rotation of $90°$ about the origin is $(0,-5)$ so its x-coordinate is 0, and the image of P under a rotation of $270°$ about the origin is $(0,5)$ so its x-coordinate is 0.

5. **C** The origin is the point $(0, 0)$. Call point P the point (x,y). Then $\left(\dfrac{0+x}{2}, \dfrac{0+y}{2}\right) = (7,-5)$. $\dfrac{x}{2} = 7 \Rightarrow x = 14$ and $\dfrac{y}{2} = -5 \Rightarrow y = -10$, so P is the point $(14,-10)$.

6. **D** If the line segment connecting points (4,1) and $(x,-3)$ has its midpoint at (8,–1), $\frac{4+x}{2} = 8 \Rightarrow 4+x = 16 \Rightarrow x = 12$.

7. **E** Find the slope of $3x - 2y = 7$ by putting the equation in slope-intercept form.

$$3x - 2y = 7$$
$$-2y = -3x + 7$$
$$y = \frac{3}{2}x - \frac{7}{2}$$

A line perpendicular to this will have a slope equal to the negative reciprocal of $\frac{3}{2}$, so the slope will be $-\frac{2}{3}$. (0,–4) is the y-intercept, so the equation of the line is $y = -\frac{2}{3}x - 4$. Since that does not appear as a choice, multiply through by 3 to get $3y = -2x - 12$.

8. **A** Since $\overrightarrow{AB}$ is parallel to the line $5x - 4y = 20$, the slope of $\overrightarrow{AB}$ is equal to the slope of $5x - 4y = 20$. Put $5x - 4y = 20$ into slope-intercept form.

$$5x - 4y = 20$$
$$-4y = -5x + 20$$
$$y = \frac{-5x + 20}{-4}$$
$$y = \frac{5}{4}x - 5$$

9. **D** A line passing through the point (0,–5), with a slope of 4, has the equation $y = 4x - 5$. Every point on the line is a solution of that equation. Testing each of the choices shows that only (–5, –5) fails to solve the equation. $y = 4x - 5 \rightarrow 5 = 4(-5) - 5 \rightarrow -5 = -20 - 5$ but $-5 \neq -25$.

10. **C** The image of the point (6,–3) under translation 4 units left and 5 units up is the point (6 – 4, –3 + 5) = (2,2).

XIII. Applications

A. Data Interpretation

Visual representations of data are often easier to understand than tables full of numbers. Read the graphs carefully to be certain you understand what they're telling you.

1. Bar Graphs

Bar graphs are used to compare different quantities. Each bar represents a quantity, and the height of the bar corresponds to its size. You may need to estimate the quantities, if exact values are not given. Be sure to read scales carefully.

EXAMPLE:

The bar graph below summarizes the sales of various lunches offered in a school cafeteria. Based upon this information, chicken outsells pasta by approximately what percent?

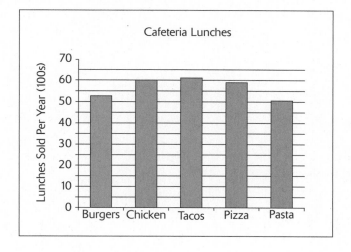

A. 10%
B. 16%
C. 20%
D. 50%
E. 60%

The bar representing sales of chicken appears to reach 60, making sales of chicken approximately 6,000 lunches, since the scale tells you that each unit on the graph is 100. Pasta is just above 50, so pasta sales are slightly more than 5,000 lunches. The difference is 1,000 lunches. Compare this to the sales of pasta, for an answer of $\frac{1,000}{5,000} = 20\%$.

2. Line Graphs

Line graphs are generally used to show the change in a quantity over time.

EXAMPLE:

The graph below shows the sales of hot dogs at Jenny's Beach Bungalow over the course of the last year. Over which period did sales have the greatest change?

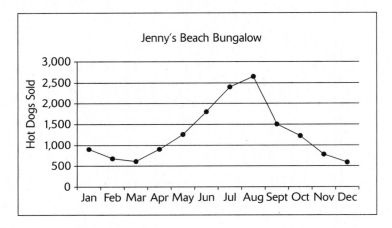

A. May to June
B. June to July
C. July to August
D. August to September
E. September to October

Estimate the sales for May, June, July, August, September, and October from the graph. May is approximately 1,250. June is approximately 1,800. The change from May to June = 1,800 − 1,250 = 550. July is approximately 2,500. The change from June to July = 2,500 − 1,800 = 700. August is approximately 2,700. The change from July to August = 2,700 − 2,500 = 200. September is approximately 1,500. The change from August to September is 1,500 − 2,700 = −1,200. October is approximately 1,200. The change from September to October = 1,200 − 1,500 = −300. Since the question does not specify whether the change must be positive or negative, the greatest change is from August to September, a decline of 1,200.

Alternatively, examine the graph. The greatest change will be represented by the line segment with the steepest slope.

3. Circle Graphs

Circle graphs, sometimes called pie charts, are used to represent quantities as fractions of a whole.

EXAMPLE:

The graph below shows the enrollment in various arts electives last year. What percent of the enrollment was in music courses?

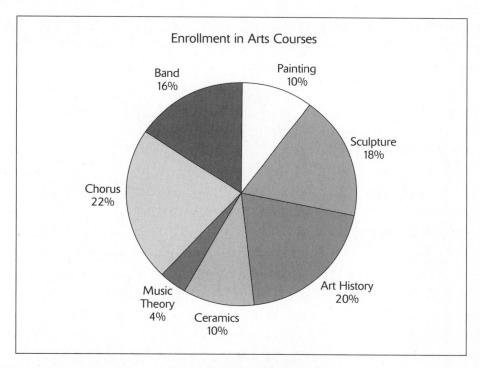

Add the percents for Band, Chorus, and Music Theory. 16% + 22% + 4% = 42%.

EXAMPLE:

If a total of 461 students signed up for arts electives, how many students took Art History?

20% of the students took Art History, and 20% of 461 is approximately 92 students.

4. Means and Medians

Statistics are numbers that represent collections of data or information. They help you to draw conclusions about the data. One of the ways you can represent a set of data is by giving an average of the data. There are three different averages in common use. The mean is the number most people think of when you say "average." The mean is found by adding all the data items and dividing by the number of items. The mode is the most common value, the one that occurs most frequently. The median is the middle value when a set of data has been ordered from smallest to largest or largest to smallest. If there is an even number of data points, and two numbers seem to be in the middle, the mean of those two is the median.

EXAMPLE:

Find the mean and median of the land in rural parks and wildlife areas in 2002 for the states shown in the table below.

Land in Rural Parks and Wildlife Areas in 2002	
State	**Acres (in thousands of acres)**
Michigan	1,436
Wisconsin	1,000
Minnesota	2,959
Ohio	372
Indiana	264
Illinois	432
Iowa	327
Missouri	649

To find the mean, add the entries for all states, and divide by 8, the number of states shown in the table: 1,436 + 1,000 + 2,959 + 372 + 264 + 432 + 327 + 649 = 7,439 and 7,439 ÷ 8 = 929.875. The states shown have a mean of 929,875 acres of land in rural parks and wildlife areas. To find the median, place the entries in order — 2,959, 1,436, 1,000, 649, 432, 372 , 327, 264—and since there are an even number of entries, average the two middle entries: (649 + 432) ÷ 2 = 1,081 ÷ 2 = 540.5 so 540,500 acres is the median.

Practice

Directions (1–2): You are given two quantities, one in Column A and one in Column B. You are to compare the two quantities and choose:

A if the quantity in Column A is greater
B if the quantity in Column B is greater
C if the two quantities are equal
D if the relationship cannot be determined from the information given

A = {2, 2, 2, 3, 3, 4, 4, 4, 4}

	Column A	Column B
1.	The mode of set A	The median of set A

Column A	Column B
2. The mean of the prime numbers less than 10	The median of the prime numbers less than 10

Directions (3–8): You are given five answer choices. Select the best choice.

The chart below shows the number of books sold each day from Monday through Friday. Use the chart to answer questions 3 and 4.

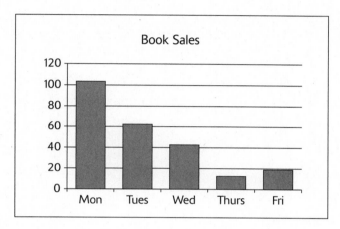

3. The largest drop in sales occurred between which two days?

   A.   Monday and Tuesday
   B.   Tuesday and Wednesday
   C.   Wednesday and Thursday
   D.   Thursday and Friday
   E.   None of these

4. Which of the following is the best estimate of the average number of books sold per day?

   A.   12
   B.   21
   C.   48
   D.   63
   E.   90

The graph below shows the number of students who were reported absent due to illness each month of the second term. Use the graph to answer questions 5 and 6.

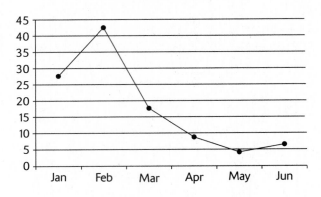

Absences Due to Illness

5. The lowest incidence of illness occurred in which month?

    A.   January
    B.   March
    C.   April
    D.   May
    E.   June

6. The largest single drop in illness occurred between which two months?

    A.   January and February
    B.   February and March
    C.   March and April
    D.   April and May
    E.   May and June

The circle graph below shows the membership of the high school honor roll, broken down by class. Use this graph for questions 7 and 8.

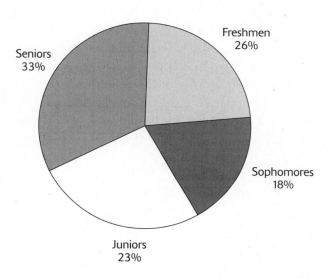

Honor Roll Membership

7. The class with the most honor roll members exceeds the class with the fewest members by what percent?

   A. 15%
   B. 18%
   C. 23%
   D. 26%
   E. 33%

8. If there are 300 students on the honor roll, how many juniors are honor roll members?

   A. 23
   B. 54
   C. 69
   D. 78
   E. 99

Directions (9–10): Give your answer as a number.

9. Find the mean of the set of numbers {34, 54, 78, 92, 101}.

10. Find the median of the set of numbers {3,4, 5, 4, 7, 8, 9, 2, 10, 1}.

Answers

1. **A** The mode of set A is 4 since there are four fours, three twos, and two threes. The median of set A is 3, since 3 is the fifth of the nine numbers.

2. **A** The prime numbers less than ten are 2, 3, 5, 7. The mean is $(2 + 3 + 5 + 7) \div 4 = 17 \div 4 = 4.25$. The median is the average of 3 and 5, which is $(3 + 5) \div 2 = 4$.

3. **A** You can eliminate Choice D immediately, because there is an increase from Thursday to Friday. The decrease from Monday to Tuesday is approximately 40, while Tuesday to Wednesday is less than 20 and Wednesday to Thursday is about 30.

4. **C** Estimate the sales each day from the chart. Add the sales for the five days and divide by 5: $(105 + 60 + 45 + 10 + 20) \div 5 = 240 \div 5 = 48$.

5. **D** The lowest point on the graph occurs in May.

6. **B** Look for the line segment with the steepest negative slope. This occurs from February to March.

7. **A** The class with the most honor roll members is the senior class with 33%. The class with the fewest members is the sophomore class with 18%. The difference is $33\% - 18\% = 15\%$.

8. **C** Juniors represent 23% of the 300 members, and $0.23 \times 300 = 69$.

9. **71.8** $(34 + 54 + 78 + 92 + 101) \div 5 = 71.8$.

10. **4.5** Arrange the numbers in order $\{1, 2, 3, 4, 4, 5, 7, 8, 9, 10 \}$. Then average the two middle numbers. The average of 4 and 5 is 4.5.

B. Functions and Invented Functions

You have probably already seen questions about functions that assume you're familiar with the $f(x)$ notation. On many tests, similar questions are slipped in without the function notation. Instead, new and sometimes odd-looking symbols are invented that do the same job. Don't be intimidated by the strange symbols. Take the time to understand how the function—whether normal or invented—is defined, and you'll be able to answer the questions.

1. Evaluation

To find the value of the function for a given input, simply replace the variable with the given value and simplify.

EXAMPLE:

If $f(x) = x^2 - 5$, find $f(3)$.

In the rule $x^2 - 5$, replace x with 3: $3^2 - 5 = 9 - 5 = 4$.

EXAMPLE:

$\lceil a$ is defined to mean $a^2 - 3a$. Find $\lceil 5$.

In the rule $a^2 - 3a$, replace a with 5: $5^2 - 3 \cdot 5 = 25 - 15 = 10$.

2. Solution

In some problems the value of the function is known and you're asked to find the value of the input. Set the expression equal to the given value and solve the equation.

EXAMPLE:

If $f(x) = \dfrac{3}{x}$, find the value of x for which $f(x) = 6$.

Set $\dfrac{3}{x} = 6$, cross-multiply and solve: $6x = 3$, and $x = \dfrac{1}{2}$.

EXAMPLE:

$[\![n]\!] = 2n - 1$. If $[\![t]\!] = 15$, find t.

Set $2t - 1 = 15$ and solve: $2t = 16$ and $t = 8$.

3. Composition

If you think of a function as a machine that takes in a number, works on it according to some rule, and gives out a new number, then composition of functions can be thought of as two machines on an assembly line. The first takes in a number, works on it, and gives an output, which it passes to the second function. The second function accepts that value, works on it according to its own rule, and puts out a new value.

EXAMPLE:

If $f(x) = 3x - 7$ and $g(x) = x^2 + 1$, find $g(f(2))$.

Work from the inside out. Put 2 in place of x in the rule for f: $f(2) = 3 \times 2 - 7 = -1$. The function f passes this value to g: $g(-1) = (-1)^2 + 1 = 2$.

EXAMPLE:

$\boxed{x} = 2x - 9$ and $\nabla y = 4y + 5$. Find the value of $\boxed{\nabla 2}$.

Work from the inside out: $\nabla 2 = 2 \cdot 2 - 9 = -5$ and then $\boxed{-5} = 4(-5) + 5 = -15$.

Practice

Directions (1–2): You are given two quantities, one in Column A and one in Column B. You are to compare the two quantities and choose:

A if the quantity in Column A is greater
B if the quantity in Column B is greater
C if the two quantities are equal
D if the relationship cannot be determined from the information given

$$f(x) = 5 - x$$

	Column A	**Column B**
1.	$f(3)$	$f(-3)$

$$\frac{\Theta}{a} = a^2 - 4a$$

	Column A	**Column B**
	Θ	Θ
2.	4	0

Directions (3–8): You are given five answer choices. Select the best choice.

3. If $g(x) = 9 - 5x$, find the value of $g(-1)$.

    A.   14
    B.   12
    C.   9
    D.   7
    E.   4

4. If $\left|\begin{matrix} a \\ b \end{matrix}\right|$ is defined to be $a^2 + b^2$, which of the following is the value of $\left|\begin{matrix} 3 \\ 9 \end{matrix}\right|$?

    A.   30
    B.   60
    C.   90
    D.   120
    E.   150

5. The function f is defined as $f(x) = 17 - 3x$. At a certain value, h, $f(h) = -1$. Find h.

   A. 3
   B. 6
   C. 12
   D. 17
   E. 20

6. Define $\dfrac{a \mid b}{c \mid d}$ to be $\dfrac{a}{b} - \dfrac{c}{d}$. Find x if $\dfrac{3 \mid 2}{x \mid 4}$ is equal to 1.

   A. 2
   B. 3
   C. 4
   D. 5
   E. 6

7. If $f(x) = 7 - 2x^2$ and $g(x) = 5x - 3$, then $f(g(1))$ is

   A. −5
   B. −3
   C. −1
   D. 1
   E. 3

8. If $℧a$ is defined to mean $\sqrt{a+9}$ and $℧p = 7$, which of the following could be the value of p?

   A. 20
   B. 30
   C. 40
   D. 50
   E. 60

Directions (9–10): Give your answer as a number.

9. When an object is thrown upward from the roof of a 90-foot building with an initial velocity of 10 feet per second, its height is a function of time. If $h(t) = 90 + 10t - 16t^2$, what is the height of the object after 1 second?

10. Define $\bigcap_b^a$ as $a^2 - b^2$ and $\boxed{x}$ as $x - 1$. Find $\boxed{\bigcap_2^3}$.

Answers

1. **B** $f(3) = 5 - 3 = 2$, but $f(-3) = 5 - -3 = 8$.

2. **C** $\overset{\Theta}{}_4 = 4^2 - 4 \cdot 4 = 0$ and $\overset{\Theta}{}_0 = 0^2 - 4 \cdot 0 = 0$.

3. **A** If $g(x) = 9 - 5x$, find the value of $g(-1) = 9 - 5(-1) = 14$.

4. **C** $\boxed{3 \atop 9} = 3^2 + 9^2 = 9 + 81 = 90$.

5. **B** $f(h) = 17 - 3h = -1$ so $-3h = -18$ and $h = 6$.

6. **A** $\dfrac{3 \mid 2}{x \mid 4} = \dfrac{3}{2} - \dfrac{x}{4} = 1$ so $-\dfrac{x}{4} = -\dfrac{1}{2}$ and $x = 2$.

7. **C** To find $f(g(1))$ evaluate $g(1)$ and then evaluate f at the resulting value: $g(1) = 5 \times 1 - 3 = 2$ and $f(2) = 7 - 2 \times 2^2 = 7 - 8 = -1$.

8. **C** $℧p = \sqrt{p+9} = 7$ so $p + 9 = 49$ and $p = 40$.

9. **84 feet** $h(1) = 90 + 10 \times 1 - 16 \times 1^2 = 90 + 10 - 16 = 84$ feet.

10. **4** $\boxed{\cap {3 \atop 2}} = \boxed{3^2 - 2^2} = \boxed{9 - 4} = \boxed{5} = 5 - 1 = 4$.

C. Combinatorics and Probability

The probability of an event is a number between 0 and 1 that indicates how likely the event is to happen. An impossible event has a probability of 0. An event with a probability of 1 is certain to happen.

1. Basic Counting Principle

In order to determine probability, you often need to count quickly the number of different ways something can happen. If, for example, you were asked about the probability of pulling a certain two-card combination from a standard deck of 52 cards, you would need to calculate the number of different ways to pull two cards. In some situations, you can quickly list all the possible outcomes, but when that isn't possible, the counting principle provides a convenient alternative.

1. **Create a slot for each choice that needs to be made.**
2. **Fill each slot with the number of options for that choice.**
3. **Multiply the numbers you have entered to find the total number of ways your choices can be made.**

EXAMPLE:

Susan has 4 skirts, 7 blouses, and 3 jackets. If all these pieces coordinate, how many different outfits, each consisting of skirt, blouse, and jacket, can Susan create?

Create a slot for each choice that needs to be made. Susan must choose three items of clothing, so three slots are needed: (___) (___) (___). Fill each slot with the number of options for that choice. There are 4 options for the skirt, 7 options for the blouse, and 3 options for the jacket: (4)(7)(3). Multiply the numbers you'ave entered to find the total number of ways the choices can be made: $4 \times 7 \times 3 = 84$ different outfits.

2. Permutations and Combinations

A *permutation* is an arrangement of items in which order matters. If you were asked, for example, how many different ways John, Martin, and Andrew could finish a race, the order of finish would matter, so you would want all the permutations of these three items.

The formula for the number of permutations of n things taken t at a time is $_nP_t = \dfrac{n!}{(n-t)!}$.

A *combination* is a group of objects in which the order does *not* matter. If you were asked to select a team of five students to represent your class of 40 students, and the order in which you chose them did not matter, the number of different such teams would be the combinations of 40 students taken 5 at a time.

The number of combinations of n things taken t at a time is $_nC_t = \dfrac{n!}{(n-t)!\,t!}$.

Factorials

In each of the formulas, the symbol $n!$ means the product of the whole numbers from n down to 1. The symbol $n!$ is read "n factorial." While the formulas for permutations and combinations may look complicated, the properties of factorials work to cut the calculations down to size.

EXAMPLE:

Find the number of permutations of 8 things taken 3 at a time.

$$_8P_3 = \frac{8!}{(8-3)!} = \frac{8!}{5!} = \frac{8 \cdot 7 \cdot 6 \cdot \cancel{5} \cdot \cancel{4} \cdot \cancel{3} \cdot \cancel{2} \cdot \cancel{1}}{\cancel{5} \cdot \cancel{4} \cdot \cancel{3} \cdot \cancel{2} \cdot \cancel{1}} = 336$$

EXAMPLE:

Find the number of combinations of 7 things taken 2 at a time.

$$_7C_2 = \frac{7!}{(7-2)!\,2!} = \frac{7!}{5!\,2!} = \frac{7 \cdot 6 \cdot \cancel{5} \cdot \cancel{4} \cdot \cancel{3} \cdot \cancel{2} \cdot \cancel{1}}{\cancel{5} \cdot \cancel{4} \cdot \cancel{3} \cdot \cancel{2} \cdot \cancel{1} \cdot 2 \cdot 1} = \frac{7 \cdot \cancel{6}^{3}}{\cancel{2} \cdot 1} = 21$$

Most of the questions you will encounter, however, are simple enough not to require a formula. You can adapt the basic counting principle.

EXAMPLE:

In how many different ways can John, Martin, and Andrew finish a race?

You could tackle this just by listing: JMA, JAM, AMJ, AJM, MJA, MAJ. There are six different orders. Alternatively, you could say there are three choices for the first place finisher, leaving 2 choices for second place, and 1 from third, so $(3)(2)(1) = 6$.

EXAMPLE:

A class of 20 students is asked to select a team of five to represent the class. How many different teams are possible?

Using the counting principle, set up five slots: (___) (___) (___) (___) (___). There are 20 choices for the first slot, 19 for the second, and so on: (20) (19) (18) (17) (16). Before you start to multiply out this extremely large number, remember that order does not matter here. To eliminate the extra arrangements of the same five people, divide by $5 \cdot 4 \cdot 3 \cdot 2 \cdot 1$ or 5!. $\frac{(20)(19)(18)(17)(16)}{5 \cdot 4 \cdot 3 \cdot 2 \cdot 1}$ is still a large number, but canceling can help to make it more manageable:

$$\frac{(20)(19)(18)(17)(16)}{5 \cdot 4 \cdot 3 \cdot 2 \cdot 1} = 19 \cdot 3 \cdot 17 \cdot 16 = 15,504$$

3. Simple Probability

The probability of an event is defined as the number of successes divided by the number of possible outcomes. The probability of choosing the ace of spades from a standard deck of 52 cards is $\frac{1}{52}$, while the probability of choosing any ace is $\frac{4}{52} = \frac{1}{13}$.

4. Probability of Compound Events

The probability of two events occurring is the product of the probability of the first and the probability of the second. The word *and* signals that you should multiply.

EXAMPLE:

A card is drawn from a standard deck of 52 cards, recorded, and replaced in the deck. The deck is shuffled and a second card is drawn. What is the probability that both cards are hearts?

The probability of drawing a heart is $\frac{13}{52} = \frac{1}{4}$. Since the first card drawn is replaced before the second draw, the probability of drawing a heart on the second try is the same, so the probability of drawing two hearts is $P(\text{heart}) \cdot P(\text{heart}) = \frac{1}{4} \cdot \frac{1}{4} = \frac{1}{16}$.

Independent and Dependent Events

Be sure to think about whether the first event affects the probability of the second. In the example above, the deck was restored to its original condition before the second card was drawn, so the two draws were independent, or unaffected by one another. If cards are drawn without replacement, however, the events are dependent. The result of the first may change the probability of the second.

EXAMPLE:

Two cards are drawn at random from a standard deck of 52 cards. The first card is not returned to the deck before the second card is drawn. What is the probability that both cards will be hearts?

The probability of the first card being a heart is $\frac{13}{52} = \frac{1}{4}$, but the probability of drawing a heart on the second try is not the same, because the removal of the first card changes the deck. The probability that the second card will be a heart is $\frac{12}{51} = \frac{4}{17}$, because there are 12 hearts left among the 51 remaining cards. The probability of drawing two hearts without replacement is $\frac{1}{4} \cdot \frac{4}{17} = \frac{1}{17}$, slightly less than with replacement.

The probability that one event or another will occur is the probability that the first will occur plus the probability that the second will occur, minus the probability that both will occur.

EXAMPLE:

A card is drawn at random from a standard deck, recorded, and returned to the deck. What is the probability that the card is either an ace or a heart?

The probability that the card is an ace is $\frac{4}{52} = \frac{1}{13}$. The probability that the card is a heart is $\frac{13}{52} = \frac{1}{4}$. One card, however, fits into both categories—the ace of hearts—so it gets counted twice. To eliminate that duplication, you need to subtract $\frac{1}{52}$. The probability that the card is an ace or a heart is $\frac{4}{52} + \frac{13}{52} - \frac{1}{52} = \frac{16}{52} = \frac{4}{13}$.

Mutually Exclusive

Two events are mutually exclusive if it's impossible for them to happen at the same time. If a card is chosen at random from a standard deck of 52 cards, it is possible for it to be a 5 or a 6, but it is not possible for it to be a 5 *and* a 6. The events "draw a 5" and "draw a 6" are mutually exclusive. By contrast, the events "draw a 5" and "draw a heart" are not mutually exclusive. It is possible to draw one card that is a 5 of hearts.

When events A and B are mutually exclusive, the probability of A and B is zero, and so the probability of A or B is simply the probability of A plus the probability of B.

Practice

Directions (1–2): You are given two quantities, one in Column A and one in Column B. You are to compare the two quantities and choose:

A if the quantity in Column A is greater
B if the quantity in Column B is greater
C if the two quantities are equal
D if the relationship cannot be determined from the information given

Column A	Column B
1. The permutations of 5 things taken 2 at a time	The combinations of 7 things taken 3 at a time

A bag contains 4 blue marbles and 3 white marbles

Column A	Column B
2. The probability of choosing a blue marble	The probability of choosing a white marble

Directions (3–8): You are given five answer choices. Select the best choice.

3. A jar contains 20 marbles, of which 2 are white, 10 are yellow, 5 are blue, and 3 are red. If one marble is selected at random, what is the probability that it is red?

   A. $\frac{1}{10}$

   B. $\frac{3}{20}$

   C. $\frac{1}{4}$

   D. $\frac{1}{2}$

   E. 1

4. If a card is selected at random from a standard deck of 52 cards, what is the probability that it is the ace of spades?

   A. $\frac{1}{52}$

   B. $\frac{1}{13}$

   C. $\frac{1}{4}$

   D. $\frac{1}{2,704}$

   E. $\frac{1}{169}$

5. Kijana has been observing the weather for several months and recording whether is was sunny, cloudy, or rainy. He has determined that there is a 38% chance that it will be cloudy, a 21% chance that it will rain, and a 41% chance that it will be sunny. What is the probability that it will not rain tomorrow?

   A. 21%
   B. 38%
   C. 41%
   D. 50%
   E. 79%

6. A bag contains 12 marbles, of which 4 are red, 3 are white, and 5 are blue. What is the probability that a marble selected at random will be red or blue?

   A. $\frac{1}{4}$

   B. $\frac{1}{3}$

   C. $\frac{5}{12}$

   D. $\frac{3}{4}$

   E. $\frac{5}{36}$

7. Two members of the science club must be selected to represent the school in a competition. Four members are seniors, 3 are juniors, 2 are sophomores, and 5 are freshmen. If the two representatives are chosen at random, what is the probability that the pair will be composed of one freshman and one senior?

   A. $\frac{1}{2}$

   B. $\frac{9}{14}$

   C. $\frac{10}{91}$

   D. $\frac{14}{91}$

   E. $\frac{20}{91}$

8. Jennifer owns a pair of "trick" dice. Each die has 6 faces, numbered 1 through 6, but one die is fair—that is, there is an equal probability of it landing on each number—and one die is not fair. The unfair die always lands on 6. What is the probability that a roll of these dice will produce a total of 10 or more?

   A. $\frac{5}{6}$

   B. $\frac{1}{4}$

   C. $\frac{1}{3}$

   D. $\frac{1}{2}$

   E. $\frac{1}{6}$

Directions (9–10): Give your answer as a number.

9. Find the probability of choosing a face card (jack, queen, or king) from a standard deck of 52 cards.

10. A fair die, numbered 1 through 6, is rolled. Find the probability that the die shows a prime number.

Answers

1. **B** The permutations of 5 things taken 2 at a time = $5 \times 4 = 20$, but the combinations of 7 things taken 3 at a time = $(7 \times 6 \times 5) \div (3 \times 2 \times 1) = 35$.

2. **A** The probability of choosing a blue marble = $\frac{4}{7}$, but the probability of choosing a white marble = $\frac{3}{7}$.

3. **B** The probability that one marble selected at random is red = $\frac{3 \text{ red marbles}}{20 \text{ marbles}} = \frac{3}{20}$.

4. **A** Since there is one ace of spades in a standard deck of 52 cards, the probability is $\frac{1}{52}$.

5. **E** The probability that it will not rain = 1– probability of rain = $100\% - 21\% = 79\%$.

6. **D** The probability that a marble selected at random will be red or blue = P(red) + P(blue) = $\frac{4}{12} + \frac{5}{12} = \frac{9}{12} = \frac{3}{4}$.

7. **E** There are $4 + 3 + 2 + 5 = 14$ people to choose from, and so the number of possible teams is the combinations of 14 people taken two at a time: $(14 \times 13) \div (2 \times 1) = 91$. The number of teams composed of a senior and a freshman is $(4 \times 5) = 20$. So the probability = $\frac{20}{91}$.

8. **D** Since one die will always land on 6, a total of 10 or more will be produced by $6 + 4$, $6 + 5$, or $6 + 6$. The question therefore becomes what is the probability of a 4, 5, or 6 on the fair die? $P(4 \text{ or } 5 \text{ or } 6) = P(4) + P(5) + P(6) = \frac{3}{6} = \frac{1}{2}$.

9. $\frac{12}{52} = \frac{3}{13}$ The probability of choosing a face card (jack, queen, or king) from a standard deck of 52 cards = $\frac{12}{52}$ since there are 12 face cards, 3 in each suit. $\frac{12}{52} = \frac{3}{13}$.

10. $\frac{3}{6} = \frac{1}{2}$ Possible prime numbers are 2, 3, and 5, so the probability that the die shows a prime number = $\frac{3}{6} = \frac{1}{2}$.

D. Common Problem Formats

1. Mixtures

Problems about mixtures can often be simplified by organizing the information into a chart.

Amount of substance	×	Cost per unit (or percent purity)	=	Value of substance

Generally, the amounts of the component substances must total the amount of the mixture, and the values of the components must total the value of the mixture.

EXAMPLE:

A merchant wants to make 10 pounds of a mixture of raisins and peanuts. Peanuts can be purchased for $2.50 per pound and raisins for $1.75 per pound. How much of the mix should be peanuts and how much should be raisins if the mixture is to be sold for $2.25 per pound?

Amount of substance	×	Cost per unit (or percent purity)	=	Value of substance
x		2.50		2.50x
y		1.75		1.75y
10		2.25		22.50

Adding down the first column, $x + y = 10$. Adding the last column, $2.50x + 1.75y = 22.50$. Solve the system by substitution, using $y = 10 - x$.

$$2.50x + 1.75y = 22.50$$
$$2.50x + 1.75(10 - x) = 22.50$$
$$2.50x + 17.50 - 1.75x = 22.50$$
$$0.75x = 5.00$$
$$x = \frac{5.00}{0.75} = 6\frac{2}{3}$$

The mixture should be made from about $6\frac{2}{3}$ pounds of peanuts and $3\frac{1}{3}$ pounds of raisins.

2. Distance, Rate, and Time

Like mixture problems, problems involving distance, rate, and time can often be simplified by organizing the information into a chart.

Rate	×	Time	=	Distance

Either the times or the distances can generally be added.

EXAMPLE:

One car leaves Chicago at noon heading east at 55 mph. One hour later another car leaves Chicago traveling west at 50 mph. When will the cars be 400 miles apart?

Let x represent the number of hours the first car travels. Then the second car travels one hour less, or $x - 1$ hours. The distances traveled by both cars must add up to 400.

Rate	×	Time	=	Distance
55		x		55x
50		x – 1		50(x – 1)
				400

Adding the distance column, $55x + 50(x - 1) = 400$. Solve for x.

$$55x + 50(x - 1) = 400$$
$$55x + 50x - 50 = 400$$
$$105x = 450$$
$$x = 4\frac{30}{105} = 4\frac{2}{7}$$

The cars will be 400 miles apart in $4\frac{2}{7}$ hours.

3. Work

When problems talk about the amount of time required to complete a job, reframe the information in terms of the part of the job that can be completed in one unit of time. This will give you a fraction less than 1. Since the entire job, the whole job, is represented by 1, the part of the job completed in one unit of time multiplied by the time spent should equal 1.

EXAMPLE:

Greg can paint a room in three hours and Harry can paint the same room in four hours. How long will it take them to paint the room if they work together?

In one hour, Greg paints $\frac{1}{3}$ of the room and Harry paints $\frac{1}{4}$ of the room. Working together they paint $\frac{1}{3} + \frac{1}{4} = \frac{4+3}{12} = \frac{7}{12}$ of the room in one hour, so it will take them x hours to paint the room, where $\frac{7}{12}x = 1$. Solving, $x = 1 \div \frac{7}{12} = \frac{12}{7} = 1\frac{5}{7}$ hours.

EXAMPLE:

When both drain pipes are opened, a tank empties in 45 minutes. When only the first drain is open, the draining process takes 60 minutes. How long will it take to drain the tank if only the second pipe is opened?

Let $x =$ the number of minutes it takes the second pipe to drain the tank. Then the first pipe can drain $\frac{1}{60}$ of the tank per minute and the second pipe can drain $\frac{1}{x}$ of the tank per minute. In order to drain the whole tank in 45 minutes when working together, they must be able to drain $\frac{1}{45}$ of the tank per minute, which means that $\frac{1}{60} + \frac{1}{x} = \frac{1}{45}$. Solve the equation to find x.

$$\frac{1}{60} + \frac{1}{x} = \frac{1}{45}$$
$$\frac{x + 60}{60x} = \frac{1}{45}$$
$$45(x + 60) = 60x$$
$$45x + 2,700 = 60x$$
$$2,700 = 15x$$
$$180 = x$$

It will take the second pipe 180 minutes or three hours to drain the tank.

Practice

Directions (1–5): Give your answer as a number.

1. A jet plane flying with the wind went 2,600 miles in 5 hours. Against the wind, the plane could fly only 2,200 miles in the same amount of time. Find the rate of the plane in calm air and the rate of the wind.

2. Flying with the wind, a plane flew 1,080 miles in 3 hours. Against the wind, the plane required 4 hours to fly the same distance. Find the rate of the plane in calm air and the rate of the wind.

3. How many liters of a 70% alcohol solution must be added to 50 liters of a 40% alcohol solution to produce a 50% alcohol solution?

4. Find the selling price per pound of a coffee mixture made from 8 pounds of coffee that sells for $9.20 per pound and 12 pounds of coffee that costs $5.50 per pound.

5. An executive drove from home at an average speed of 30 mph to an airport where a helicopter was waiting. The executive boarded the helicopter and flew to the corporate offices at an average speed of 60 mph. The entire distance was 150 miles; the entire trip took three hours. Find the distance from the airport to the corporate offices.

Answers

1. **The speed of the plane is 480 mph, and the wind speed is 40mph.**

Rate	×	Time	=	Distance
$x + y$		5		2,600
$x - y$		5		2,200

$\begin{matrix} 5(x+y)=2,600 \\ 5(x-y)=2,200 \end{matrix} \Rightarrow \begin{matrix} 5x+5y=2,600 \\ 5x-5y=2,200 \end{matrix} \Rightarrow 10x=4,800 \Rightarrow 480$. Then substitute $5(x + y) = 2600 \rightarrow 5(480 + y) = 2600 \rightarrow 480 + y = 520 \rightarrow y = 40$.

2. **325 mph and 45 mph** Flying with the wind, a plane flew 1,080 miles in 3 hours, so $x + y = 1,080 \div 3 = 360$. Since $3(x + y) = 4(x - y)$, $3x + 3y = 4x - 4y$, and $x = 7y$. Substituting, $7y + y = 360$ so $y = 45$ and $x = 315$.

3. **25 liters**

Amount of substance	×	percent purity	=	Value of substance
x		0.70		$0.70x$
50		0.40		20
$x + 50$		0.50		$0.50(x + 50)$

$0.70x + 20 = 0.50x + 25 \rightarrow 0.20x = 5 \rightarrow x = 25$.

4. **$6.98**

Amount of substance	×	Cost per unit (or percent purity)	=	Value of substance
8		9.20		73.60
12		5.50		66.00
20		x		139.60

$20x = 139.60 \rightarrow x = 6.98$.

5. **120 miles** Let x represent the number of hours she drove and $3 - x$ represent the number of hours she flew. $30x + 60(3 - x) = 150 \rightarrow 30x + 180 - 60x = 150 \rightarrow -30x = -30$ so $x = 1$. She drove 1 hour and flew for 2, so the offices were $2(60) = 120$ miles from the airport.

E. Set Theory

1. Sets and Set Notation

A *set* is simply a collection of objects, but in math we are generally concerned with sets of numbers. A set can be denoted by listing the elements, or members, of the set between a set of braces, and often the set is named by an uppercase letter; for example $P = \{2, 3, 5, 7, 11, 13, 17, 19\}$. The elements of the set can also be described verbally or by a formula. Set P might also be indicated as {prime numbers less than 20}. The notation $t \in P$ says "t is an element of set P."

Set A is a subset of set B if every element of A is also an element of B. Set A is contained in set B and B contains A.

EXAMPLE:

Which of the following is a subset of $P = \{2, 3, 6, 7, 11, 13, 17, 19\}$?

A. $\{2, 3, 4\}$
B. $\{6, 7, 16, 17\}$
C. $\{11, 13, 19\}$
D. $\{2, 3, 6, 7, 8\}$
E. $\{17, 18, 19\}$

Choice A contains 4, which is not in P, and Choice B includes 16, which is also not in P. Each of the elements of Choice C is also an element of P, so this is a subset. Choice D contains 8 and Choice E contains 19, neither of which is in P, so only Choice C is a subset of P.

2. Venn Diagrams

A Venn diagram can be a convenient way of understanding set relationships. The Venn diagram consists of a rectangle, representing the universe, that is, all items being considered. Inside this rectangle, circles represent different sets. They may overlap if they have elements in common or not overlap if they're disjoint.

EXAMPLE:

A group of 100 people was surveyed and asked what pets they owned. Of the group, 28 said they did not own a pet, 38 said they owned a cat, and 9 of those said they owned both a dog and a cat. If all the members of the group gave some response, how many owned dogs?

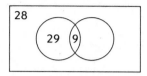

The rectangle represents the 100 people surveyed and the two circles represent cat owners and dog owners. The circles overlap because 9 people own both a dog and a cat. The 38 cat owners include 9 who own a dog and a cat and 29 others who own only a cat. This accounts for 28 + 29 + 9 = 66 people, so there are 100 − 66 = 34 people still uncounted. There is only one answer they could have given, which is that they owned a dog. Those 34 plus the 9 people who own both dogs and cats make a total of 43 dog owners.

3. Intersection

The intersection of two sets is the set of elements that belong to both sets. It represents the overlap of the two sets. If there is no overlap, the intersection is an empty set and the two sets are disjoint. The symbol for the intersection of A and B is $A \cap B$.

EXAMPLE:

If P = {prime numbers less than 20} and Q = {odd numbers less than 20}, find $P \cap Q$.

P = {2, 3, 5, 7, 11, 13, 17, 19} and Q = {3, 5, 7, 9, 11, 13, 15, 17, 19}. The elements that appear in both sets are 3, 5, 7, 11, 13, 17, and 19 so $P \cap Q$ = {3, 5, 7, 11, 13, 17, 19}.

4. Union

The union of two sets is a new set formed by combining the elements of the two sets. If an element appears in both sets, it does not need to be duplicated in the union. The symbol for the union of A and B is $A \cup B$.

EXAMPLE:

If R = {perfect squares less than 30} and T = {multiples of 5 less than 20}, find $R \cup T$.

R = {1, 4, 9, 16, 25} and T = {5, 10, 15} so $R \cup T$ = {1, 4, 5, 9, 10, 15, 16, 25}.

Practice

Directions (1–2): You are given two quantities, one in Column A and one in Column B. You are to compare the two quantities and choose:

A if the quantity in Column A is greater
B if the quantity in Column B is greater
C if the two quantities are equal
D if the relationship cannot be determined from the information given

$$A = \{2, 7, 10, 15, 22\}$$
$$B = \{2, 10, 22\}$$

	Column A	**Column B**
1.	The number of elements in A	The number of elements in $A \cap B$

$$P = \{\text{prime numbers between 20 and 30}\}$$
$$R = \{\text{odd numbers between 20 and 30}\}$$

	Column A	**Column B**
2.	The number of elements in $P \cup R$	The number of elements in $P \cap R$

Directions (3–5): You are given five answer choices. Select the best choice.

3. If $A = \{\text{multiples of 3 less than 25}\}$ and $B = \{\text{multiples of 4 less than 25}\}$, then $A \cap B =$

   A. $\{12\}$
   B. $\{12, 24\}$
   C. $\{4, 8, 12, 16, 20, 24\}$
   D. $\{3, 6, 9, 12, 15, 18, 21, 24\}$
   E. $\{3, 4, 6, 8, 9, 12, 15, 16, 18, 20, 24\}$

4. A survey of 50 people found that 28 people liked vanilla ice cream, 37 people liked chocolate ice cream, and 8 did not like either. How many people liked both vanilla and chocolate?

   A. 15
   B. 23
   C. 30
   D. 42
   E. 65

5. P = {red, blue, yellow}, C = {red, white, blue} and M= {blue, yellow, green}. Find $C \cup (P \cap M)$.

    A.   {blue, yellow}

    B.   {red, blue}

    C.   {blue}

    D.   {red, white, blue, yellow}

    E.   {red, blue, yellow, green}

Answers

1. **A** $A \cap B$ = {2, 10, 22}. The number of elements in A is 5 and the number of elements in $A \cap B$ is 3.

2. **A** P = {23, 29}, R = {21, 23, 25, 27, 29}, $P \cup R$ = {21, 23, 25, 27, 29}, and $P \cap R$ = {23, 29}. The number of elements in $P \cup R$ = 5 and the number of elements in $P \cap R$ = 2.

3. **B** A = {3, 6, 9, 12, 15, 18, 21, 24} and B = {4, 8, 12, 16, 20, 24}, so $A \cap B$ = {12, 24}.

4. **B** 28 + 37 > 50 so clearly some people liked both vanilla and chocolate. Let x represent that number. Then 8 + (28 − x) + x + (37 − x) = 50 → 73 − x = 50 and x = 23.

5. **D** $P \cap M$ = {blue, yellow} and $C \cup (P \cap M)$ = { red, white, blue, yellow }.

F. Sequences

A sequence is an ordered list of numbers. Questions about sequences generally involve predicting the value of terms not shown. This requires that you determine a pattern underlying the terms shown. Commonly, sequences are *arithmetic* (which means that each new term is found by adding a set value to the previous term) or *geometric* (in which each term is multiplied by a number to produce the next term).

The sequence 3, 7, 11, 15, 19, . . . is an example of an arithmetic sequence. Each term is 4 more than the previous term. The terms in the sequence can be denoted a_1, a_2, a_3, . . . and if the common difference, in this case 4, is d, then $an = a_1 + (n − 1)d$.

EXAMPLE:

    Find the 100th term of the sequence 9, 6, 3, 0, –3, . . .

The first term is 9 and the common difference is –3. To find the 100th term, you need to add –3 to each term, and do that a total of 99 times. $a_{100} = a_1 + (100 − 1)d = 9 + (99)(−3) = 9 − 297 = −288$. The 100th term is –288.

The geometric sequence 7, 35, 175, 875, . . . has a common ratio of 5. The common ratio can be found by dividing two adjacent terms. To calculate later terms, you need to multiply repeatedly by 5, which means multiplying the first term by a power of 5: $an = a_1 r^{(n−1)}$.

EXAMPLE:

    Find the eighth term of the sequence 40, 20, 10, 5, . . .

The common ratio is $\frac{1}{2}$ and the first term is 40, so the eighth term will be $a_8 = a_1 r^{(8−1)} = 40 \left(\frac{1}{2} \right)^7 = \frac{5}{32}$.

Sequences can be formed with patterns that are variations and combinations of these. The sequence 3, 5, 12, 14, 21, 23, 30, . . . alternates between adding 2 and adding 7. The sequence 8, 16, 19, 38, 41, 82, 85, . . . combines multiplying by 2 with adding 3. A famous sequence known as the Fibonacci sequence adds two adjacent terms to create the next term, starting with two ones: 1, 1, 2, 3, 5, 8, 13, . . .

Practice

Directions (1–2): You are given two quantities, one in Column A and one in Column B. You are to compare the two quantities and choose:

A if the quantity in Column A is greater
B if the quantity in Column B is greater
C if the two quantities are equal
D if the relationship cannot be determined from the information given

	Column A	Column B
1.	The tenth term in the sequence 3, 7, 11, 15, 19, . . .	The eighth term in the sequence 3, 6, 12, 24, . . .

	Column A	Column B
2.	The twelfth term in the sequence 20, 17, 14, 11, 8, . . .	The seventh term in the sequence 18, 16, 14, 12, 10, . . .

Directions (3–5): You are given five answer choices. Select the best choice.

3. Find the tenth term in the sequence 1,024, 512, 256, 128, . . .

   A. 0
   B. 1
   C. 2
   D. 4
   E. 8

4. Find the twelfth term in the sequence 7, 9, 3, 5, –1, 1, . . .

   A. –3
   B. –5
   C. –7
   D. –8
   E. –11

5. Find the product of the eighth and ninth terms of the sequence 40, 20, 18, 9, 7, . . .

    A.   5.25

    B.   0.75

    C.   −1.25

    D.   −0.9375

    E.   1.125

Answers

1. **A** The sequence 3, 7, 11, 15, 19, . . . has a common difference of 4, so the tenth term will be $3 + 9 \times 4$ = 39. The sequence 3, 6, 12, 24, . . . has a common difference of 3 so the eighth term is $3 + 7 \times 3$ = 24.

2. **B** The twelfth term in the sequence 20, 17, 14, 11, 8, . . . is $20 + 11(-3) = -13$. The seventh term in the sequence 18, 16, 14, 12, 10, . . . is $18 + 6(-2) = 6$.

3. **C** The sequence 1,024, 512, 256, 128, . . . is a geometric sequence with a common ratio of $\frac{1}{2}$, so the tenth term is $1,024\left(\frac{1}{2}\right)^9 = 1,024\left(\frac{1}{512}\right) = 2$.

4. **E** Two rules are at work here $\underbrace{7, 9,}_{} \underbrace{3, 5,}_{+2} \underbrace{-1, 1,}_{+2}$ ... and $7, \underbrace{9, 3,}_{-6} \underbrace{5, -1,}_{-6} 1,$ ... so continue the sequence to the twelfth term: 7, 9, 3, 5, −1, 1, −5, −3, −9, −7, −13, −11.

5. **D** Two rules are at work. $\underbrace{40, 20,}_{\times \frac{1}{2}} \underbrace{18, 9,}_{\times \frac{1}{2}} 7,...$ and $40, \underbrace{20, 18,}_{-2} \underbrace{9, 7,}_{-2}....$ Continue the sequence to the ninth term: 40, 20, 18, 9, 7, 3.5, 1.5, 0.75, −1.25. Then the product of the eighth and ninth terms is 0.75×-1.25 = −0.9375.

XIV. Full-Length Practice Test with Answer Explanations

The total time for the entire exam is 2 hours and 15 minutes.

Answer Sheet

Section 1

Essay 1

_____

_____

_____

_____

_____

_____

_____

_____

_____

_____

_____

_____

_____

_____

_____

_____

_____

_____

CUT HERE

CUT HERE

Essay 2

CUT HERE

CUT HERE

CUT HERE

Section 2

1 Ⓐ Ⓑ Ⓒ Ⓓ Ⓔ		21 Ⓐ Ⓑ Ⓒ Ⓓ Ⓔ		
2 Ⓐ Ⓑ Ⓒ Ⓓ Ⓔ		22 Ⓐ Ⓑ Ⓒ Ⓓ Ⓔ		
3 Ⓐ Ⓑ Ⓒ Ⓓ Ⓔ		23 Ⓐ Ⓑ Ⓒ Ⓓ Ⓔ		
4 Ⓐ Ⓑ Ⓒ Ⓓ Ⓔ		24 Ⓐ Ⓑ Ⓒ Ⓓ Ⓔ		
5 Ⓐ Ⓑ Ⓒ Ⓓ Ⓔ		25 Ⓐ Ⓑ Ⓒ Ⓓ Ⓔ		
6 Ⓐ Ⓑ Ⓒ Ⓓ Ⓔ		26 Ⓐ Ⓑ Ⓒ Ⓓ Ⓔ		
7 Ⓐ Ⓑ Ⓒ Ⓓ Ⓔ		27 Ⓐ Ⓑ Ⓒ Ⓓ Ⓔ		
8 Ⓐ Ⓑ Ⓒ Ⓓ Ⓔ		28 Ⓐ Ⓑ Ⓒ Ⓓ Ⓔ		
9 Ⓐ Ⓑ Ⓒ Ⓓ Ⓔ		29 Ⓐ Ⓑ Ⓒ Ⓓ Ⓔ		
10 Ⓐ Ⓑ Ⓒ Ⓓ Ⓔ		30 Ⓐ Ⓑ Ⓒ Ⓓ Ⓔ		
11 Ⓐ Ⓑ Ⓒ Ⓓ Ⓔ				
12 Ⓐ Ⓑ Ⓒ Ⓓ Ⓔ				
13 Ⓐ Ⓑ Ⓒ Ⓓ Ⓔ				
14 Ⓐ Ⓑ Ⓒ Ⓓ Ⓔ				
15 Ⓐ Ⓑ Ⓒ Ⓓ Ⓔ				
16 Ⓐ Ⓑ Ⓒ Ⓓ Ⓔ				
17 Ⓐ Ⓑ Ⓒ Ⓓ Ⓔ				
18 Ⓐ Ⓑ Ⓒ Ⓓ Ⓔ				
19 Ⓐ Ⓑ Ⓒ Ⓓ Ⓔ				
20 Ⓐ Ⓑ Ⓒ Ⓓ Ⓔ				

Section 3

1 Ⓐ Ⓑ Ⓒ Ⓓ Ⓔ		21 Ⓐ Ⓑ Ⓒ Ⓓ Ⓔ		
2 Ⓐ Ⓑ Ⓒ Ⓓ Ⓔ		22 Ⓐ Ⓑ Ⓒ Ⓓ Ⓔ		
3 Ⓐ Ⓑ Ⓒ Ⓓ Ⓔ		23 Ⓐ Ⓑ Ⓒ Ⓓ Ⓔ		
4 Ⓐ Ⓑ Ⓒ Ⓓ Ⓔ		24 Ⓐ Ⓑ Ⓒ Ⓓ Ⓔ		
5 Ⓐ Ⓑ Ⓒ Ⓓ Ⓔ		25 Ⓐ Ⓑ Ⓒ Ⓓ Ⓔ		
6 Ⓐ Ⓑ Ⓒ Ⓓ Ⓔ		26 Ⓐ Ⓑ Ⓒ Ⓓ Ⓔ		
7 Ⓐ Ⓑ Ⓒ Ⓓ Ⓔ		27 Ⓐ Ⓑ Ⓒ Ⓓ Ⓔ		
8 Ⓐ Ⓑ Ⓒ Ⓓ Ⓔ		28 Ⓐ Ⓑ Ⓒ Ⓓ Ⓔ		
9 Ⓐ Ⓑ Ⓒ Ⓓ Ⓔ		29 Ⓐ Ⓑ Ⓒ Ⓓ Ⓔ		
10 Ⓐ Ⓑ Ⓒ Ⓓ Ⓔ		30 Ⓐ Ⓑ Ⓒ Ⓓ Ⓔ		
11 Ⓐ Ⓑ Ⓒ Ⓓ Ⓔ		31 Ⓐ Ⓑ Ⓒ Ⓓ Ⓔ		
12 Ⓐ Ⓑ Ⓒ Ⓓ Ⓔ		32 Ⓐ Ⓑ Ⓒ Ⓓ Ⓔ		
13 Ⓐ Ⓑ Ⓒ Ⓓ Ⓔ		33 Ⓐ Ⓑ Ⓒ Ⓓ Ⓔ		
14 Ⓐ Ⓑ Ⓒ Ⓓ Ⓔ		34 Ⓐ Ⓑ Ⓒ Ⓓ Ⓔ		
15 Ⓐ Ⓑ Ⓒ Ⓓ Ⓔ		35 Ⓐ Ⓑ Ⓒ Ⓓ Ⓔ		
16 Ⓐ Ⓑ Ⓒ Ⓓ Ⓔ		36 Ⓐ Ⓑ Ⓒ Ⓓ Ⓔ		
17 Ⓐ Ⓑ Ⓒ Ⓓ Ⓔ		37 Ⓐ Ⓑ Ⓒ Ⓓ Ⓔ		
18 Ⓐ Ⓑ Ⓒ Ⓓ Ⓔ		38 Ⓐ Ⓑ Ⓒ Ⓓ Ⓔ		
19 Ⓐ Ⓑ Ⓒ Ⓓ Ⓔ				
20 Ⓐ Ⓑ Ⓒ Ⓓ Ⓔ				

Section 4

1 Ⓐ Ⓑ Ⓒ Ⓓ Ⓔ		21 Ⓐ Ⓑ Ⓒ Ⓓ Ⓔ		
2 Ⓐ Ⓑ Ⓒ Ⓓ Ⓔ		22 Ⓐ Ⓑ Ⓒ Ⓓ Ⓔ		
3 Ⓐ Ⓑ Ⓒ Ⓓ Ⓔ		23 Ⓐ Ⓑ Ⓒ Ⓓ Ⓔ		
4 Ⓐ Ⓑ Ⓒ Ⓓ Ⓔ		24 Ⓐ Ⓑ Ⓒ Ⓓ Ⓔ		
5 Ⓐ Ⓑ Ⓒ Ⓓ Ⓔ		25 Ⓐ Ⓑ Ⓒ Ⓓ Ⓔ		
6 Ⓐ Ⓑ Ⓒ Ⓓ Ⓔ		26 Ⓐ Ⓑ Ⓒ Ⓓ Ⓔ		
7 Ⓐ Ⓑ Ⓒ Ⓓ Ⓔ		27 Ⓐ Ⓑ Ⓒ Ⓓ Ⓔ		
8 Ⓐ Ⓑ Ⓒ Ⓓ Ⓔ		28 Ⓐ Ⓑ Ⓒ Ⓓ Ⓔ		
9 Ⓐ Ⓑ Ⓒ Ⓓ Ⓔ		29 Ⓐ Ⓑ Ⓒ Ⓓ Ⓔ		
10 Ⓐ Ⓑ Ⓒ Ⓓ Ⓔ		30 Ⓐ Ⓑ Ⓒ Ⓓ Ⓔ		
11 Ⓐ Ⓑ Ⓒ Ⓓ Ⓔ				
12 Ⓐ Ⓑ Ⓒ Ⓓ Ⓔ				
13 Ⓐ Ⓑ Ⓒ Ⓓ Ⓔ				
14 Ⓐ Ⓑ Ⓒ Ⓓ Ⓔ				
15 Ⓐ Ⓑ Ⓒ Ⓓ Ⓔ				
16 Ⓐ Ⓑ Ⓒ Ⓓ Ⓔ				
17 Ⓐ Ⓑ Ⓒ Ⓓ Ⓔ				
18 Ⓐ Ⓑ Ⓒ Ⓓ Ⓔ				
19 Ⓐ Ⓑ Ⓒ Ⓓ Ⓔ				
20 Ⓐ Ⓑ Ⓒ Ⓓ Ⓔ				

Section 5

1 Ⓐ Ⓑ Ⓒ Ⓓ Ⓔ		21 Ⓐ Ⓑ Ⓒ Ⓓ Ⓔ		
2 Ⓐ Ⓑ Ⓒ Ⓓ Ⓔ		22 Ⓐ Ⓑ Ⓒ Ⓓ Ⓔ		
3 Ⓐ Ⓑ Ⓒ Ⓓ Ⓔ		23 Ⓐ Ⓑ Ⓒ Ⓓ Ⓔ		
4 Ⓐ Ⓑ Ⓒ Ⓓ Ⓔ		24 Ⓐ Ⓑ Ⓒ Ⓓ Ⓔ		
5 Ⓐ Ⓑ Ⓒ Ⓓ Ⓔ		25 Ⓐ Ⓑ Ⓒ Ⓓ Ⓔ		
6 Ⓐ Ⓑ Ⓒ Ⓓ Ⓔ		26 Ⓐ Ⓑ Ⓒ Ⓓ Ⓔ		
7 Ⓐ Ⓑ Ⓒ Ⓓ Ⓔ		27 Ⓐ Ⓑ Ⓒ Ⓓ Ⓔ		
8 Ⓐ Ⓑ Ⓒ Ⓓ Ⓔ		28 Ⓐ Ⓑ Ⓒ Ⓓ Ⓔ		
9 Ⓐ Ⓑ		29 Ⓐ Ⓑ Ⓒ Ⓓ Ⓔ		
10 Ⓐ Ⓑ Ⓒ Ⓓ Ⓔ		30 Ⓐ Ⓑ Ⓒ Ⓓ Ⓔ		
11 Ⓐ Ⓑ Ⓒ Ⓓ Ⓔ		31 Ⓐ Ⓑ Ⓒ Ⓓ Ⓔ		
12 Ⓐ Ⓑ Ⓒ Ⓓ Ⓔ		32 Ⓐ Ⓑ Ⓒ Ⓓ Ⓔ		
13 Ⓐ Ⓑ Ⓒ Ⓓ Ⓔ		33 Ⓐ Ⓑ Ⓒ Ⓓ Ⓔ		
14 Ⓐ Ⓑ Ⓒ Ⓓ Ⓔ		34 Ⓐ Ⓑ Ⓒ Ⓓ Ⓔ		
15 Ⓐ Ⓑ Ⓒ Ⓓ Ⓔ		35 Ⓐ Ⓑ Ⓒ Ⓓ Ⓔ		
16 Ⓐ Ⓑ Ⓒ Ⓓ Ⓔ				
17 Ⓐ Ⓑ Ⓒ Ⓓ Ⓔ				
18 Ⓐ Ⓑ Ⓒ Ⓓ Ⓔ				
19 Ⓐ Ⓑ Ⓒ Ⓓ Ⓔ				
20 Ⓐ Ⓑ Ⓒ Ⓓ Ⓔ				

CUT HERE

Section 1: Analytical Writing

Essay 1: Present Your Perspective on an Issue

Time: 45 minutes

First you'll see two issue topics; each will appear as a short quotation implying or directly stating a general topic. Before you decide upon a topic, read each carefully. Choose a topic on which you can write a logical and well-substantiated essay.

You will have 45 minutes to organize and write a response that shows your point of view on the topic you select. You will receive a zero if you write about another topic. You can support, deny, or qualify the claim made in the topic you select, as long as the concepts you present are relevant to the topic. Substantiate your ideas or views with strong reasons and solid examples based on general knowledge, direct experience, and/or academic studies.

The GRE readers will grade your writing based on how well you:

- Recognize the intricacies and implications of the issue
- Organize your thoughts in a coherent outline in your essay
- Substantiate your response of the topic with strong, relevant examples
- Edit and proofread your writing

Organize your thoughts, write out a quick outline, make sure you have strong examples, and analyze the argument from different angles. Think logically. Then compose your critique of the argument. Give yourself a few minutes to edit and proofread to avoid careless errors.

Present your perspective on *one* of the issues below, using relevant reasons and/or examples to support your views.

Choice 1: "In this day and age, specialists are overrated because they cannot give broader viewpoints like generalists. Our society needs more generalists rather than experts."

Choice 2: "In modern civilizations, depression is on the rise due to the technological innovations and the manner in which we use these advances."

You can use the rest of this page to plan your response.

Essay 2: Analyze an Argument

Time: 30 minutes

You will have 30 minutes to prepare and compose a critique of a particular argument presented as a short passage about the size of a paragraph or less. You must write a critique on that argument or you will receive a score of zero.

Scrutinize the logic and reasoning in the argument. Think about and write down notes about the evidence needed to refute or support the argument, as well as any questionable assumptions.

It is important to organize and write using strong examples or evidence that supports your case. The evidence should either support or refute the argument. *This is not about your personal views, but an objective critique of an argument.*

The GRE readers will grade your writing based on how well you:

- Recognize or list the significant aspects of the argument that need to be analyzed
- Organize your thoughts in a coherent outline in your critique
- Substantiate your critique of the argument with strong examples
- Edit and proofread your writing

Organize your thoughts, write out a quick outline, make sure you have strong examples, and analyze the argument from different angles. Think logically. Then compose your critique of the argument. Give yourself a few minutes to edit and proofread to avoid careless errors.

Discuss how well reasoned you find this argument.

Approximately 80 percent of people who visit emergency rooms after a skateboarding accident did not use protective gear or light-reflecting material. The risk of injury could be avoided by wearing protective gear with light reflectors when skateboarding, so clearly this statement proves that taking these precautions will reduce the risk of being hurt in a skateboarding accident.

You can use the rest of this page to plan your response.

IF YOU FINISH BEFORE TIME IS CALLED, CHECK YOUR WORK ON THIS SECTION ONLY. DO NOT WORK ON ANY OTHER SECTION IN THE TEST.

Section 2: Quantitative

Time: 30 minutes

30 questions

Numbers: All numbers used are real numbers.

Figures: Figures are intended to provide useful positional information, but they are not necessarily drawn to scale. Unless a note states that a figure is drawn to scale, you should not solve these problems by estimating sizes or by measurements. Use your knowledge of math to solve the problems. Angle measures can be assumed to be positive. Lines that appear straight can be assumed to be straight. Unless otherwise indicated, figures lie in a plane.

Directions (1–15): You are given two quantities, one in Column A and one in Column B. You are to compare the two quantities and choose:

A if the quantity in Column A is greater
B if the quantity in Column B is greater
C if the two quantities are equal
D if the relationship cannot be determined from the information given

Column A	Column B
1. $(3^2)^2$	$(2^3)^2$

$$5x - y = 3$$
$$3x + y = 13$$

Column A	Column B
2. x	y

$$a \, \Xi \, b = a^2 - ab$$

Column A	Column B
3. $4 \, \Xi \, 3$	$3 \, \Xi \, 4$

248

	Column A	**Column B**
4.	$\frac{121}{31}$ rounded to the nearest tenth	$\frac{121}{31}$ rounded to the nearest hundredth

$$7x - 6y > 4$$

	Column A	**Column B**
5.	$18y - 21x$	-12

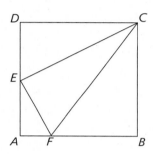

ABCD is a square with side length 12. $\angle CEF$ is a right angle. DE = 5. FB = 9.

	Column A	**Column B**
6.	Perimeter of $\triangle DEC$	Perimeter of $\triangle FEC$

p, q, and r are prime numbers less than 10, and $p < q < r$.

	Column A	**Column B**
7.	$q - p$	$r - q$

x and y are positive integers and $\left(\dfrac{x}{y}\right)^2 > \left(\dfrac{y}{x}\right)^2$.

	Column A	**Column B**
8.	x	y

	Column A	**Column B**
9.	The time needed to drive a miles at $\dfrac{b}{a}$ miles per hour	The time needed to drive $\dfrac{b}{a}$ miles at b miles per hour

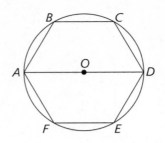

ABCDEF is a regular hexagon inscribed in circle O. $\overline{AD}$ is a diameter of circle O.

	Column A	Column B
10.	The length of $\overline{OD}$	The length of $\overparen{FE}$

A television with a list price of $300 is advertised at 15% off. The final cost reflects that discount and a 6% sales tax.

	Column A	Column B
11.	The final cost	$273

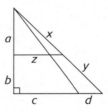

	Column A	Column B
12.	$(x + y)^2$	$a^2 + b^2 + c^2 + d^2$

A manufacturer produces plastic boxes that are cubes, 2 inches on each edge.

	Column A	Column B
13.	The number of cubes that can be packed into a shipping carton that is a cube 1 foot on each edge	The number of cubes that can be packed into a shipping carton 2 feet long, 1 foot wide, and 6 inches high

Column A

Column B

14. $\dfrac{2}{5}(0.001)$

$\dfrac{1}{5}(0.002)$

Yvonne bought a refrigerator at 15% off the regular price. Alicia bought the same refrigerator at 95% of what Yvonne paid.

Column A

Column B

15.   The cost of the refrigerator at 20% off regular price

The price Alicia paid for the refrigerator

Directions (16–30): You are given five answer choices. Select the best choice.

16. $\triangle ABC$ is an equilateral triangle. If $m\angle DAC = m\angle DCA = 40°$, which of the following is *not* true?

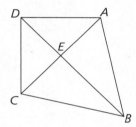

A. $AD = DC$
B. $AD < BC$
C. $m\angle DAB = m\angle DCB$
D. $m\angle ADC > m\angle DCB$
E. $CE = EA$

17.   If $|a| = b$ and $a + b = 0$, then $b - 2a =$

A. $3a$
B. $2a$
C. 0
D. $2b$
E. $3b$

18. If $2x - 5 = y + 4$, then $x - 2 =$

    A. $\dfrac{y+5}{2}$

    B. $y + 5$

    C. $\dfrac{y+9}{2}$

    D. $y + 9$

    E. $\dfrac{y-1}{2}$

19. The sides of equilateral $\triangle ABD$ are tangent to circle O. If $AB = 12\sqrt{3}$ and $OD = 12$, the circumference of the circle is

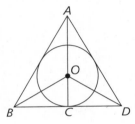

    A. 6π
    B. 12π
    C. $6\pi\sqrt{3}$
    D. $12\pi\sqrt{3}$
    E. 24π

20. If a and b are positive integers and $a \times b$ is odd, which of the following statements must be true?

    A. a and b are prime numbers.
    B. ab^2 is even.
    C. $a - b$ is odd.
    D. $a + b$ is even.
    E. b is a multiple of a.

21. Alberto saves $12 each week. Dahlia has already saved $270 and each week she spends $15 of that savings. When they both have the same amount in savings, they combine their money. What is the combined amount?

    A. $120
    B. $216
    C. $240
    D. $390
    E. $432

22. Each week, Sharon earns 2% of the first $2,500 she sells and 5% of sales beyond $2,500. How much does she earn in a week she sells $3,000?

    A. $60
    B. $75
    C. $125
    D. $150
    E. $200

23. To choose a committee, the names of all possible members are written on identical cards, and five cards are drawn at random. If there are 14 men and 16 women among the possible members, what is the probability that all committee members are women?

    A. $\dfrac{1}{2}$

    B. $\dfrac{1}{32}$

    C. $\dfrac{8}{15}$

    D. $\left(\dfrac{8}{15}\right)^5$

    E. $\dfrac{8}{261}$

24. Each member of the chorus must wear a shirt, slacks, and a sweater, but no two people should have the same outfit. If sweaters are available in 5 different colors, shirts in 6 different colors, and slacks in 3 different colors, how many different costumes are possible?

    A. 6
    B. 14
    C. 30
    D. 90
    E. 196

25. In a hexagon, the total number of diagonals that can be drawn exceeds the total number of sides by

    A. 1
    B. 2
    C. 3
    D. 4
    E. 5

Questions 26–30 refer to the graphs of Land Use in Urban Areas shown below.

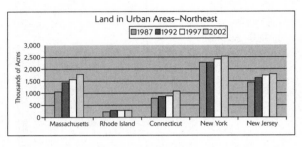

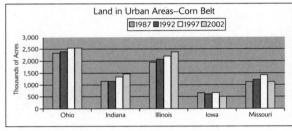

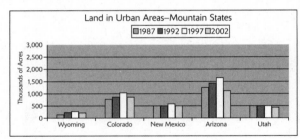

26. Which two states have the most similar amounts of land in urban areas?

    A. Massachusetts and Arizona
    B. Colorado and Missouri
    C. New York and Ohio
    D. Utah and Iowa
    E. Indiana and New Jersey

27. From 1987 to 2002 the land in urban areas in Massachusetts increased by approximately

   A.   20%
   B.   39%
   C.   56%
   D.   64%
   E.   90%

28. In 2002, the land in urban areas in Ohio exceeded the land in urban areas in New Mexico by approximately

   A.   2,000 acres
   B.   20,000 acres
   C.   200,000 acres
   D.   2 million acres
   E.   20 million acres

29. The average number of acres in urban areas in Arizona over the years from 1987 to 2002 was approximately

   A.   0.6 million
   B.   1.1 million
   C.   1.3 million
   D.   1.5 million
   E.   1.8 million

30. Based on the graphs, which of the following statements are true in 2002?

   I. Urban land in Iowa and New Mexico was approximately equal.

   II. Urban land in Rhode Island exceeded that in Wyoming.

   III. Urban land in Connecticut and Colorado was approximately equal.

   A.   I only
   B.   I and II
   C.   I and III
   D.   II and III
   E.   I, II, and III

IF YOU FINISH BEFORE TIME IS CALLED, CHECK YOUR WORK ON THIS SECTION ONLY. DO NOT WORK ON ANY OTHER SECTION IN THE TEST.

STOP

Section 3: Verbal

Time: 30 minutes

39 questions

Directions: Each blank in the following sentences indicates that something has been omitted. Considering the lettered words beneath the sentence, choose the word or set of words that best fits the whole sentence.

1. The _____ student's _____ behavior toward the teacher just before report cards came out annoyed his fellow classmates.

    A. diligent . . . floundering
    B. insipid . . . smug
    C. eclectic . . . pestering
    D. lethargic . . . cursory
    E. sycophantic . . . fawning

2. The delegates made every attempt to _____ the leader but to no avail, his demands were _____.

    A. pacify . . . untenable
    B. propitiate . . . intractable
    C. assiduate . . . complaisant
    D. abnegate . . . acerbic
    E. encumber . . . craven

3. The anonymous donor's _____ allowed him to attend college on a full scholarship.

    A. largess
    B. levity
    C. rancor
    D. relief
    E. frugality

4. The child _____ fish oil capsules and dreaded the dose every night.

    A. venerated
    B. rescinded
    C. abhorred
    D. placated
    E. extolled

5. The extreme heat caused the tourists to move in a(n) _____ manner; they were not adapted to the southern climate at all.

   A. inhibited
   B. torpid
   C. frenetic
   D. refined
   E. headlong

6. Although the new leader had _____ the democratic ideals of a free press and religious freedom, his reign quickly became _____.

   A. availed . . . beneficent
   B. abrogated . . . enlightened
   C. advocated . . . egalitarian
   D. espoused . . . despotic
   E. negated . . . unequivocal

7. Her enthusiasm for the project _____ as soon as she found out that the budget had been cut in half and the deadline had been moved up by a month.

   A. dissipated
   B. retained
   C. elevated
   D. exalted
   E. disparaged

8. Leo Tolstoy was known for _____ on the subject of land use and peasants in many of his novels.

   A. rescinding
   B. expatiating
   C. attenuating
   D. placating
   E. nullifying

Directions: Each of the following questions gives you a related pair of words or phrases. Select the lettered pair that best expresses a relationship similar to that in the original pair of words.

9. DEFER : ACCEPTANCE ::

   A. key : security
   B. snooze : alarm
   C. mute : silence
   D. indict : conviction
   E. score : victory

10. QUINTET : FIVE ::

    A.   decade : century

    B.   score : twenty

    C.   gram : pound

    D.   dozen : gross

    E.   gallon : quart

11. INORDINATE : SENSIBLE ::

    A.   illicit : legal

    B.   prohibitive : safe

    C.   colossal : mammoth

    D.   visceral : key

    E.   salient : surprise

12. COMMODIOUS : SPACE ::

    A.   recalcitrant : authority

    B.   spurious : validity

    C.   succinct : brief

    D.   maudlin: grief

    E.   profuse : paucity

13. ACME : MOUNTAIN ::

    A.   nadir : pit

    B.   query : platitude

    C.   penury : poverty

    D.   peak : mesa

    E.   tenacity : range

14. INSURGENT : SUBSERVIENCE ::

    A.   salubrious : health

    B.   sedulous : diligence

    C.   astringent : wound

    D.   immutable : changeability

    E.   culpable : blame

15. RASH : FORESIGHT ::

    A.   inimical : injury

    B.   contiguous : border

    C.   profligate : restraint

    D.   presumptuous : liberty

    E.   archaic : prescience

16. PRIVATE : GENERAL ::

   A.   chef : cook
   B.   iconoclast : traditionalist
   C.   officer : chief
   D.   teacher : student
   E.   judge : clerk

17. INACTIVE : DORMANT ::

   A.   eccentric : normal
   B.   subtle : obvious
   C.   terse : prolific
   D.   chary: wary
   E.   trenchant : weak

18. PHARMACY : MEDICINE ::

   A.   hospital : bandage
   B.   stationer : envelope
   C.   school : paper
   D.   grocery : cashier
   E.   diner : table

19. SCHOOL : FISH ::

   A.   university : faculty
   B.   pack : horses
   C.   pound : dogs
   D.   gaggle : geese
   E.   country : people

Directions: Questions follow each of the passages. Using only the stated or implied information in each passage, answer the questions.

The earliest form of painting, used by Egyptian artists, was with colors ground in water. Various mediums, such as wax and mastic, were added as a fixative. Today, this is known as tempera painting. The Greeks acquired their knowledge of the art from the Egyptians, and later the Romans dispersed it throughout Europe; they probably introduced tempera painting for decoration of the walls of their houses. The English monks visited the Continent and learned the art of miniature painting for illuminating their manuscripts by the same process. Owing to opaque white being mixed with the colors, the term of painting in *body-color* came in use. Painting, in this manner, was employed by artists throughout Europe in making sketches for their oil paintings.

Two such drawings by Albrecht Dürer, produced with great freedom in the early part of the 16th century, are in the British Museum. The Dutch masters also employed the same means. Holbein introduced the painting of miniature portraits into this country, for although the monks inserted figures in their illuminations, little attempt was made in producing likenesses. As early as the middle of the 17th century, the term *water colors* came into use.

20. An appropriate title for this passage could be:

    A.   The History of Drawing
    B.   The Origins of Watercolor
    C.   The Origins of Painting and Watercolor
    D.   The Difference between Painting and Drawing
    E.   The Complexities of Art

21. The passage states that:

    A.   The Romans introduced tempura painting minimally.
    B.   The Greeks dispersed tempura painting throughout the region.
    C.   Tempura painting in color was employed by artists in Europe.
    D.   The English monks used portraits as a means of communication.
    E.   Artists disagreed about the effects of tempura painting.

22. Which of the following is a true statement based on this passage?

    A.   There was minimal attempt to produce realistic portraits by the monks.
    B.   There was critical acclaim about the production-realistic portraits by the monks.
    C.   There was a strong attempt to produce realistic portraits by the monks.
    D.   There was minimal attention of realistic portraits by the European artists.
    E.   There was a fervor about using tempura painting methods by all artists at the turn of the century.

The remains of pueblo architecture are found scattered over thousands of square miles of the arid region of the southwestern plateaus. This vast area includes the drainage of the Rio Pecos on the east and that of the Colorado on the west, and extends from central Utah on the north beyond the limits of the United States southward, in which direction its boundaries are still undefined.

The descendants of those who at various times built these stone villages are few in number and inhabit about 30 pueblos distributed irregularly over parts of the region formerly occupied. Of these, the greater number are scattered along the upper course of the Rio Grande and its tributaries in New Mexico; a few of them, comprised within the ancient provinces of Cibola and Tusayan, are located within the drainage of the Little Colorado. From the time of the earliest Spanish expeditions into the country to the present day, a period covering more than three centuries, the former province has been often visited by whites, but the remoteness of Tusayan and the arid and forbidding character of its surroundings have caused its more complete isolation. The architecture of this district exhibits a close adherence to aboriginal practices, still bears the marked impress of its development under the exacting conditions of an arid environment, and is but slowly yielding to the influence of foreign ideas. The architecture of Tusayan and Cibola embraces all of the inhabited pueblos of those provinces, and includes a number of the ruins traditionally connected with them.

23. The remoteness and the arid and forbidding character of its surroundings have caused its more complete isolation. This relates to the:

A. Tusayan
B. Cibola
C. Tusayan and Cibola
E. Rio Pecos
D. Neither

24. The passage suggests that:

A. Pueblo architecture shows organized structures within a small region.
B. Pueblo architecture gives clues to certain people reacting to their environment.
C. The influence of pueblo architecture is worldwide.
D. The Tusayan and Cibola were rivals.
E. The Tusayan and Cibola were fighting nomads.

The Panama Canal conflict is due to the fact that the Governments of Great Britain and the United States do not agree upon the interpretation of the Hay-Pauncefote Treaty of September 18, 1901, which stipulates as follows: "The Canal shall be free and open to the vessels of commerce and of war of all nations . . . , on terms of entire equality, so that there shall be no discrimination against any such nation, or its citizens or subjects, in respect of the conditions and charges of traffic, or otherwise. Such conditions and charges of traffic shall be just and equitable." By Section 5 of the Panama Canal Act of August 24, 1912, the President of the United States is authorized to prescribe, and from time to time to change, the tolls to be levied upon vessels using the Panama Canal, but the section orders that no tolls whatever shall be levied upon vessels engaged in the coasting trade of the United States, and also that, if the tolls to be charged should be based upon net registered tonnage for ships of commerce, the tolls shall not exceed $1.25 per net registered ton nor be less, for other vessels than those of the United States or her citizens, than the estimated proportionate cost of the actual maintenance and operation of the Canal.

As regards the enactment of Section 5 of the Panama Canal Act that the vessels of the Republic of Panama shall be entirely exempt from the payment of tolls. Now Great Britain asserts that since these enactments set forth in Section 5 of the Panama Canal Act are in favor of vessels of the United States, they comprise a violation of Article III, No. 1, of the Hay-Pauncefote Treaty, which stipulates that the vessels of all nations shall be treated on terms of entire equality. This assertion made by Great Britain is met by the memorandum which, when signing the Panama Canal Act, President Taft left to accompany the Act. The President contends that, in view of the fact that the Panama Canal has been constructed by the United States wholly at her own cost, upon territory ceded to her by the Republic of Panama, the United States possesses the power to allow her own vessels to use the Canal upon such terms as she sees fit. Therefore, vessels pass through the Canal either without the payment of any tolls, or on payment of lower tolls than those levied upon foreign vessels.

25. Which of the following statements could logically follow the last sentence of the second paragraph?

    A. The Republic of Panama is exempt from the payment of tolls.
    B. The President denies that Article III, No. 1, of the Hay-Pauncefote Treaty.
    C. In other words, the privilege to use the Canal is a conditional most-favored-nation.
    D. Any factors may have been levied upon them for the use of the Canal.
    E. The Republic of Panama may remit to her own vessels.

26. Which of the following could best describe the organization of the passage:

    A. An objective investigation into the conflict between Great Britain and the United States regarding the Panama Canal
    B. A critical debate into the conflict between Great Britain and the United States regarding the Panama Canal
    C. A biased opinion into the conflict between Great Britain and the United States regarding the Panama Canal
    D. A biased query into the conflict between Great Britain and the United States regarding the Panama Canal
    E. A critique into the conflict between Great Britain and the United States regarding the Panama Canal

Directions: Each word in capital letters is followed by five words or phrases. The correct choice is the word or phrase whose meaning is most nearly *opposite* the meaning of the word in capitals. You may be required to distinguish fine shades of meaning. Look at all choices before marking your answer.

27. GRANDILOQUENT

    A. bombastic
    B. elegant
    C. clear
    D. understated
    E. simple

28. QUIESCENT

    A. still
    B. rough
    C. rapid
    D. unsettled
    E. cacophonous

29. INSOUCIANT

    A. transparent
    B. solvent
    C. conscientious
    D. vexed
    E. carefree

30. INTONE

    A. recite
    B. sing
    C. chant
    D. act
    E. exclaim

31. HEPATIC

    A. light
    B. hued
    C. sporadic
    D. blanched
    E. honored

32. RECIDIVISTIC

    A. vapid
    B. chaotic
    C. relativistic
    D. reproachable
    E. corrigible

33. UNCTUOUS

    A. daring
    B. dry
    C. voluble
    D. smooth
    E. sibilant

34. CLOY

    A. satiate
    B. crave
    C. strengthen
    D. surfeit
    E. weary

35. DISSEMBLE

    A. disabuse
    B. disguise
    C. create
    D. crave
    E. rarefy

36. INFELICITOUS

    A. malapropos
    B. appropriate
    C. melancholic
    D. luxurious
    E. injurious

37. OCCLUDE

    A. liberate
    B. imprison
    C. collect
    D. abandon
    E. abhor

38. APPROBATION

    A. criticism
    B. ejection
    C. chicanery
    D. ennui
    E. critique

IF YOU FINISH BEFORE TIME IS CALLED, CHECK YOUR WORK ON THIS SECTION ONLY. DO NOT WORK ON ANY OTHER SECTION IN THE TEST.

Section 4: Quantitative

Time: 30 minutes

30 questions

Numbers: All numbers used are real numbers.

Figures: Figures are intended to provide useful positional information, but they are not necessarily drawn to scale. Unless a note states that a figure is drawn to scale, you should not solve these problems by estimating sizes or by measurements. Use your knowledge of math to solve the problems. Angle measures can be assumed to be positive. Lines that appear straight can be assumed to be straight. Unless otherwise indicated, figures lie in a plane.

Directions (1–15): You are given two quantities, one in Column A and one in Column B. You are to compare the two quantities and choose:

A if the quantity in Column A is greater
B if the quantity in Column B is greater
C if the two quantities are equal
D if the relationship cannot be determined from the information given

p, q, and r are positive integers.
$p = 3q$ and $q = 5r$.

	Column A	**Column B**
1.	The remainder when pq is divided by r	The remainder when pr is divided by q

	Column A	**Column B**
2.	$(6 + 3) \times 5 - 6 \div 2 + 3^2$	$6 + 3 \times 5 - 6 \div 2 + 3^2$

	Column A	**Column B**
3.	x if $x^3 = 125$	y is $y^2 = 25$

	Column A	**Column B**
4.	The number of weeks in 427 days	The number of months in 5 years

	Column A	**Column B**
5.	$\frac{1}{2} \div \frac{3}{4} + \frac{1}{3}$	$\frac{1}{2} + \frac{3}{4} \div \frac{1}{3}$

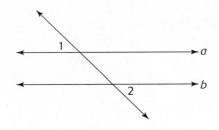

Line a is parallel to line b.

Column A	Column B
Column A	**Column B**
6. The measure of $\angle 1$	The measure of $\angle 2$

Column A	Column B
Column A	**Column B**
7. $(0.1)^5$	10^{-5}

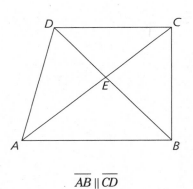

$$\overline{AB} \parallel \overline{CD}$$

Column A	Column B
Column A	**Column B**
8. Area of $\triangle AED$	Area of $\triangle BEC$

$$a \boxtimes b = a^2 - b$$
$$a \odot b = a + b^2$$

Column A	Column B
Column A	**Column B**
9. $(3 \boxtimes 4) \odot 5$	$3 \boxtimes (4 \odot 5)$

Column A	Column B
Column A	**Column B**
10. $\sqrt{18} \cdot \sqrt{50}$	90

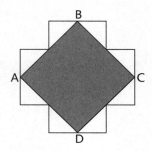

Square *ABCD* has a side of 12 units.

All unshaded triangles are congruent isosceles right triangles.

Column A	Column B
Column A	**Column B**
11. The shaded area	The unshaded area

$$\frac{x}{3} = \frac{4}{y}$$

Column A	**Column B**
12. $\dfrac{xy}{6}$	$\dfrac{60}{xy}$

Column A	**Column B**
13. The number of square units in the area of a circle with diameter π units	The number of units in the circumference of a circle with area of π^3 square units

A right circular cylinder has a volume of 175π cubic units.

Both the radius and the height of the cylinder are positive integers.

Column A	**Column B**
14. The radius of the cylinder	The height of the cylinder

a, *b*, and *c* are positive integers.

Column A	**Column B**
15. $\dfrac{45a^7b^3c^5}{\left(6a^3b^2c^2\right)\left(15a^3b^{-4}c^2\right)}$	$\dfrac{48a^9b^2c^{-7}}{\left(4a^3b^{-3}c^{-3}\right)^2\left(9a^2b^3c^{-2}\right)}$

Directions (16–30): You are given five answer choices. Select the best choice.

Distances between Cities				
	Springfield	**Fort Wayne**	**Toledo**	**Indianapolis**
Springfield	–	254	343	186
Fort Wayne	254	–	89	101
Toledo	343	89	–	183
Indianapolis	186	101	183	–

16. If the distance in miles between cities is shown in the table above, which of the following statements are true?

   I. Springfield, Fort Wayne, and Toledo lie on a line.
   II. Indianapolis is the midpoint of the line segment connecting Toledo and Springfield.
   III. Indianapolis, Toledo, and Fort Wayne are the vertices of an equilateral triangle.

   A. Only I is true.
   B. Only II is true.
   C. Only III is true.
   D. I and II are true.
   E. II and III are true.

Life Expectancy by Age, Race, and Gender								
	All Races			**White**			**Black**		
Age	Total	Male	Female	Total	Male	Female	Total	Male	Female
0	77.8	75.2	80.4	78.3	75.7	80.8	73.1	69.5	76.3
20	78.8	76.2	81.2	79.1	76.6	81.5	74.6	71.2	77.7
40	79.9	77.6	81.9	80.1	77.9	82.1	76.3	73.4	78.8
60	82.5	80.8	84.0	82.6	80.9	84.1	80.4	78.2	82.2
80	89.1	88.2	89.8	89.1	88.1	89.7	89.1	88.0	89.6

17. The life expectancy for 40-year-old black females exceeds that for 40-year-old white males by

   A. 0.9 years
   B. 1.3 years
   C. 3.8 years
   D. 4.5 years
   E. 5.9 years

18. Life expectancy for 60-year-old females is what percent higher than that for males of the same age?

   A. 0.12%
   B. 1.20%
   C. 3.96%
   D. 5.12%
   E. 8.97%

19. In right triangle $\triangle ABC$, $\angle C$ is a right triangle, $\overline{DE}$ is parallel to $\overline{AB}$, and D and E are the midpoints of $\overline{CA}$ and $\overline{CB}$, respectively. Each shaded triangle is similar to the $\triangle ABC$ and the shaded triangles are congruent to one another. What fraction of the area of $\triangle ABC$ is shaded?

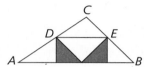

   A. $\dfrac{1}{8}$

   B. $\dfrac{1}{4}$

   C. $\dfrac{1}{3}$

   D. $\dfrac{1}{2}$

   E. $\dfrac{3}{4}$

20. If S is the point $(4,1)$, T is the point $(-2,y)$, and the slope of $\overrightarrow{ST} = \dfrac{2}{3}$, find y.

   A. 5
   B. 2
   C. 0
   D. -3
   E. -8

21. If $2x + 3y = 12$ find the value of $12x + 18y$.

   A. 30
   B. 60
   C. 72
   D. 144
   E. 448

22. If $a^2 + 2ab + b^2 = 9$, then $(2a + 2b)^3 =$

A. 3
B. 6
C. 9
D. 27
E. 216

23. Two pools in the shape of rectangular prisms are being filled with water by pumps. The first pump fills its pool completely in 1 hour. The second pumps water twice as fast as the first pump, and fills a pool that is twice the width, twice the length, and the same depth of the first pool. How many hours does it take the second pump to fill its pool?

A. 1
B. 2
C. 4
D. 8
E. 16

24. Two cars started from the same point and traveled on a straight course in opposite directions for exactly 3 hours, at which time they were 330 miles apart. If one car traveled, on average, 10 miles per hour faster than the other car, what was the average speed of the slower car for the 3-hour trip?

A. 40
B. 45
C. 50
D. 55
E. 60

25. In the chart below, 40 people reported their age on their last birthday. Find the median age.

Age on Last Birthday	
Age	Frequency
30	5
31	7
32	3
33	12
34	9
35	4

A. 6
B. 6.666
C. 32.5
D. 32.625
E. 33

26. A theater sells children's tickets for two-thirds of the adult ticket price. If 7 adult tickets and 3 children's tickets cost a total of $108, what is the cost of an adult ticket?

    A. $8.00
    B. $10.80
    C. $15.50
    D. $12.00
    E. $36.00

27. A particular stock is valued at $50 per share. If the value increases 25 percent and then decreases 20 percent, what is the value of the stock per share after the decrease?

    A. $55.00
    B. $52.50
    C. $50.00
    D. $47.50
    E. $45.00

28. If the mean of 6 consecutive integers is 8.5, what is the product of the first and the last?

    A. 80
    B. 72
    C. 70
    D. 66
    E. 56

29. If $xy \neq 0$ and $y = 3x$, then $\dfrac{x^2 + 2xy + y^2}{xy} =$

    A. $1\dfrac{1}{3}$

    B. $2\dfrac{4}{9}$

    C. $3\dfrac{1}{9}$

    D. $3\dfrac{1}{3}$

    E. $5\dfrac{1}{3}$

30. If $x > 0$ and $y > 0$, which of the following is equivalent to $\dfrac{y^2}{x}\sqrt{\dfrac{x^2}{y^4}}$

   A. $\dfrac{1}{y}\sqrt{x}$

   B. $\dfrac{1}{y}$

   C. $\sqrt{x}$

   D. $\dfrac{y^4}{x^2}$

   E. 1

IF YOU FINISH BEFORE TIME IS CALLED, CHECK YOUR WORK ON THIS SECTION ONLY. DO NOT WORK ON ANY OTHER SECTION IN THE TEST.

Section 5: Verbal

Time: 30 minutes

35 questions

Directions: Each blank in the following sentences indicates that something has been omitted. Considering the lettered words beneath the sentences, choose the word or set of words that best fits the whole sentence.

1. The doctor's _____ temperament made her ideally suited to work in the hospital's emergency room.

   A. apathetic
   B. phlegmatic
   C. insensate
   D. churlish
   E. peevish

2. The prosecuting attorney's argument proved to be _____; the defendant was ultimately _____ of the crime.

   A. untenable . . . acquitted
   B. salacious . . . exonerated
   C. indefensible . . . accused
   D. specious . . . convicted
   E. peevish . . . guilty

3. The new parents were so exhausted by their twins' refusal to sleep for more than two hours at a time that they found themselves longing for the _____ days before they had children.

   A. importune
   B. halcyon
   C. esoteric
   D. assiduous
   E. restive

4. Her _____ interest in classical music led her to buy subscription tickets to the philharmonic's spring season.

   A. lassitude
   B. proviso
   C. inopportune
   D. nascent
   E. felicitous

5. The aspirin _____ his migraine but only slightly.

   A. attenuated
   B. alleviated
   C. intensified
   D. ameliorated
   E. impinged

6. In hindsight, Michelle realized that her _____ decision to pursue her master's degree and her Ph.D. _____ may have been a mistake, as the workload was staggering.

   A. rash . . . exclusively
   B. scrupulous . . . serially
   C. perspicacious . . . audaciously
   D. unequivocal . . . resolutely
   E. extemporaneous . . . concurrently

7. America's foreign policy is _____, as it represents the views of both _____ political parties.

   A. bilateral . . . important
   B. bilingual . . . major
   C. bipartisan . . . competitive
   D. bipartisan . . . major
   E. bilateral . . . significant

Directions: Questions follow each of the passages. Using only the stated or implied information in each passage, answer the questions.

The majority of plants are adaptable to a terrestrial environment indoors, even if they are epiphytic in the wild, and thus must be contained to propagate roots. When the nutrients in the houseplant's soil become depleted, it is necessary to artificially replace them with fertilizers that contain the essential chemical elements (macronutrients) of potassium, phosphorous and nitrogen. Fertilizers for indoor plants are commercially available in crystalline, liquid, granular, or tablet forms and contain trace minerals as well.

Potassium (K), in the form of potash, engenders the production of fruit and flowers and aids the overall health and heartiness of the plant. Phosphorous (P), in the form of phosphate or phosphoric acid, is crucial for healthy root production. Nitrogen (N) is essential for the growth of the plant's stems and leaves and for the production of chlorophyll.

Fertilizers vary in their composition, but the majority of commercial fertilizers contains a 20-20-20 (N-P-K) formula. They are suitable for most indoor plants. Those containing more N are best for particularly leafy plants and plants nearing the peak of leaf production. If more P is prevalent it results in a slightly slower growth rate but will aid in a well developed root system. Fertilizers high in potash are ideal for plants that have just completed flowering and need fortifying as they prepare for the next flowering cycle.

Over-fertilization can result in an excess of soluble salts, which accumulate on the top layer of the soil, around the drainage holes in the pots or build up on the exterior of clay pots. When water evaporates from soil, the minerals remain and over time become more and more concentrated, resulting in a plant being unable to effectively absorb water. Houseplants need only be fertilized during periods of active growth.

8. The main purpose of this passage is to explain

    A.   what occurs if a houseplant is over-fertilized
    B.   why it is important to supplement the soil of houseplants with fertilizer
    C.   what the best fertilizer is for a leafy plant
    D.   None of the above
    E.   All of the above

9. A plant that is gearing up for its next flowering should be fed a fertilizer high in:

    A.   potassium
    B.   phosphorous
    C.   nitrogen
    D.   nitrogen and phosphorous
    E.   None of the above

10. If salts are accruing on the top layer of the soil, it is a sign that:

    A.   The plant is undernourished.
    B.   The salts are not water soluble.
    C.   There are too many nutrients in the soil.
    D.   There is a lack of trace minerals in the soil.
    E.   The plant needs water.

11. A fertilizer composition of 16-20-12 contains:

    A.   More potassium than nitrogen
    B.   More nitrogen than potassium
    C.   More phosphoric acid than phosphate
    D.   Less potassium than phosphorus
    E.   More phosphorus than nitrogen or potassium

Directions: Each of the following questions gives you a related pair of words or phrases. Select the lettered pair that best expresses a relationship similar to that in the original pair of words.

12. IRREVOCABLE : ALTER ::

    A.   unique : match
    B.   disputable : question
    C.   tractable : manage
    D.   feasible : complete
    E.   inconsequential : defer

13. BENEFACTOR : MALICE ::

    A. perpetrator : offense
    B. fledging : experience
    C. beneficiary : assistance
    D. tutor : instruction
    E. curator : museum

14. IMPUNITY : PUNISHMENT ::

    A. merit : reward
    B. insecurity : anxiety
    C. susceptibility : disease
    D. frailty : injury
    E. infallibility : error

15. CHARLATAN : MALEFACTOR ::

    A. writer : subscriber
    B. consumer : manufacturer
    C. physician : pediatrician
    D. infant : dependent
    E. columnist : publisher

16. GLUTTONOUS: DEVOUR ::

    A. lavish : conserve
    B. dissident : agree
    C. determined : waver
    D. withdrawn : socialize
    E. avaricious : hoard

17. DISPASSIONATE : PARTIALITY ::

    A. merciless : cruelty
    B. maltreated : resentment
    C. malevolent : spite
    D. indecisive: hesitation
    E. indifferent : interest

18. MALNUTRITION : HEALTH ::

    A. scandal : reputation
    B. misinformation : inconvenience
    C. enlightenment : knowledge
    D. exercise : appetite
    E. commendation : promotion

19. IRRATIONAL : LOGIC ::

    A. loyal : allegiance
    B. corrupt : ethics
    C. contentious : controversy
    D. facetious : laughter
    E. sturdy : stamina

20. INCESSANT : INTERMITTENT ::

    A. slovenly : untidy
    B. robust : strong
    C. permanent : transient
    D. dormant : sluggish
    E. meek : acquiescent

21. IMMACULATE : BLEMISH ::

    A. airtight : weakness
    B. noxious : harm
    C. imperfect : flaw
    D. versatile : use
    E. valuable : worth

Directions: Each word in capital letters is followed by five words or phrases. The correct choice is the word or phrase whose meaning is most nearly *opposite* the meaning of the word in capitals. You may be required to distinguish fine shades of meaning. Look at all choices before marking your answer.

22. IMPORTED

    A. alien
    B. pliable
    C. pertinent
    D. foreign
    E. native

23. PROTRACT

    A. curtail
    B. sojourn
    C. dawdle
    D. travel
    E. dispute

24. CONTINUOUS

    A. perennial

    B. unruly

    C. essential

    D. obstinate

    E. intermittent

25. DISPENSABLE

    A. pliable

    B. arrogant

    C. disciplined

    D. essential

    E. necessary

26. INCARCERATE

    A. impugn

    B. indict

    C. confine

    D. refine

    E. free

27. RENEGADE

    A. adversary

    B. recalcitrant

    C. opponent

    D. adherent

    E. postgraduate

28. ABHOR

    A. adverse

    B. love

    C. admire

    D. respect

    E. vote

29. ADJACENT

    A. penultimate

    B. distant

    C. next

    D. near

    E. primary

30. DEFAULT

    A. pay
    B. fail
    C. win
    D. ignore
    E. attend

31. INADVERTENT

    A. remiss
    B. careful
    C. lax
    D. thoughtless
    E. overlook

32. SOLICITUDE

    A. anxiety
    B. examination
    C. inquiry
    D. indifference
    E. vigilance

33. INORDINATE

    A. moderate
    B. superabundant
    C. multitude
    D. pliable
    E. powerful

Directions: Questions follow each of the passages. Using only the stated or implied information in each passage, answer the questions.

Scandinavian migration to the United States at the turn of the 19th century differed from other European migration patterns in that the bulk of people who made the journey were not fleeing religious or political persecution. Rather, they were abandoning an agrarian way of life threatened by an increase in the standard of living that led to huge population surges. Rural areas were greatly impacted by this increase, which was due to a decrease in infant mortality, more food production, and a lack of famine and war, which historically caused migration from other European countries to the U.S. to soar. The population growth strained social structures and exacerbated social issues as a surplus of laborers resulted in not enough work, a shrinking amount of tillable land and an increase in landless citizens resulting in social upheaval. Rural people attracted to land rich America moved primarily to the upper Midwest and had a strong proclivity to re-create their traditional ways of life in their new world. The Scandinavians tended to migrate within cohesive family groups and, thus, the balance of the sexes was even. These people clung to their religious traditions and languages and rural ways of life.

34. Scandinavians emigrated to America largely due to:

    A.   an inability to practice their religion in their native land

    B.   an increase in the rural population

    C.   a decrease in the rural population

    D.   famine

    E.   political upheaval

35. The primary point of this passage is

    A.   to describe how Scandinavian migration differed from other migration patterns

    B.   to highlight why Scandinavians settled in the Midwest

    C.   to explain the surge in Scandinavian migration to the U.S. at the turn of the 19th century

    D.   to explain the changing social structures in Scandinavia

    E.   to explain why most people migrating from Scandinavia to the U.S. came from rural rather than industrial areas

IF YOU FINISH BEFORE TIME IS CALLED, CHECK YOUR WORK ON THIS SECTION ONLY. DO NOT WORK ON ANY OTHER SECTION IN THE TEST.

Answer Key

Section 2: Quantitative

1. A	9. D	17. E	25. C
2. B	10. B	18. A	26. C
3. A	11. B	19. B	27. D
4. C	12. A	20. D	28. D
5. B	13. C	21. C	29. C
6. B	14. C	22. B	30. B
7. D	15. B	23. E	
8. A	16. D	24. D	

Section 3: Verbal

1. E	11. A	22. A	32. E
2. B	13. A	23. A	33. B
3. A	14. D	24. B	34. B
4. C	15. C	25. A	35. A
5. B	16. C	26. A	36. B
6. D	17. D	27. D	37. A
7. A	18. B	28. D	38. A
8. B	19. D	29. D	
9. B	20. B	30. A	
10. B	21. C	31. A	

Section 4: Quantitative

1. C	9. A	17. A	25. E
2. A	10. B	18. C	26. D
3. D	11. A	19. B	27. C
4. A	12. B	20. D	28. D
5. B	13. B	21. C	29. E
6. C	14. B	22. E	30. E
7. C	15. A	23. B	
8. D	16. A	24. C	

Section 5: Verbal

1.	B	10.	C	19.	B	28.	B
2.	A	11.	E	20.	C	29.	B
3.	B	12.	A	21.	A	30.	A
4.	D	13.	B	22.	E	31.	B
5.	A	14.	E	23.	A	32.	D
6.	E	15.	D	24.	E	33.	A
7.	D	16.	E	25.	D	34.	B
8.	D	17.	E	26.	E	35.	C
9.	A	18.	A	27.	D		

Answer Explanations

Section 1: Analytical Writing

In this section, we provide sample score-6 essays. For more information on scoring the essays, see Chapter 9. For more sample essays, visit www.ets.org.

Sample Issue Essay

Today, specialists are necessary but overrated; we need generalists as well as specialists in our society as it becomes increasingly complex with both positive and negative effects from the innovative social and technological advances.

Today there are high-speed social and technological changes with innovative ways of communication moves, which contributes to the intricacies and psychological shifts, both positive and negative effects among persons in Western cultures, demand for an equilibrium in which there are both non-experts and specialists.

Specialists are critical. Without them, society in this day and age could not properly function nor could we digest or incorporate the heaps of new information. There is a convergence of technology and knowledge can only be formed out of research after it's digested by specialists. In today's shrinking global world or flattening playing field, information is disseminated through mass global media at a speed hardly anyone can decipher. I paraphrase from a writer who I heard give a talk at my educational institute: "I am able to research only because so many individuals whom I know are reliable and I can turn to them for basic knowledge. Each person whom I rely on has a sharp focus in a given area so that at each step we can gain a full and true perspicacious understanding of the complexities of life. Each one of us adds to the tree of knowledge, leaf by leaf, and together we can reach the stars." This demonstrates the point that our society's level of knowledge and technology is in a phase now in which there simply must be experts or specialists in order for our society to use information effectively.

To state this point simply, without experts, our civilization would find itself overwhelmed in the ocean of information that piles up in excess. While it worked okay for early thinkers to learn and to comprehend the concrete laws and concepts that existed then, now, no one individual can possibly absorb and learn all of the knowledge in any given field.

On the contrary, too much specialization means narrow-mindedness or too tight of a focus or lens. Then people can lose the macro ideas or larger picture. No one can wish to appreciate beauty by only viewing one's artistic masterpiece. What we study or observe from the perspective of a narrow focus may be logically coherent or sound, but may be immaterial or fallacious within the broader framework. More so, if we inspect only one masterpiece, Monet's Gardens for example, we may conclude that all Impressionist painting is similar. Another example to illustrate my point: If I only read one of my student's papers all year long, I would make a fallacious conclusion about his or her writing style and skill. So, useful conclusions and positive inventions must come by sharing among specialists perhaps. Simply throwing out various discoveries means we have a heap of useless discoveries, it is only when one can make with them a montage or medley that we can see that they may form a picture.

Overspecialization be risky in terms of the accuracy, clarity, and cohesion of critical knowledge because it may serve to obfuscate universal or ethical issues. Only generalists can interpret a broad individual focuses on their independent research and then industrialization, development, and advances

283

forge ahead in society. At the same time, it is challenging for one to see the holistic view on a global scale. In that scenario, meaningful progress may be debilitating to specialists for the benefit of society.

Furthermore, over-specialization in society would unfortunately rush people into making important decisions too early in life (at least by university), thus compartmentalizing their lives. It would be easier to feel isolated and on one's own. Not only does this hypothetical view create a less progressive view-point, but also it would generate many narrowly focused individuals who may be able to regurgitate information, but not necessarily process it well. Problem solving would suffer with people who would be generally poorly educated individuals with information but not able to use it effectively. Also it would assure a sense of loss of community, often followed by a feeling of general dissatisfaction. Without generalists, society becomes myopic and less efficient. Thus, society needs both specialists and generalists because specialists drive us forward in the world series as in baseball, while generalists make sure we have our bases covered and apply good field strategies.

Reader Response: This is a superb response because it shows strong reasoning skills and the language is sophisticated and gets its point across with both solid examples along with figurative language. The issue is twofold: It presents a compelling case for specialization as well as an equally compelling, well-organized case against overspecialization. Again, this example is an exceptional written response to the topic.

Sample Argument Essay

In the faulty argument, there are two separate kinds of gear: preventive and protective, but it does not take into account other significant factors. Helmets are an example of protective gear whereas light-reflecting material is considered to be preventive or to warn other people. What is the warning? A skate-boarder is near a person driving a vehicle. The argument falls apart if the motorist is irresponsible or infringes upon the space of the person on the skateboard. The intention of protective gear is to decrease the margin of potential accident, whether it's caused by someone else, by the skateboarder, or by some other factor. Protective gear does little, though, to stop an accident from happening or to prevent it. However, in this argument, it is presumed to reduce the injuries. There are many statistics on injuries suffered by skateboarders showing people who were injured with protective and preventive gear. These statistics could give us a better understanding of which kinds of gear are more of assistance in a precarious situation between a motorist and skateboarder.

Thus, the idea that protective gear greatly reduces the injuries suffered in accidents is not a logical conclusion. At first glance, it sounds logical but it is not. The argument is weakened by the patent fact that it does not take into account the vast differences between skaters who wear gear and those who do not use protective or preventive gear. Are the people who wear it more safety-conscious individuals or not? The skaters who invest in gear may be less likely to cause an accident through careless or dangerous behavior. So, it's not the gear that saves them but their attitude or cautious approach when skateboarding. It's critical to take the locale into this argument. Are people who are safety conscious by nature skating on busy streets or in the safe venues such as quiet roads or their own driveway? This is an important factor overlooked in this argument, and it needs to be taken into consideration.

This argument does not allow for one to analyze the seriousness of an injury. Not all injuries can be lumped into one category. The conclusion that safety gear prevents severe injuries implies that it is presumed that individuals who go to the hospital only suffer from severe injuries. That line of reasoning is unrealistic. It may be the fact that people are skateboarding during leisure hours when a doctor is only available in an emergency room so their injuries are not severe, but their general-care practitioner is unavailable at the time of the injury.

Furthermore, there is insufficient evidence that proves high-quality or expensive gear works better than less expensive models. Possibly a person did not put on their gear correctly and a wristband would not protect a break in the wrist effectively.

The case that safety gear based on emergency-room statistics could give us critical information and potentially save lives is not sound.

Reader response: This fine response shows the writer's strong reasoning and ability to analyze an argument, introducing holes or faulty assumptions. It allows the reader to see that there are missing pieces to a declarative statement because (1) individuals do not share common approaches to skateboarding, (2) the venue is significant, and (3) the statistics do not differentiate by the severity of the injuries nor the different types of gear. All these points substantiated this essay very well even though it could have been written with more eloquence.

Section 2: Quantitative

1. **A** $(3^2)^2 = 9^2 = 81$ but $(2^3)^2 = 8^2 = 64$.

2. **B** Adding the equations eliminates y and gives $8x = 16$ or $x = 2$. Substituting 2 for x in the first equation gives $10 - y = 3$, so $y = 7$.

3. **A** $4 \boxminus 3 = 4^2 - 4 \times 3 = 16 - 12 = 4$ but $3 \boxminus 4 = 3^2 - 3 \times 4 = 9 - 12 = -3$.

4. **C** $\frac{121}{31} \approx 3.903225. \ldots$ Rounded to the nearest tenth, 3.903225 becomes 3.9. Rounded to the nearest hundredth, it becomes 3.90.

5. **B** $18y - 21x = -3(7x - 6y)$ so we can gain information about its value by multiplying both sides of the given inequality by -3. That multiplication will reverse the direction of the inequality. $-3(7x - 6y) < -3 \times 4$ and $18y - 21x < -12$.

6. **B** Since $DE = 5$ and $DC = 12$, $\triangle DEC$ is a 5-12-13 right triangle, with $EC = 13$; it has a perimeter of 30. Since $FB = 9$ and $BC = 12$, the sides of $\triangle FBC$ are multiples of a 3-4-5 right triangle, specifically 9-12-15, with $FC = 15$. The third side of $\triangle FEC$, EF, is the hypotenuse of $\triangle FEA$ and so is longer than either of the legs; therefore, $EF > 7$. The perimeter of $\triangle FEC = EC + FC + EF > 13 + 15 + 7$; therefore, the perimeter of $\triangle FEC > 35$.

7. **D** The primes less than 10 are 2, 3, 5, and 7. Four possibilities exist for the values of p, q, and r. In two cases, $q - p < r - q$; in one case $q - p > r - q$ and in the last, $q - p = r - q$

p	q	r	q-p	r-q
2	3	5	1	2
2	3	7	1	4
2	5	7	3	2
3	5	7	2	2

8. **A** If x and y were equal, both $\left(\frac{x}{y}\right)^2$ and $\left(\frac{y}{x}\right)^2$ would equal 1. Since $\left(\frac{x}{y}\right)^2 > \left(\frac{y}{x}\right)^2$, $x \neq y$. Since the numbers are not equal, one of the ratios, $\frac{x}{y}$ or $\frac{y}{x}$, will be greater than 1 and the other less than 1. The square of a number larger than 1 is larger than 1, and the square of a number less than 1 is less than 1. The given information that $\left(\frac{x}{y}\right)^2 > \left(\frac{y}{x}\right)^2$ tells us that $\frac{x}{y} > 1$, so $x > y$.

9. **D** Using the relationship *distance = rate × time*, the time needed to drive a miles at $\frac{b}{a}$ miles per hour is $a \div \frac{b}{a} = \frac{a}{1} \cdot \frac{a}{b} = \frac{a^2}{b}$. The time needed to drive $\frac{b}{a}$ miles at b miles per hour is $\frac{b}{a} \div b = \frac{b}{a} \cdot \frac{1}{b} = \frac{1}{a}$. It is impossible to determine which is larger without more information.

10. **B** In the regular hexagon, if $\overline{OE}$ and $\overline{OF}$ are drawn, $\triangle OEF$ is an equilateral triangle, and so $\overline{FE} \cong \overline{OE} \cong \overline{OD}$. Since $\overparen{FE}$ is longer than $\overline{FE}$, however, $\overparen{FE}$ is longer than $\overline{OD}$.

11. **B** The final cost = $300 - (15\%$ of $300) + (6\%$ of the discounted price). The discount is $0.15 \times 300 = \$45$, so the discounted price is \$255. The tax is $0.06(255) = \$15.30$, so the final cost is $\$255 + \$15.30 = \$270.30$.

12. **A** $(x + y)^2 = (a + b)^2 + (c + d)^2$ but $(a + b)^2 + (c + d)^2$ does not equal $a^2 + b^2 + c^2 + d^2$. $(a + b)^2 + (c + d)^2 = a^2 + 2ab + b^2 + c^2 + 2cd + d^2$. Since a, b, c, and d are all positive, $2ab$ and $2cd$ are positive, and so $(a + b)^2 + (c + d)^2$ is larger than $a^2 + b^2 + c^2 + d^2$; therefore, $(x + y)^2$ is greater than $a^2 + b^2 + c^2 + d^2$.

13. **C** A shipping carton that is a cube 1 foot on each edge has a volume of 1 ft.³ or 1,728 in.³. The 2-inch cubes can be packed into the carton in 6 layers, each with 36 cubes, arranged 6 by 6. It holds a total of 216 cubes. A shipping carton 2 feet long, 1 foot wide, and 6 inches high can hold layers of 12 by 6 cubes, 72 cubes in each layer, but it can only hold 3 layers. It holds a total of 216 cubes.

14. **C** $\frac{2}{5}(0.001) = 0.4(0.001) = 0.0004$ and $\frac{1}{5}(0.002) = 0.2(0.002) = 0.0004$.

15. **B** The cost of the refrigerator at 20% off regular price is 80% of the original price. The price Yvonne paid for the refrigerator is 85% of the original price. The price Alicia paid for the refrigerator is 95% of 85% of the original price. Since $0.95 \times 0.85 = 0.8075$, or 80.75%, the price Alicia paid is greater than 20% off regular price.

16. **D** Since $m\angle DAC = m\angle DCA = 40°$, $AD = DC$. $m\angle ADC = 180 - 2(40) = 100°$, so $m\angle ADE = 50°$, and $m\angle ABE = 30°$. In $\triangle ADE$, $AD < BC$. Adding equals to equals tells us that $m\angle DAB = m\angle DCB$. $m\angle ADC = 100°$ and $m\angle DCB = m\angle DCE + m\angle ECB = 40° + 60° = 100°$. So $m\angle ADC$ is equal to $m\angle DCB$, rather than larger.

17. **E** If $|a| = b$, then either $a = b$ or $a = -b$. The fact that $a + b = 0$ tells us that $a = -b$. Then $b - 2a = b - 2(-b) = b + 2b = 3b$.

18. **A** If $2x - 5 = y + 4$, then $2x - 4 = y + 5$, so $2(x - 2) = y + 5$ and $x - 2 = \frac{y + 5}{2}$.

19. **B** $\triangle ACB$ is a 30°-60°-90° right triangle with hypotenuse $AB = 12\sqrt{3}$, so $BC = 6\sqrt{3}$, and $AC = 6\sqrt{3} \cdot \sqrt{3} = 18$. $OA = OB = OD = 12$, and $OC = AC - OA = 6$, so the radius of the circle is 6, and its circumference is $C = 2\pi r = 12\pi$.

20. **D** Since $a \times b$ is odd, both a and b must be odd. They need not be prime, simply odd, but the difference between two odd numbers will be even, and since $ab^2 = a \times b \times b$ (so the product of three odd numbers), it will be odd, not even. The sum $a + b$ of two odd numbers will be even.

21. **C** Alberto's savings can be represented by $12w$, where w is the number of weeks. Dahlia's savings can be represented by $270 - 15w$. Solve $12w = 270 - 15w$ to find that $27w = 270$ and $w = 10$. After 10 weeks, they have equal savings of $120 each, which they combine for $240.

22. **B** In a week when she sells $3,000, Sharon earns 2% of the first $2,500 and 5% of the additional $500. So, $0.02(2,500) + 0.05(500) = 50 + 25 = \$75$.

23. **E** The probability that all committee members are women is $\frac{16}{30} \cdot \frac{15}{29} \cdot \frac{14}{28} \cdot \frac{13}{27} \cdot \frac{12}{26}$
$= \frac{16}{30} \cdot \frac{15}{29} \cdot \frac{14}{28} \cdot \frac{13}{27} \cdot \frac{12}{26} = \frac{16 \cdot 4}{2 \cdot 29 \cdot 2 \cdot 9 \cdot 2} = \frac{8}{261}$.

24. **D** The number of different costumes is $5 \times 6 \times 3 = 90$.

25. **C** In a hexagon, the total number of diagonals that can be drawn is $\frac{6 \times 3}{2} = 9$, which exceeds the total number of sides by $9 - 6 = 3$.

26. **C** Massachusetts increases each year, while Arizona declined in 2002. Colorado and Missouri have a similar shape, but values for Missouri are higher. New York and Ohio are very similar. Utah is lower and more constant than Iowa. Indiana has lower values and is not increasing as quickly as New Jersey.

27. **D** From 1987 to 2002 the land in urban areas in Massachusetts increased from about 1,100,000 to about 1,800,000, an increase of about 700,000. Percent change is $\dfrac{700,000}{1,100,000} = \dfrac{7}{11}$, which is 63.6%. The best answer is (D) 64%.

28. **D** In 2002, the land in urban areas in Ohio was slightly more than 2,500,000 acres, while the land in urban areas in New Mexico was just about 500,000 acres. The difference is 2,500,000 − 500,000 = 2,000,000 or 2 million acres.

29. **C** The land in urban areas in Arizona, in thousands of acres, was approximately 1,200 in 1987, 1,400 in 1992, 1,700 in 1996, and 1,000 in 2002. Averaging these gives $\dfrac{1,200 + 1,400 + 1,700 + 1,000}{4}$ $= \dfrac{5,300}{4} = 1,325$ thousand acres or 1.325 million acres.

30. **B** In 2002, urban land in Iowa and New Mexico was approximately equal, and urban land in Rhode Island did exceed that in Wyoming, but urban land in Connecticut and Colorado was not approximately equal.

Section 3: Verbal

1. **E** The correct answer is Choice E, *sycophantic . . . fawning*. Both *sycophantic* and *fawning* mean "to be obsequious; to seek favor or attention." The key in the sentence is *annoyed*.

2. **B** The correct answer is Choice B, *propitiate . . . intractable*. *Propitiate* means "to conciliate" or "to appease." *Intractable* means "to be obstinate and stubborn." So the delegates were unable to appease the leader because he was too stubborn. The clue in the sentence is the phrase *to no avail*.

3. **A** The correct answer is Choice A, *largess*. *Largess* means "the bestowal of generous gifts or monies." The key in the sentence is "allowed" and "full scholarship," indicating a generous donation. Choice D is close but not as good.

4. **C** The correct answer is Choice C, *abhorred*. To abhor something is to loathe it, to absolutely detest it. The key in the sentence is "dreaded"; it's the only word that fits with Choice C.

5. **B** The correct answer is Choice B, *torpid*. *Torpid* means "sluggish" and "lethargic." In the sentence, the tourists are "not adapted" to the weather, which is a context clue to help you choose Choice B.

6. **D** The correct answer is Choice D. To espouse is "to advocate and defend something." Someone who rules in a despotic way is "tyrannical and autocratic," not a democratic rule. The key word is *although*, making D the best choice. If you just look at the second words in other answer choices, you can see most words are positive in meaning and would not work.

7. **A** The correct answer is Choice A, *dissipated*. A secondary meaning of *dissipate* is "to disintegrate." Two context clues in the sentence are "the budget had been cut" and "deadline had been moved up" thus making it an unappealing situation. Choices B, C, and D are all positive words, so they don't fit. That leaves you with A and E. E doesn't fit because *disparage* means "to belittle" and doesn't make sense.

8. **B** The correct answer is Choice B. To expatiate is to speak or write about something at length. In this question, the context clue of "Leo Tolstoy" helps you to be able to choose the correct answer, because Tolstoy's novels are notoriously long.

9. **B** To snooze an alarm is to put it off; to defer is to put off an acceptance. In Choice A, a key does not put off or delay security; in Choice C, to mute does not delay the silence; in Choice D, to indict means "to accuse," not delay a conviction. Choice E also doesn't work; to score would do the opposite of delay or put off a victory.

10. **B** A quintet is a group of 5 and a score is a group of 20. Choice A does not work because a decade is not "a group of a century"; the ratio is 1:10 here. Choice C does not work because the measurements for ounce and pound are not the same as the keywords. The same applies for choices D and E.

11. **A** The correct answer is Choice A. Something inordinate is not sensible and illicit is not legal. Both key words are antonyms. The other answer choices are not opposite in meaning.

12. **D** Something that is commodious has an excess of space, just as someone who is maudlin has an excess of grief. The relationship between the key words is a matter of degree.

13. **A** The acme is the extreme point of a mountain, just as the nadir is the extreme aspect of a pit. Choice C is close, but penury is not the extreme degree of poverty. The relationship between the key words is a matter of degree.

14. **D** An insurgent person lacks subservience. The relationship between the key words is a matter of "lack of." In Choice D, immutability lacks changeability.

15. **C** A rash person lacks foresight, just as a profligate person lacks restraint or is excessively wasteful. The relationship between the key words is a matter of "lack of."

16. **C** Private is to general or people of opposite rank as an officer is to a chief. A private reports to the general, taking orders, which is a similar relationship between an officer and a chief.

17. **D** Something inactive is dormant or lethargic just as something chary is wary. The relationship between the key words is synonymous.

18. **B** A pharmacy is a store where you buy medicine, just as a stationer is a store where you buy an envelope. The relationship between the key words is related to place and specifically the purposes of a different types of stores.

19. **D** A school is a group of fish just as a gaggle is group of geese. The relationship between the key words is categorizing types according to group.

20. **B** The correct answer is Choice B because the narrative discusses the origins of watercolor from the use of tempura thousands of years ago.

21. **C** The correct answer is Choice C because it is stated explicitly in the passage about color and tempura. The other choices are incorrect.

22. **A** Choice A is stated explicitly in the passage about how the monks gave a minimal attempt for realism in portraiture in the second paragraph. The other answer choices do not make sense.

23. **A** It is stated explicitly in the passage so Choice A is correct.

24. **B** Choice B is correct. It is logical, unlike the other answer choices, and implied throughout the passage.

25. **A** Choice A is correct because it continues the idea. The key word is "tolls," which is not in any other answer choices. It fits logically into this paragraph.

26. **A** Choice A is correct because it is an objective point of view, without any biased opinion about the topic of the Panama Canal and the conflict between the United States and Great Britain.

27. **D** *Grandiloquent* means "long-winded, copious, and even bombastic," which is the opposite of Choice D, understated. Choice E, simple, is close but not good enough. Grandiloquent implies a degree of overstatement making Choice D the best answer.

28. **D** *Quiescent* means "calm" and Choice D, unsettled, works better than choices B, C, and E. Choice E, cacophonous, doesn't work as an antonym because its opposite would be harmonious.

29. **D** *Insouciant* means "calm and unbothered" and the antonym is Choice D, vexed, which means "troubled or irritated."

30. **A** *Intone* means "to chant in a monotonous voice." The other answer choices are in the category of speech, but Choice E, exclaim, is not quite as appropriate as Choice A. In this case, it's a matter of degree.

31. **D** *Hepatic* means liver-colored or a reddish, brown, or dark hue. So the antonym that fits best here is Choice D, *blanched,* meaning "pale or ashen."

32. **E** A recidivistic individual often repeats or goes back to their former behavior. Choice E is the most opposite in meaning, because a corrigible person is stable or not recidivistic.

33. **B** *Unctuous* means smug, but in this case, it means greasy or like an unguent. Therefore, Choice B, dry works best as an antonym.

34. **B** To cloy is to tire of excess sweets and certain foods and the only answer choice that is close to an antonym is Choice B, crave.

35. **A** To dissemble means "to give a false or misleading appearance to or to conceal the truth or real nature of" which is clearly the opposite of answer Choice A, disabuse, or "to reveal the truth or to clarify or tell."

36. **B** *Infelicitous* means "inappropriate; inapt; or awkward." Choice B works best as an antonym: "appropriate." Choice A is a synonym.

37. **A** *Occlude* means" to close or to shut." Choice A, *liberate*, is the best of all the choices as a word in opposite meaning.

38. **A** Approbation is praise and Choice A, criticism, is the opposite in meaning. The other answer choices do not fit.

Section 4: Quantitative

1. **C** $\dfrac{pq}{r} = \dfrac{3q \cdot q}{r} = \dfrac{3(5r)^2}{r} = \dfrac{75r^2}{r} = 75r$. Since 75 and r are both positive integers, the remainder is 0.

   $\dfrac{pr}{q} = \dfrac{3q \cdot r}{5r} = \dfrac{3(5r) \cdot r}{5r} = \dfrac{15r^2}{5r} = 3r$. Here too, the denominator is a factor of the numerator, so the remainder is 0.

2. **A** $(6+3) \times 5 - 6 \div 2 + 3^2 = 9 \times 5 - 6 \div 2 + 3^2 = 9 \times 5 - 6 \div 2 + 9 = 45 - 3 + 9 = 42 + 9 = 51$ but $6 + 3 \times 5 - 6 \div 2 + 3^2 = 6 + 3 \times 5 - 6 \div 2 + 9 = 6 + 15 - 3 = 9 = 21 - 3 + 9 = 18 + 9 = 27$.

3. **D** If $x^3 = 125$, then $x = 5$, but if $y^2 = 25$, y may be equal to 5 or –5.

4. **A** The number of weeks in 427 days is $427 \div 7 = 61$, and the number of months in 5 years is $5 \times 12 = 60$.

5. **B** Order of operations is a concern here, as are the fractions. $\dfrac{1}{2} \div \dfrac{3}{4} + \dfrac{1}{3} = \left(\dfrac{1}{2} \div \dfrac{3}{4}\right) + \dfrac{1}{3} = \left(\dfrac{1}{\cancel{2}} \cdot \dfrac{\cancel{4}^2}{3}\right) + \dfrac{1}{3}$
   $= \dfrac{2}{3} + \dfrac{1}{3} = 1$ while $\dfrac{1}{2} + \dfrac{3}{4} \div \dfrac{1}{3} = \dfrac{1}{2} + \left(\dfrac{3}{4} \div \dfrac{1}{3}\right) = \dfrac{1}{2} + \left(\dfrac{3}{4} \cdot \dfrac{3}{1}\right) = \dfrac{2}{4} + \dfrac{9}{4} = \dfrac{11}{4}$.

6. **C** $\angle 1$ and $\angle 2$ are alternate exterior angles, and when parallel lines are cut by a transversal, alternate exterior angles are congruent.

7. **C** $(0.1)^5 = 0.00001$ and $10^{-5} = \dfrac{1}{10^5} = \dfrac{1}{10}^5 = (0.1)^5 = 0.00001$.

8. **D** *ABCD* is a trapezoid, but no information is available about its dimensions. If the trapezoid were isosceles, it would be possible to show that $\triangle AED \cong \triangle BEC$, so the areas would be equal, but without that information, the relationship cannot be determined.

9. **A** $(3 \boxtimes 4) \odot 5 = (3^2 - 4) \odot 5 = (9 - 4) \odot 5 = 5 \odot 5 = 5 + 5^2 = 5 + 25 = 30$ but
   $3 \boxtimes (4 \odot 5) = 3 \boxtimes (4 + 5^2) = 3 \boxtimes (4 + 25) = 3 \boxtimes 29 = 3^2 - 29 = 9 - 29 = -20$.

10. **B** $\sqrt{18} \cdot \sqrt{50} = 3\sqrt{2} \cdot 5\sqrt{2} = 15 \cdot 2 = 30 < 90$.

11. **A** The shaded area is $12^2 = 144$ square units. Each isosceles right triangle has a hypotenuse equal to half the side of the square, so 6 units long. Each leg is $\dfrac{6}{\sqrt{2}}$ or $\dfrac{6\sqrt{2}}{2} = 3\sqrt{2}$. The unshaded area is made up of 8 right triangles each with an area of $\dfrac{1}{2}(3\sqrt{2})^2$, so the unshaded area is $8 \cdot \dfrac{1}{2}(3\sqrt{2})^2 = 4(9 \cdot 2) = 72$ square units.

12. **B** Since $\dfrac{x}{3} = \dfrac{4}{y}$, $xy = 12$. Then $\dfrac{xy}{6} = 2$ and $\dfrac{60}{xy} = 5$.

13. **B** Since the radius is half the diameter, the number of square units in the area of a circle with diameter π units is $\pi r^2 = \pi \left(\dfrac{\pi}{2}\right)^2 = \dfrac{\pi^3}{4}$. Estimate that value as $\dfrac{27}{4}$. A circle with area of π^3 square units has a radius equal to π, since $\pi^3 = \pi r^2$ and $\pi^2 = r^2$ so $\pi = r$. The circle has a circumference equal to $C = 2\pi r = 2\pi \times \pi = 2\pi^2$, which is greater than 18.

14. **B** Since the volume of the cylinder is 175π cubic units, you can determine that $175\pi = \pi r^2 h$ and $175 = r^2 h$. At first it may seem that you cannot determine the value of radius or height, but since both are positive integers, consider the prime factorization of $175 = 5 \times 5 \times 7 = r^2 h$. The radius of the cylinder is 5 and the height is 7.

15. **A** $\dfrac{45a^7b^3c^5}{\left(6a^3b^2c^2\right)\left(15a^3b^{-4}c^2\right)} = \dfrac{45a^7b^3c^5}{90a^6b^{-2}c^4} = \dfrac{ab^5c}{2}$ and $\dfrac{48a^9b^2c^{-7}}{\left(4a^3b^{-3}c^{-3}\right)^2\left(9a^2b^3c^{-2}\right)} = \dfrac{48a^9b^2c^{-7}}{\left(16a^6b^{-6}c^{-6}\right)\left(9a^2b^3c^{-2}\right)}$

$= \dfrac{48a^9b^2c^{-7}}{144a^8b^{-3}c^{-8}} = \dfrac{ab^5c}{3}$. Since the numerators are the same and a, b, and c are positive integers, the fraction with the smaller denominator is the larger number.

16. **A** If three points lie on a line, the distance from the first to the second plus the distance from the second to the third will equal the distance from the first to the third. Reading the distances from the table, you can see that $254 + 89 = 343$, so Statement I is true. The distance from Toledo to Springfield is 343. The midpoint of the segment connecting them would be 171.5 miles from each. Indianapolis is 186 miles from Springfield and 183 miles from Toledo, so it is not the midpoint, and Statement II is false. Indianapolis, Toledo, and Fort Wayne are the vertices of a triangle, but the triangle is not equilateral. Its sides measure 89, 183, and 186, so Statement III is not true.

17. **A** The life expectancy for 40-year-old black females is 78.8, while that for 40-year-old white males is 77.9. So, $78.8 - 77.9 = 0.9$ years

18. **C** Life expectancy for 60-year-old females is 84.0, while that for males of the same age is 80.8. The difference of $84.0 - 80.8 = 3.2$ years as a percent of the life expectancy for males is $\dfrac{3.2}{80.8} = \dfrac{32}{808} = \dfrac{4}{101}$ or slightly less than 4%.

19. **B** The shaded triangles have heights equal to half the height of $\triangle ABC$, and their combined bases are equal to $\overline{DE}$. Since it connects the midpoints of the sides, $\overline{DE}$ is half as long as $\overline{AB}$. If the area of $\triangle ABC$ is $\dfrac{1}{2}bh$, the area of one shaded triangle is $\dfrac{1}{2}\left(\dfrac{1}{4}b\right)\left(\dfrac{1}{2}h\right) = \dfrac{1}{16}bh$, so the shaded area of the two triangles is $\dfrac{1}{8}bh$. Since $\dfrac{1}{8}bh \div \dfrac{1}{2}bh = \dfrac{1}{4}$, one-fourth of $\triangle ABC$ is shaded.

20. **D** The slope of $\overline{ST} = \dfrac{1-y}{4--2} = \dfrac{1-y}{6} = \dfrac{2}{3}$. Cross-multiplying, $3(1-y) = 2 \times 6$, so $3 - 3y = 12$. Solving, $-3y = 9$ and $y = -3$.

21. **C** $12x + 18y = 6(2x + 3y) = 6(12) = 72$.

22. **E** Since $a^2 + 2ab + b^2 = (a+b)^2 = 9$, $a + b = \pm3$. $2a + 2b = \pm6$ and $(2a + 2b)^3 = (\pm6)^3 = \pm216$. The best answer choice is 216.

23. **B** If the dimensions of the first pool are l, w, and h, the dimensions of the second pool are $2w$, $2l$, and h. The volume of the first pool is lwh, and the volume of the second is $(2l)(2w)(h)$ or $4lwh$. The second pool holds four times as much as the first. If the first pool's pump were used to fill the second, it would take four hours to fill; however, since the second pump fills twice as fast, it will take two hours.

24. **C** Since the two cars were traveling in opposite directions, the distance between them is the sum of the distances traveled by each car. They were 330 miles apart after 3 hours, so the distance between them increased by 110 miles per hour. Because one car traveled, on average, 10 miles per hour faster than the other car, their speeds can be represented as x and $x + 10$. Then $x + x + 10 = 110$, so the slower car traveled at 50 mph and the faster car at 60 mph.

25. **E** The median of the 40 data points will be the average of the 20th and 21st values. Since both the

20th and 21st value are 33, the median is 33.

26. **D** If c is the price of a child's ticket and a is the price of an adult's ticket, $c = \frac{2}{3}a$. Seven adult tickets and 3 children's tickets cost \$108, so $7a + 3\left(\frac{2}{3}a\right) = 108$ or $9a = 108$ and $a = 12$.

27. **C** The stock begins at \$50. A 25% increase will be an increase of \$12.50, raising the price to \$62.50. A 20% decrease — 20% of \$62.50 — is a decrease of \$12. 50, taking the price back to \$50.

28. **D** Represent the six consecutive integers as x, $x + 1$, $x + 2$, $x + 3$, $x + 4$, and $x + 5$. If the mean is 8.5, the sum of the six integers is $6(8.5) = 51$. Then $6x + 15 = 51$, $6x = 36$, and $x = 6$. The six integers are 6, 7, 8, 9, 10, and 11, so the product of the first and the last is 66.

29. **E** If $xy \neq 0$ and $y = 3x$, then $\dfrac{x^2 + 2xy + y^2}{xy} = \dfrac{x^2 + 2x(3x) + (3x)^2}{x(3x)} = \dfrac{x^2 + 6x^2 + 9x^2}{3x^2} = \dfrac{16x^2}{3x^2} = \dfrac{16}{3}$.

30. **E** If $x > 0$ and $y > 0$, $\dfrac{y^2}{x}\sqrt{\dfrac{x^2}{y^4}} = \dfrac{y^2}{x}\dfrac{x}{y^2} = 1$.

Section 5: Verbal

1. **B** *Phlegmatic* means calm and unemotional, someone who isn't excitable. If a doctor is working in an emergency room, you can infer that he or she would act calmly under stressful circumstances making Choice B correct.

2. **A** An untenable argument is one that cannot be defended. The defendant was acquitted, which means not able to be convicted. This sentence works like a syllogism or a logical sequence.

3. **B** *Halcyon* means peaceful and calm. The demands of new children stated explicitly in the sentence make Choice B, halcyon, the best choice. Choice E, restive, means impatient, not restful.

4. **D** Something that is nascent is developing or flowering. The key word in the sentence is *interest* indicating a new or developing hobby.

5. **A** To attenuate means to weaken, to lessen the force or amount. The key words in the sentence are *only slightly,* meaning the migraine is still a problem, so the other answer choices are not as good a fit as A.

6. **E** An extemporaneous decision is one made on the spur of the moment, and *concurrently* means occurring at the same time. The key words in the sentence are *mistake* and *staggering,* indicating that her quick decision was a mistake in judgment.

7. **D** The correct is Choice D, bipartisan and major, because both words fit logically. The word *bipartisan,* works with the context clue, *both,* in the sentence.

8. **D** The answer is D, none of the above. While all of the statements may be true or are mentioned in the passage, none describe what the main or central purpose of the passage is.

9. **A** The answer is A. The passage states that if a plant has just completed one flowering cycle and is preparing for the next one a fertilizer high in K, or potassium, is best.

10. **C** The correct answer is C. Visible salt on the top layer of the soil is a sign that the plant has an over-abundance of nutrients in the soil indicating that it has been over-fertilized.

11. **E** The correct answer is E. The composition of 16-20-12 means there are 16 units of N (nitrogen), 20 units of P (phosphate or phosphoric acid) and 12 units of K (potassium). Therefore, there is more phosphorous than nitrogen or potassium.

12. **A** A is the correct answer. If something is irrevocable, you cannot alter it. The same relationship is true for unique and match. You cannot match something that is unique. Choice D does not work because if something is feasible you can complete it. Choices B and C do not work for the same reason as Choice D. Choice E does not work because there is no connection.

13. **B** B is the correct answer. A benefactor does not have malice, or a kindly helper does not wish harm or injury just as a fledgling does not have experience. The other answer choices do not share this relationship.

14. **E** E is the correct answer. If you have impunity, you are exempt from punishment. If you have infallibility, you do not err or make any errors. The other answer choices do not share this relationship.

15. **D** D is the correct answer. A charlatan is a type of malefactor, a person who does harm or evil. An infant is a type of dependent. The other answer choices do not share this relationship.

16. **E** E is the correct answer. If you are gluttonous, you devour. If you are avaricious or greedy, you will hoard. The other answer choices do not share this relationship.

17. **E** E is the correct answer. The key words are antonyms because dispassionate means lacking passion or impartial and calm. This is the opposite of partiality. If you are partial, you favor another. The same relationship holds true for Choice E. If you are indifferent, you lack interest. The other answer choices do not share this relationship.

18. **A** A is the correct answer. Both A and C fit because a scandal affects one's reputation and enlightenment affects one's knowledge, but A is a better choice since it has a negative connotation just like the key words. Malnutrition negatively affects one's health. The other answer choices do not share this relationship.

19. **B** B is the correct answer. An irrational act lacks logic just as a corrupt act lacks ethics. The other answer choices do not share this relationship.

20. **C** C is the correct answer. Incessant is practically the opposite of intermittent because incessant means never-ending or ceasing and intermittent is stopping or ceasing and starting again. The antonym of *permanent* is *transient,* reflecting a similar relationship between words. The other answer choices do not share this relationship.

21. **A** A is the correct answer. Something immaculate cannot have a blemish just as something airtight does not have a weakness. The other answer choices do not share this relationship.

22. **E** *Imported* indicates goods coming from another country, which is the opposite of native.

23. **A** To protract is to lengthen and Choice A, curtail, is the best antonym, because it means "to shorten."

24. **E** *Continuous* means never stopping, which is the opposite in meaning of Choice E, intermittent.

25. **D** *Dispensible* means it's not necessary and the opposite is necessary or Choice D, essential.

26. **E** To incarcerate means to confine or jail, making Choice E, free, the word opposite in meaning.

27. **D** A *renegade* is a person who deserts a party or cause for another. Choice D, adherent, is the opposite, meaning someone who sticks with something.

28. **B** *Abhor* means to hate or not respect so Choice B, love, is a better fit than Choice C, admire, in this antonym.

29. **B** *Adjacent* means "next to" and the word most opposite in meaning is Choice B, distant.

30. **A** If you default on a bill, you do not pay it. Therefore, Choice A works best.

31. **B** *Inadvertent* means careless and Choice B, careful, would be the best word among the answer choices when looking for the antonym.

32. **D** *Solicitude* is anxiety or concern, the opposite of Choice D, indifferent.

33. **A** *Inordinate* means excessive or unrestrained, making Choice A the best antonym choice.

34. B The correct answer is Choice B. The large wave of migration at the turn of the 19th century was largely to the increase in the rural population and the ensuing problems that caused in rural Scandinavia.

35. C The correct answer is Choice C. Though some of the other answers are mentioned or explained in the passage, the primary point of this brief history is to explain why so many Scandinavians emigrated to the United States at the turn of the 19th century.